FRESH WINDS
OF THE SPIRIT

BOOK 2

FRESH WINDS OF THE SPIRIT

BOOK 2

Liturgical Resources for Year A

Lavon Bayler

The Pilgrim Press
Cleveland, Ohio

The Pilgrim Press, Cleveland, Ohio 44115

© 1992 by The Pilgrim Press

Book design by Jim Gerhard. Cover design by Jo Caress.

Printed in the United States of America on acid-free paper

97   96   95   94   93   92   5   4   3   2   1

Library of Congress Cataloging-in-Publication Data

(Revised for volume/Open)

Bayler, Lavon, 1933–
  Fresh Winds of the spirit.

  Includes indexes.
  1. Worship programs. I. Title.
BV18.B29   1986   264   86-21191
ISBN 0-8298-0736-5 (bk. 1)
ISBN 0-8298-0927-9 (bk. 2)

*Dedicated to the clergy
and lay leaders
of Northern Association
with whom I have worked for many years
and to the promise of a new day
in the Illinois Conference
of the United Church of Christ*

CONTENTS

INTRODUCTION

The untamed, irresistible sweep of the wind has long suggested to human-kind the mysterious power of God. In the biblical narratives, whirlwinds and storms usually accompanied a theophany. The coming of the Holy Spirit at Pentecost was like a mighty wind. Indeed, the words for wind, breath, and spirit are interchangeable in the languages of the Bible. The Spirit is an agent of creation, breathing life into the inanimate form fashioned from dust to bring humanity into being. Through the centuries, people have looked to the Spirit for inspiration. Prophets spoke with authority as agents of the Spirit. Apostles conveyed the Spirit's blessing through baptism and the laying on of hands. The gospel has been proclaimed and individuals drawn into commu-nity by the Spirit's energizing presence. So we, in our day, seek fresh winds of the Spirit to strengthen our faith and witness.

Fresh Winds of the Spirit, Book 2 is an entirely new resource with a call to worship, invocation, call to confession, prayer of confession, assurance of for-giveness, collect, offertory invitation, offertory prayer, and commission and blessing based on the Scriptures for each Sunday and for special days of Year A, using the ecumenical lectionary. In addition, at least one new hymn text is provided for each worship occasion.

All may be copied in church bulletins for use in worship, according to in-structions on the copyright page. Pastors and laity are encouraged to employ the prayers in their personal devotions and worship preparation. They may be adapted to fit your needs. It is my hope that they may inspire your own creativity. Because liturgy is meant to be "the work of the people," the more who are involved in worship preparation and participation, the better.

Indexes may be helpful in directing worship leaders to topical materials. One focuses on themes and words in the main text and another on the hymns. They are intended especially to assist nonlectionary preachers and persons preparing worship for groups in the church.

The beginning and ending of each set of materials is designed for respon-sive use. Most are written in such a way that the leader's part may be used without the responses, if desired. You probably will not often use both the invocation and the confessional service. The collect is a special prayer, usu-ally appearing before the reading of the Scriptures. It lifts up gospel themes and often phrases from some of the other texts for the day as well. All four readings, including the Psalms, have inspired the liturgy for the day.

Some lectionary occasions are omitted from this book. These include Monday, Tuesday, and Wednesday of Holy Week, Presentation, Annunciation, Visitation, and Holy Cross. Few congregations observe these days. However, because the same Scriptures are used each year, you can find resources suggested for Year A in my previous books, *Whispers of God* (Year B) and *Refreshing Rains of the Living Word* (Year C). Because of the changing position of Easter, there are more Epiphany and/or Pentecost resources than you will need in any one year. Usually the Epiphany materials follow straight through from the beginning and then skip to the last Sunday after Epiphany just before Lent begins on Ash Wednesday. Pentecost resources are skipped at the beginning of the season after Trinity Sunday. This means you may be using Pentecost 12 materials for the tenth Sunday after Pentecost, for example. Dates are provided for your guidance.

It has been a joy to me to spread the writing of this book over the weeks of Year A as a part of my daily devotions and preparation for Sunday worship. My thanks to family and friends who have tolerated those times when writing has spilled over into their space. Special gratitude is expressed to Pat Kitner, who once again prepared the manuscript from my handwritten notebooks.

Far beyond the reach of this book, may all of us be open to God's surprises as we continue to encounter fresh winds of the Spirit.

LITURGICAL
RESOURCES FOR YEAR A

THE ADVENT SEASON

First Sunday of Advent

Lesson 1:   Isaiah 2:1–5
               Psalm 122
Lesson 2:   Romans 13:11–14
Gospel: Matthew 24:36–44

CALL TO WORSHIP

The God of peace calls us to this season of anticipation;
the God of love summons us to this time of worship.
   I was glad when they said to me,
   Let us go to the house of our God.
Let all people and all nations bow together in praise.
Let us wake from sleep to welcome our salvation.
   Here we will seek the light God offers us;
   here we will prepare to walk in God's path.
Let us conduct ourselves becomingly as in the day.
Let us watch for the One who makes all things new.
   We will equip ourselves as Jesus' disciples,
   watching and waiting and serving in Christ's name.

INVOCATION

Gracious God, make this the hour of your coming to us. Break into our routines, transform our vision, equip us to hear and see you at work among us. Take away our lust for dominating, that we may meet one another as equals in your sight. Remove our warring spirits, to open us to your peaceful ways. Send your light to illuminate our thinking and warm our responses. Amen.

CALL TO CONFESSION

Before the light of God's presence, we seek to cast off the works of the night. The wrong we embrace and the evil we condone are revealed in the silence of this place. God knows our intentions and is aware of our self-deception. Let us turn to God for cleansing, for healing, for the power to change our attitudes and actions.

PRAYER OF CONFESSION

God of peace, we confess that our own poor choices tear us up inside. Quarreling and jealousy poison our relationships with others. We polish our swords rather than beating them into plowshares. We battle, not for just causes, but for unjust advantage. We pursue our own agendas rather than the well-being of all your children. We seek your forgiveness, O God, and the strength to amend our ways. Help us to live in peace, within ourselves and among all your children. Amen.

ASSURANCE OF FORGIVENESS

Salvation is nearer than we have reason to hope. God leads us to peaceful mountaintops out of the valleys of our despair. God's day is at hand, a time when we are made new. What is destructive no longer attracts us as a better day dawns. Give thanks to the one who creates wholeness out of our broken spirits.

COLLECT

While we are standing within your gates, we long to hear your word in fresh ways, O God of our ancestors. Open our eyes to the dawn of new possibilities among us. Move us from desire for self-gratification to eager anticipation of Christ's coming into our lives. Fill us with expectation and hope. Amen.

OFFERTORY INVITATION

We have prospered and found security in the gracious bounty of our God. Now we seek the good of all God's people as we share the abundance entrusted to us. Let those who rob God to satisfy their own desires find instead the unexpected joy of giving.

OFFERTORY PRAYER

With these gifts, we seek to accomplish the good you intend, O God. With these offerings, we commit ourselves anew to your way of peace. Prosper the work of your church in this place and link us with all who watch and wait for your revelation. Amen.

COMMISSION AND BLESSING

Know the peace of God in this Advent season;
God's peace go with you through your busy days.
We take the peace of this worship time
into the clamor of our daily lives.
Be alert to signs of God's presence wherever you go;
God comes to you at times you least expect.
We carry the anticipation of this season
into our work and study and leisure.
Accept God's healing and salvation,
for they are gifts meant for you to have and share.
We believe that God is shaping a new world
where nation shall not lift up sword against nation.
Amen. **Amen.**

(See hymn no. 1.)

Second Sunday of Advent

Lesson 1:   Isaiah 11:1–10
                Psalm 72:1–8
Lesson 2:   Romans 15:4–13
Gospel: Matthew 3:1–12

CALL TO WORSHIP

Welcome one another as Christ welcomes you;
let all together sing praise to the glory of God.
   Blessed be the God who brings us together,
   whose amazing wonders fill the universe.
We are greeted by a voice beyond our hearing,
welcomed by a presence far greater than we can know.
   All creation speaks to us of our Creator,
   who calls us into this community of caring people.
Listen, people of God, for a message of hope;
look around you for opportunities to share good news.
   The God of hope fills us with joy and peace;
   the Holy Spirit empowers us to serve in humble trust.

INVOCATION

Defender of the poor and needy, meet us here in our own poverty and need. Prepare your way within us and among us. We want to lay aside all pretense and selfish ambition that cut us off from you and the people around us. Grant us here a vision of your realm in which harmony prevails and peace abounds. Amen.

CALL TO CONFESSION

We who have known the refreshing waters of baptism recognize out continuing need to be cleansed. We have not heeded the voice of love, which seeks the highest good of all. We have ignored the wonders of God to live in fear, not hope. Our Creator calls us back to a relationship of trust and obedience. Let us seek to respond.

PRAYER OF CONFESSION

Righteous God, we confess that we have not looked up to claim the riches of your love. We have not listened to your voice of truth in the wilderness of our despair. We have not acknowledged your presence amid the loneliness of our struggles. We have been too busy with our own agendas to reach out in concern to those who carry burdens far greater than our own. Baptize us anew, we pray, with a passion for justice and righteousness. Amen.

ASSURANCE OF FORGIVENESS

God does not judge by what our eyes see or decide by what our ears hear. The needy are delivered from their oppressors. The righteous flourish and peace abounds. Even now, God's realm is among us, making all things new. We are freed to bear fruit befitting repentance.

COLLECT

Let us hear your voice, Sovereign God, beyond the clamor of our surroundings. Let us see the paths of life made straight for our guidance. Let us feel the purifying fires of your love, summoning us into joyous harmony and peace and hope. Amen.

OFFERTORY INVITATION

The mountains of God offer prosperity for all people. We have been blessed that we might be a blessing to others. Now we are invited to employ the resources God grants us, to hasten the day when the wolf shall live with the lamb and a little child shall lead them. We give in the name of One whose coming we seek anew in this Advent season.

OFFERTORY PRAYER

Out of the roots you have provided, O God, we seek to be branches whose fruit glorifies Christ. Multiply the harvest of these gifts to feed your hungry people in body and spirit. We rejoice in the hope of these days as your realm unfolds its promise among us. Keep us faithful in our receiving and in our giving. Amen.

COMMISSION AND BLESSING

Our God who has blessed us in this time of praise
goes with us in steadfast love through all our days.
Our eyes have been opened to a larger vision,
and our ears are attuned in new ways to God's voice.
Go out as a caring, generous people,
eager to live the good news and pass it on.
We have been empowered by a hope that lifts us up;
now we want to encourage others to claim that hope.
Be on fire with the Holy Spirit,
that God's promises may be confirmed in you.
As the earth is filled with the knowledge of God,
we offer to all the joy and peace of our faith.
Amen. **Amen.**

(See hymn no. 2.)

Third Sunday of Advent

Lesson 1:   Isaiah 35:1–10
              Psalm 146:5–10
Lesson 2:   James 5:7–10
Gospel: Matthew 11:2–11

CALL TO WORSHIP

Come once more, with eager longing,
to receive the promises of God.
> **Out of the desert places of our lives,**
> **we gather with joy and gladness.**

Come expectantly, with all your questions.
Bring to this place all your hopes and dreams.
> **Out of our weaknesses and fears,**
> **we assemble to gain new strength and courage.**

Come to behold the majesty of our God.
Draw near to God's Holy Way.
> **Out of all circumstances that imprison us,**
> **we come to claim the joy of freedom in Christ.**

INVOCATION

God of all generations, we are impatient for your coming to save our generation. We are ready for a word of hope in the wilderness where we live. We want to see as we have not seen before. We long to hear the message we have previously ignored. We are eager to join in the singing that announces good news to the world. Amen.

CALL TO CONFESSION

Sometimes this season of expectation finds us among the cynics. We distrust the prophets and their message. We shrink from any judgment on our way of living. We grumble against others. There is so much within us that blinds our eyes and stops up our ears. Yet God invites us once more to let down the barriers, to confess all that cuts us off from our own best selves. Come to this time of prayer, seeking salvation.

PRAYER OF CONFESSION

Where are you, God? For we have not seen your face or heard your voice or felt your healing touch. We have doubted the credentials of those who claim to be your messengers. Horrible events in our world leave us shaken and hopeless. We are offended by promises unrealized and good news unfulfilled. Yet even as we confess our anger with conditions in the world, we must also acknowledge our own blindness, deafness, and resistance to change. O God, we do not want to go on this way. Come to save us, we pray. Amen.

ASSURANCE OF FORGIVENESS

The One who has come and is coming announces good news that turns our lives around. There is sight for all who have turned away from seeing, and truth for those who have covered their ears. In Christ, the lame walk, the sick are healed, and the dead are raised. God reigns, forgives us, and strengthens us for greatness as we serve in God's realm, which is already here.

COLLECT

Meet us in the message we are about to experience so we too may go and tell what we have heard and seen. Redeem us to walk in your Holy Way, that with patience, joy, and gladness we may share your good news. Amen.

OFFERTORY INVITATION

In gratitude to the Creator of heaven and earth, who waters the parched places in our lives, we now bring our offerings with joy and singing. Join in the happiness of those who share in the transforming work of God.

OFFERTORY PRAYER

We lift up our gifts so that people who are bowed down by life's burdens may be lifted up to new hope. May there be justice for the oppressed and food for the hungry, freedom for the enslaved and wholeness for the blind, lame, deaf, and suffering. We pray that all we share will strengthen our ministry to one another and to many of fearful hearts in every land. Amen.

COMMISSION AND BLESSING

The Christ who is coming offers hearing and sight
to those of closed ears and blinded eyes.
> **We are open to receive the gifts Christ brings,**
> **for we want to see and hear more clearly**.
There is good news for sojourners and oppressed,
for widows, orphans, and those bowed down.
> **We embrace the freedom Christ offers us,**
> **and seek to walk in the Holy Way set before us.**
Go forth with joy and singing, with gladness and hope,
proclaiming to all the majesty of our God.
> **We will establish our hearts for Christ's coming,**
> **and prepare the way for others to receive this gift.**
Amen. **Amen.**

(See hymns nos. 3, 4.)

Fourth Sunday of Advent

Lesson 1:   Isaiah 7:10–16
                 Psalm 24
Lesson 2:   Romans 1:1–7
Gospel: Matthew 1:18–25

CALL TO WORSHIP

Welcome, saints of God, to this time of celebration;
come with clean hands and pure hearts to worship God.
We come to this holy place seeking a blessing.
We gather as apostles to renew our faith.
Let us together prepare to greet the child of Mary,
the one called Emmanuel, God with us.
We remember the story of God's greatest gift.
We lift up our heads to share the good news.
Be still, that the Holy Spirit may be known to us;
be open to the grace and peace of salvation.
We affirm that God loves us and all people;
we seek to live that love among all we meet.

INVOCATION

Creator of all worlds, we lift up our souls to you. All the earth is yours, and all who dwell here are your children. We seek once more to experience your truth, to receive your blessing, to ascend above the limitations we have known. You are strong and mighty beyond our imagining. We aspire to become more than we have believed ourselves to be, individually and together. Amen.

CALL TO CONFESSION

We have surely wearied God when we live as if there were no God. How often have we been deceitful, skeptical, disobedient? Have we not turned away from God's presence, choosing evil instead of good? When we ascend the hill of God, has it been with closed minds and hearts instead of openness to the Ruler of glory?

PRAYER OF CONFESSION

Our hands are dirty, God, not from toil for you, but from falsehood and deceit. Our hearts are stained, God, not from faithful apostleship, but from the evil we have accepted as part of life. Our lives are less than they could be, God, not because of outward circumstances, but because of our disobedience to your will. Draw us back to yourself, Gracious God, and turn us from our fears and failures to receive the new life you promise. Amen.

ASSURANCE OF FORGIVENESS

All who honestly seek forgiveness will receive vindication from the God of their salvation. All who are open to the grace that comes with faith will receive the blessing of God. Lift up your heads, O gates! and be lifted up, O ancient doors! that the Ruler of glory may come in.

COLLECT

We are waiting, God of all worlds, for the celebration of Jesus' birth. We anticipate the Coming One, not just as an event of past history, but as a part of our own story here and now. Help us to encounter your Word as a living message for our own day. Amen.

OFFERTORY INVITATION

The earth is God's, and all that is in it, the world, and all those who live in it. We have been blessed by God with the stewardship of many resources. God has asked us to use them for the benefit of all with whom we share this planet. The church is a most important channel for faithfulness to this mandate. Let us give to the glory of God.

OFFERTORY PRAYER

Reveal yourself to many, O God, through these offerings. May our gifts proclaim the gospel of Christ and strengthen your faithful apostles. Grant us all to know Emmanuel, God with us. Amen.

COMMISSION AND BLESSING

Go without fear into life's difficult places,
for the earth is God's, and you are God's own.
We have been blessed, reassured, and prepared;
our hearts have been cleansed and our faith renewed.
The dawn of God's truth greets us once more
as we celebrate the birth of Emmanuel.
We know God is with us wherever we go.
God's strength and might sustain us always.
Be alert for the signs that our salvation nears.
Choose the good, and receive its blessing.
We lift up our hearts in faith and obedience,
for we bear the name of Jesus Christ.
Amen. **Amen.**

(See hymn no. 5)

THE CHRISTMAS SEASON

Christmas Eve/Day

Lesson 1:   Isaiah 9:2–7
                 Psalm 96
Lesson 2:   Titus 2:11–14
Gospel: Luke 2:1–20

CALL TO WORSHIP

O sing to God a new song;
sing to God, all the earth.
We sing of light that reduces shadows,
and joy that comes with promises fulfilled.
Declare the marvelous works of God among all people;
worship God in the beauty of the sanctuary.
We gather to greet the Child of Peace,
born for God's rule of justice and righteousness.
Let the heavens be glad and the earth rejoice,
for our hopes find fulfillment beyond the manger.
Here we know Christ's presence among us,
and commit ourselves anew to living the good news.

INVOCATION

You are great, O God, and greatly to be praised. You welcome us when no one else has a place for us. Your gifts reach us amid life's deepest shadows, and your light shows us new paths. Free our voices to sing with angels and our feet to run with shepherds. Open our hearts to ponder great mysteries, and our mouths to glorify you. Make us zealous for good deeds. Amen.

CALL TO CONFESSION

Where have we chosen to journey through life? Have we pursued the difficult paths of justice and peace for all, or have we been primarily concerned with our own security? Is Christmas, for us, a sentimental story or a reawakening of transforming faith? Let us confess to God the gaps in our relationship with the One welcomed anew in this service.

PRAYER OF CONFESSION

Judge of all people, we confess that we have often chosen to walk without light. We have worn the boots of trampling warriors, pursuing national idols instead of your global reign. Our religion has been tainted with worldly passions, ignoring the search for truth to which you invite us. We have not dared to believe the Wonderful Counselor, who has come to lift our burdens and establish justice. Forgive us, God, and help us walk in your light. Amen.

ASSURANCE OF FORGIVENESS

The grace of God has appeared for the salvation of all who aspire to sober, upright, godly lives. God will judge the world with righteousness, and its nations with equity and truth. Rejoice, and tell of God's salvation from day to day. Glory to God in the highest, and on earth peace among those whom God favors!

COLLECT

Grant us your revelation, Mighty God, and with it the courage to go ourselves and search. Overcome our resistance to the unexpected, our rejection of the unusual, our refutation of the unexplainable. Help us to recognize ourselves as chosen and valued bearers of good news to a wondering world. Then make us zealous for the good deeds for which you call us. Amen.

OFFERTORY INVITATION

Ascribe to God the glory due God's name, bring an offering as you come into God's courts. Let your giving say to the world: Christ has come; God reigns among us. We have been saved from our iniquity to serve wherever there is need.

OFFERTORY PRAYER

We rejoice before you, O God, as with joy at the harvest. Your gifts to us are too numerous to count. Your grace in Christ offers wholeness and meaning for our lives. We count it a privilege to give in joyous response. We would be generous in our support of Christ's body on earth and all the redeeming work the church seeks to do. Grant that we may be faithful in praising you for all we have seen and heard, and in working for peace and justice in your world. Amen.

COMMISSION AND BLESSING

Let us go into the world to see what God reveals;
let us be open to good news of great joy.
We go forth with gladness and singing,
proclaiming to all the earth: God reigns!
By the grace of God, we are being saved;
by the zeal of God, nations are transformed.
We announce to all that Christ has come,
bearing God's righteousness and peace.
Let the heavens be glad and the earth rejoice.
Let us return, glorifying and praising God.
In response to the greatest of all God's gifts,
we give ourselves in witness to the world.
Amen. **Amen.**

(See hymns nos. 6, 7.)

Lesson 1:	Isaiah 62:6–7, 10–12
	Psalm 97
Lesson 2:	Titus 3:4–7
Gospel:	Luke 2:8–20

CALL TO WORSHIP

God reigns; let the earth rejoice;
let the many coastlands be glad!
   The goodness of God has been revealed once more;
   the day for which we prepared has come.
The heavens proclaim God's righteousness;
and all the people behold God's glory.
   The mercy of God has been poured out on us;
   the Holy Spirit reclaims and renews us.
Rejoice in God, O you righteous,
and give thanks to God's holy name!
   The loving-kindness of God has sent us a Savior;
   the light dawns, and our hearts are filled with joy.

INVOCATION

Amazing God, once more you have sought us out and brought us to the manger. You have interrupted our routines to penetrate our dreariness with your good news. You have gathered this unlikely assortment of folk to become a transforming community of faith, a holy people. We want to respond. Show us how, and equip us with renewed purpose and energy. Amen.

CALL TO CONFESSION

Like exiles from the holy city, we have wandered far from home. We have pursued images of pleasure and success, which hang like dark clouds between ourselves and God. Sometimes, when the lightning of God's presence penetrates our darkness, we are filled with fear. How will the Creator of the universe deal with our misplaced loyalties?

PRAYER OF CONFESSION

Merciful God, we lay before you all the idols that have kept us from true worship. We have been so distracted by our own concerns and destructive pleasures that we have not heard the songs of angels or seen your activity in the common place. You have brought light to the world, and we have chosen to live in darkness. O God, we need the Savior you have sent to deliver us from our self-destructive ways. We want to be led to a new day by the good news of great joy. Amen.

ASSURANCE OF FORGIVENESS

There is good news for all who are open to receive it. God has prepared a way for us to come home. There is healing for all who welcome the Seeking One, deliverance from the evil that oppresses us. Washing and renewal are gifts of God's grace. Light and joy and peace are here for us to receive. Rejoice in God, and give thanks.

COLLECT

Let the heavens sing and the earth rejoice, Glorious God. Attune our ears and hearts to the melodies that transcend all our doing. Meet us once more, in our faithful pursuits and in our faithless wandering, with good news of great joy. Set your vision before us now and awaken our feet to follow your path to unlikely places where your saving grace is revealed. Amen.

OFFERTORY INVITATION

We are called to be watchers for God, alert to human need, partners in building God's community. As personal representatives of God's grace and rule, we also support others who work on our behalf where we cannot go. Our offerings assist many faithful efforts to share good news. Even more, they are expressions of our thanks for the gift of new life this Christmas.

OFFERTORY PRAYER

We are amazed and overwhelmed, Gracious God, when we ponder the strange gift in a manger. Your investment in human life puts our idols to shame. We want to be part of your redeeming work. Inspire us to be giving people every day as we share the hope of Christmas. Bless these offerings as a down payment on the larger gifts of self and service we intend to invest. Amen.

COMMISSION AND BLESSING

God reigns: call all the earth to rejoice with us;
carry the message wherever you go this week.
We have met the One who comes to save,
and have sensed the wholeness God intends.
Light and joy are gifts to be shared;
take them to both loved ones and strangers.
At the manger, we become friends in Christ,
common seekers after love and peace.
Go, then, into the shadowed places to bring light;
carry hope among all who have lost their way.
For all we have seen and heard, we glorify God.
For the grace we have experienced, we sing a new song.
Amen. **Amen.**

(See hymn no. 8.)

Christmas Day (Additional Lections, Second Set)

Lesson 1:   Isaiah 52:7–10
              Psalm 98
Lesson 2:   Hebrews 1:1–12
Gospel: John 1:1–14

CALL TO WORSHIP

Sing a new song to God,
who has done marvelous things.
God has spoken to us through a Child;
let us all worship at the manger.
Make a joyful noise to God, all the earth;
break forth into joyous song and sing praises.
God has given us a song to sing;
let our voices soar with good tidings.
With trumpet and lyre and joyous clapping,
greet the One who judges the earth with equity.
God upholds the universe with love
and meets us here with unending faithfulness.

INVOCATION

Reigning God, whose rule extends to the farthest stars, come to rule within
us on this glorious day when the Word becomes flesh once more to dwell
among us. We open ourselves to the light and long to offer our lives as
a dwelling place for your truth. Speak to us again through the Child of
Bethlehem. Reach out to the child in all of us, and hold us in the warmth
of love's embrace. Amen.

CALL TO CONFESSION

God who judges earth with righteousness invites us to examine ourselves
once more. Our Creator, who loves virtuousness and hates lawlessness,
encourages us to confess the self-centeredness in which we have lived. The
Majesty on high, who has spoken to the world in the Word made flesh,
summons us to the cleansing waters of confession.

PRAYER OF CONFESSION

We shrink from your judgment, Mighty God, for we have often broken
your law of love. We have rejected your Word and hidden from your Light.
We have not responded to your offers of salvation with clapping hands or
joyous spirits. Forgive us, God, for halfhearted commitments and muted
witness. Move within and among us to bring your new day in our lives.
Amen.

ASSURANCE OF FORGIVENESS

God judges the world with equity; all the ends of the earth shall see the salvation of God. There is comfort amid our sorrow, grace to cover all our brokenness, purification from all our sin. God empowers us with flames of fire to become servants of the highest and best. God anoints us with the oil of gladness and fills our hearts with song.

COLLECT

Eternal God, whose Word invaded time in Jesus of Nazareth, and whose Light comes to us today, enlighten us now with a new vision of your presence and your grace. Comfort and direct us that we may walk faithfully in the paths where you lead and bear witness to the ends of the earth. Amen.

OFFERTORY INVITATION

Let us worship the Child of God with our offerings. Let us recognize the victories of God among us in a spirit of celebration and praise. Let us respond with a new song of peace as we reach out to the ends of the earth with our gifts.

OFFERTORY PRAYER

Through these gifts we reach out to share good tidings of peace, to publish salvation. As we experience the joy of giving, free our lips to witness to your grace. Direct our feet to walk in your way. Harness our creative energies to spread the oil of gladness beyond our comrades to all the world. To that end we dedicate our offering and ourselves. Amen.

COMMISSION AND BLESSING

Proclaim tidings of joy; publish good news:
God has spoken. God dwells with us. God reigns.
We have heard God's voice and have good news to tell.
We have felt God's presence, so we reach out to share.
Sing songs of praise; speak of salvation;
God comforts. God loves. God is faithful.
We have joined our voices with sisters and brothers.
We have been anointed and surrounded by saving grace.
Bear witness to light and peace. Share the Word:
God walks with us. God gives. God empowers.
We have seen light shining into our darkness;
we would now share the Word in all we do.
Amen. **Amen.**

(See hymn no. 9.)

First Sunday After Christmas

Lesson 1:   Isaiah 63:7–9
               Psalm 111
Lesson 2:   Hebrews 2:10–18
Gospel: Matthew 2:13–15, 19–23

CALL TO WORSHIP

Come, give thanks to God with your whole heart;
join your voice with a congregation of seekers.
Great are the works of our God;
we will remember and take pleasure in them.
We have known God's mercy and steadfast love;
we have been fed both physically and spiritually.
God has given us a precious heritage;
we will celebrate God's faithfulness.
God has entered into covenant with us.
We are both heard and led by our Creator.
The works of God's hands are just and upright.
We will put our trust in God.

INVOCATION

We praise you, God, for the love that surrounds us in this place and everywhere we go. Lift us up once more to that glory you intend for us. Link us
with one another in the sharing of good news and the doing of good deeds.
We meet in the name of Jesus, who shared our common lot and is able to
deliver us from temptation. Fill us with expectation, that all our senses may
be fully attuned to you in this hour. Amen.

CALL TO CONFESSION

Come, all who have been overwhelmed by temptation. Come, all who have
dealt falsely with one another. Come, all who walk in the bondage of fear.
Come, all who cut yourselves off from others out of pride or contempt or
timidity. God is waiting to hear our confession and heal our brokenness.

PRAYER OF CONFESSION

Loving God, you know our sins before we confess them. You know how we
withdraw from you and are less than honest in our dealings with others.
You know the fears that hold us captive and the lack of faith that paralyzed us. We resent suffering, but take good times for granted. We want
the fruits of faithfulness without following in the paths where you would
lead us. Open us to a fuller vision of life's possibilities, and lead us to a
better way. Amen.

ASSURANCE OF FORGIVENESS

In mercy and steadfast love, God joins us in our affliction. God lifts us up and carries us when our inner resources are spent. Salvation comes in the midst of trials and suffering, for Christ claims us as sisters and brothers. In Christ, evil is destroyed and life triumphs over death. Remember the power of God's works, and give thanks. Praise God!

COLLECT

God, our Protector and Guide, we remember how you directed Joseph in unexpected ways. We ask you to lead us through the dangers and temptations of this life, feeding us in every way and saving us from all that is false and destructive. Speak to us now, that we may respond in faithfulness to your redeeming love and do what you would have us do. Amen.

OFFERTORY INVITATION

Consider once more our covenant with God. The One for whom and by whom all things exist has blessed us with abundance, mercy, and steadfast love. We are called to respond with our whole being in an outpouring of thanksgiving. Let us worship God with our offerings.

OFFERTORY PRAYER

Thank you, God, for all we have, for all we are. Thank you for the faithfulness of your love, mediated to us through Jesus and through all who have taught us, cared for us, and led us to you. Thank you for the privilege of responding to your generosity with these gifts and with our lives. Amen.

COMMISSION AND BLESSING

God sends us forth into our everyday world,
and blesses us on our journeys near and far.
We dare to go where we are sent,
knowing that God is with us wherever we go.
God seeks to communicate with us,
and comes to us day by day in unexpected ways.
We open ourselves more fully to God's message,
confident that God will lead us, in love.
God strengthens us against the powers of death,
and offers, in every moment, the blessing of new life.
We commit ourselves to a new affirmation of life,
trusting in God to grant wisdom and understanding.
Amen. **Amen.**

(See hymns nos. 10, 11, 12.)

New Year's Day – A

Lesson 1: Deuteronomy 8:1–10
Psalm 117
Lesson 2: Revelation 21:1–6a
Gospel: Matthew 25:31–46

CALL TO WORSHIP

A bright new year reminds us of God's promise:
There shall be a new heaven and a new earth.
Praise God, who is Alpha and Omega;
praise God, who surrounds our life with good.
This time of celebrating new possibilities
recalls for us the fertile land we have inherited.
Praise God for brooks, fountains, and springs,
for grain and fruit and abundant food.
This day of renewed commitment offers nourishment,
for we know we cannot live by bread alone.
Praise God for steadfast love and mercy.
Praise God for new beginnings.
Amen. **Amen.**

INVOCATION

Renewing God, we are discovering once more that you dwell with us. We need you in our deepest thoughts, in the eyes of a friend, in the embrace of loved ones. You act in us as we wipe away one another's tears. You make yourself known in quiet talks and enthusiastic revelry. We are your people; let us know you more fully in this hour. Amen.

CALL TO CONFESSION

Christ invites us to be a self-disciplined people. We know the commandments by which God tests us. We are aware of temptations that lead us astray. We can acknowledge the poor choices we have made, and enter into a new day. Let us confess our sin and seek God's forgiveness.

PRAYER OF CONFESSION

We come to you, all-knowing God, aware of our neglect of your law and our misuse of resources you entrust to us. We cling to ways of doing things that no longer serve your purposes. We ignore sisters and brothers who need the witness and affirmation we can provide. We turn away from the cries of persons in need whom we consider not worthy of our help. We forget to talk to you or to listen for your word for us. Help us, God, for we cannot forgive ourselves. Amen.

ASSURANCE OF FORGIVENESS

The God who separates the sheep from the goats wants all within the fold of divine grace. So God invites us once more to put off former things, to let go of past failures, to adopt the new ways that God is opening up for us. To all who humbly turn away from self-centered agendas, God promises, "See, I am making all things new." Let us rejoice in God's renewing love.

COLLECT

God of new opportunities, you have opened for us a fresh calendar and vast possibilities for new experiences. Fill us now with your word of life, that we may dwell in your realm in this new year. Open our eyes to the new Jerusalem in our midst, that all who hunger and thirst and dwell in loneliness may gather as one family, loving and serving you. Amen.

OFFERTORY INVITATION

How good it is to eat and be full! How privileged we are to have shelter and clothing! How wonderful that there are friends to greet us and freedom to pursue activities that interest us! How marvelous, too, that we can share in the work of God through our tithes and offerings! Let us give as we have been blessed.

OFFERTORY PRAYER

We offer our gifts with thanksgiving for all whose labor provides the good things we enjoy. We bring from our abundance these tokens of gratitude to you for granting us life and all that we need to sustain it. Thank you for the privilege of sharing with those who are hungry, thirsty, naked, sick, imprisoned, or friendless. We reinvest our lives, with our money, in your renewing, transforming work. Amen.

COMMISSION AND BLESSING

Go forth as members of God's realm;
God grants new life to the world through you.
We will proclaim God's steadfast love
to the poor, the stranger, and the prisoner.
Listen to the mourning and crying and pain;
proclaim good news that heals and empowers.
We will embrace God's steadfast love
for ourselves, and have plenty to give away.
God, who is Alpha and Omega, blesses us
and sends us out as care-givers to one another.
We will accept God's steadfast love
and let it make a difference in our lives.
Amen. **Amen.**

(See hymn no. 13.)

Lesson 1:	Numbers 6:22–27
	Psalm 67
Lesson 2:	Galatians 4:4–7 *or* Philippians 2:9–13
Gospel:	Luke 2:15–21

CALL TO WORSHIP

Praise God, who came to us in the Child of Bethlehem,
who rescues us from slavery and claims us as family.
Let all the people praise you, O God;
let all the people praise you, O Christ.
Give thanks for God's guidance to our forebears,
who planned and sacrificed to bring us to this hour.
Let the nations be glad and sing for joy;
let all the people praise you, O God.
Celebrate the name of Jesus our Sovereign,
who calls us to wholeness and obedience.
Let all your namesakes rejoice in their salvation;
let all the people praise you, O Christ.

INVOCATION

Gracious God, whose face shines upon us and whose saving power is experienced on every hand, bless us once more as we gather in Jesus' name. Write your law in our hearts and guide our footsteps in your way. In awe and wonder, we seek the peace you promise and proclaim the joy you have poured out on us in Christ. Amen.

CALL TO CONFESSION

Children of God, come once more to confess your disobedience. How often we have turned away from the awkward places to which God calls us! How easily we forget the one whose name identifies us! Let us come with fear and trembling to the God revealed to us in Jesus Christ.

PRAYER OF CONFESSION

God of lonely hillsides and busy city streets, we confess that we have not looked for you in the commonplace. Our doubts keep us from hearing angels' songs, and our fears keep us from leaving our security to meet you at the manger. We do not glorify and praise you nor do we share the good news with our friends, for we have not yet allowed the message to claim us. Forgive us, God, and make your story our own. Amen.

ASSURANCE OF FORGIVENESS

God judges us with equity and guides all who respond in gratitude and love. God is at work in us even now, bringing good news to the world through us. Let us glorify and praise God for all we have seen and heard.

COLLECT

God of wonder, you come to us in unexpected ways. Adopt us as heirs, with Christ, of your light and joy. So fill us with a vision for us to ponder that we may be moved to glorify your name and to praise you for all we have seen and heard. Amen.

OFFERTORY INVITATION

The earth has yielded its increase. We have been blessed with an outpouring of good things: food to sustain the lives God has given us, gifts to enrich our enjoyment of life, the coming of Christ to empower our full humanity. How shall we show our thanks? How shall we glorify and praise God for all we have heard and seen?

OFFERTORY PRAYER

We, your children, return to you, Gracious God, for the work of your church some of the blessings we have received from your hands. Your face shines on us. You have set your way before us. You have embraced us with your love. Now we invest these offerings and ourselves in the joyous work of sharing the good news with the world. Amen.

COMMISSION AND BLESSING

God bless you and keep you;
God's face shine on you, and God be gracious to you.
   May God be gracious to us and bless us.
   May light surround us and reveal God's way.
Carry God's saving power into the world;
share the peace of Christ with all you meet.
   In humble obedience, we will go where God sends us.
   In joyous response, we will praise God.
See the world anew through the eyes of faith;
serve the world with renewed commitment and trust.
   God is at work in us to change the world.
   God sends us out with good news of great joy.
Amen. **Amen.**

(See hymn no. 14.)

Second Sunday After Christmas

Lesson 1:   Jeremiah 31:7–14
               Psalm 147:12–20
Lesson 2:   Ephesians 1:3–6, 15–18
Gospel: John 1:1–18

CALL TO WORSHIP

Return to the one who gathers us together,
who blesses us in Christ with spiritual blessings.
Blessed be the God who enlightens our hearts
and comforts us in times of pain and sorrow.
In the beginning was the Word, God's Word,
which is life today for all who believe.
In Christ, we see life as God intends it to be.
In Christ, we are equipped to live as God's children.
Proclaim, give praise, and welcome your salvation.
Sing aloud, and be radiant over God's goodness.
We rejoice in the winds of God's Spirit,
and praise God for grace freely given.

INVOCATION

We praise you, O God, for fresh winds of the Spirit, for warmth in the winters of our lives, for refreshment in the midst of our weary toil. Thank you, God, for the consolation of your Word, the blessing of your peace, the riches of your grace. Shine on us now with the light of your presence and the power of your truth. Meet us here with a fresh revelation of life's possibilities in your service. Amen.

CALL TO CONFESSION

As the fascination of Christmas fades and the faint echoes of good news are lost amid our frantic activities, God calls us once more to examine ourselves. Are we holy and blameless as God intends? Do we live as people of light and hope, even in the deepest night? Have we listened each day to the call of God's Word and looked for the signs of God's active presence? Come, let us confess our sins.

PRAYER OF CONFESSION

Loving Parent, we shrink from admitting all the ways we have been disobedient children. We have taken your goodness for granted and have failed to live thankfully. We have not turned with eager longing to be enlightened by your Word. Instead, we have pursued our own half-truths. We neglect our prayers and forget to bear witness to good news. As the songs of Christmas fade, we turn away from Christ and from your call to service. Lead us back, Gracious God, for life apart from you is drained of meaning. Amen.

ASSURANCE OF FORGIVENESS

To all who receive God's Word, there comes the assurance of power to become children of God. We are born anew, and filled with the grace and truth that dwelt in Christ Jesus. Spiritual blessings are poured out on us. We are forgiven. We are filled with wisdom and hope. Rejoice and be merry. Dance and sing aloud, for God's salvation comes to us once more.

COLLECT

Light of the World, whose Word offers life to all who receive you, grant us power to live as your children. Reveal once more the glorious inheritance to which you have called us, that our work and worship may be a beacon of light, a sign of hope, in all the dark places that surround us. Dwell with us, so we may not falter or cease to give thanks for your abundant goodness. Amen.

OFFERTORY INVITATION

God brings among us the blind and lame, the battered child, the mourning widow. God summons us to give ourselves and our wealth to those who have no bread or pure water or shelter from the cold. God calls us to dry one another's tears, to be healers and peacemakers. Join in thanksgiving for the privilege of sharing what God has so richly entrusted to us.

OFFERTORY PRAYER

Thank you, God, for the abundance you have given us. Thank you for your goodness to us year after year. Out of the riches of your grace, we return to you resources of time and talents and treasure. Use these gifts within and beyond your church to accomplish your intention for the world. Use all we have and all we are in the service of your will. Amen.

COMMISSION AND BLESSING

The grace and truth of Jesus Christ empower you;
the fresh winds of the Spirit inspire you.
> **Our work will be as worship,**
> **and our prayers will transform our work.**
God grant you wisdom and gladness every day,
enlightening your hearts with hope and joy,
> **We will seek the light that we might witness to it,**
> **and embrace hope, that it might strengthen us.**
Go forth to sing and serve and share God's Word.
Praise the God of love in all you do.
> **Praise be to God who blesses our work and worship.**
> **Praise be to God who sends us on a mission.**
Amen. **Amen.**

(See hymns nos. 15, 16)

THE EPIPHANY SEASON

Epiphany – A, B, C

Lesson 1:   Isaiah 60:1–6
               Psalm 72:1–14
Lesson 2:   Ephesians 3:1–12
Gospel: Matthew 2:1–12

CALL TO WORSHIP

Where is the One whose rule we accept?
Who is the One whom we have come to worship?
   God, whose dominion is over all creation, is with us.
   We worship God, who acts in human history.
What are the signs of God's presence?
When shall we know we have found the truth we seek?
   God is revealed in the commonplace, even in a child.
   When we share our gifts, God is made known.
Why do weary travelers gather to worship?
How will our prayers and praise make a difference?
   The grace of God has come to us once more.
   We will let God change us in our daily routines.

INVOCATION

Interrupt our lives, O God, with stars we cannot refuse to see. Set before us today those life-changing possibilities which will send us on better paths than we have known. Go with us as we explore the mysteries of Christ. Fill us with awe and wonder, with joy and confidence, with generosity and praise. Reveal to us in new ways the promises of the gospel, that we may be bold to proclaim good news by the way we live. Amen.

CALL TO CONFESSION

As the glory of God shines around us once more, our mistakes and unfaithfulness are revealed in ways we cannot escape. We come to recognize that we have failed to act with God to show forth Christ to the world. We have resisted communion with God, who seeks to expand the narrow circles of interest and attention that constrict us. May our confession express an earnest desire for change.

PRAYER OF CONFESSION

God of all people, we cry out to you from the prisons of our own self-concern. We have sought to create you in our own image, to serve people like us. We shrink from your righteousness and justice. We participate in acts of oppression and violence, sometimes actively, often through neglect. Forgive us, we pray, and lead us out of the shadows. Help us to hear your prophets, to see the signs of your activity among us, to feel the pain of sisters and brothers who need our compassion, not our judgment. Amen.

ASSURANCE OF FORGIVENESS

The grace of God comes to us. The stars by which God would lead us still shine. The mysteries of God are yet revealed. We are forgiven. We are accepted. We are empowered to minister. Let the light of God shine in you, and the joy of serving fill you with a bright radiance.

COLLECT

God of Magi and common people, before whom all distinctions of rank and worth melt away, draw us into the larger community you are creating. Help us join the search for your revelation, that we may discover anew the joy of worship, the satisfaction of responsible stewardship, the exhilaration of selfless service. We long for the day when all your children emerge from the shadows into your light, into the fullness of life you intend for us all. Amen.

OFFERTORY INVITATION

The wealth of the nations has come to us. What are we doing with it? Prosperity is ours. How shall we share it? We are invited to join the Magi at the feet of Christ, offering whatever gifts are entrusted to us. Let us equip the church to make known "the wisdom of God in its rich variety."

OFFERTORY PRAYER

Use our offerings, Glorious God, to defend the poor, deliver the needy, and crush oppression. We praise you with our gifts and with our lives, that the unsearchable riches of Christ might be opened for all to experience. We share the joy of the Magi, for we too have seen the star and known the joy of giving. Amen.

COMMISSION AND BLESSING

Where are the shadowed places, needing light?
Who needs the good news you have found here?
   God will brighten our homes, our work, our play.
   When the gospel rules, our shadows disappear.
What joys have you discovered to share with others?
When will you present the gifts you have to offer?
   It is a joy to be alive and to worship God.
   In Christ, we will find ways to use our gifts.
Why do you go forth to minister in Christ's name?
How will others know the grace of God through you?
   We have been empowered by God to do God's work.
   We cannot keep the light from shining through us.
Amen. **Amen.**

(See hymn no. 17.)

First Sunday After Epiphany (Baptism of Jesus)

Lesson 1:   Isaiah 42:1–9
               Psalm 29
Lesson 2:   Acts 10:34–43
Gospel: Matthew 3:13–17

CALL TO WORSHIP

Hear the voice of God, powerful and majestic;
know the presence of God in whirlwind and flames.
God speaks to us in thunder and fire;
God is revealed in a quiet voice within us.
See the works of God in the life of Jesus;
feel the Spirit gently descending on our gathering.
God calls us to ministries of healing.
God accepts and affirms us and fills us with light.
Remember your baptism and sense God's benediction;
recall God's covenant and dare to live by it.
God takes us by the hand and keeps us.
God grants us a spirit of caring and service.

INVOCATION

God of the covenant, before whom the mighty prostrate themselves, we bow in humble gratitude that you have called us to be your servants. We have come to receive the light you promise and to equip ourselves to carry your salvation to the ends of the earth. Hear our cries and draw us out of the pits of desolation. Place our feet on solid rock and help us to step forward with patient trust. Baptize us anew with your Spirit as we seek to realize and live out the community you intend.

CALL TO CONFESSION

In the midst of an unjust world, we have been chosen to bring light and comfort and healing to the oppressed. But we have turned away from this mandate and from those persons who seem unacceptable to us. Often we ourselves cry out as broken people, unable to fulfill God's righteous intention for us. Let us confess all that separates us from God.

PRAYER OF CONFESSION

God of the poor, we confess that we have followed after false gods. We have become easily discouraged and have failed to live up to our baptism. We have trampled over the bruised of the earth, leaving devastation in our wake. We have blown out the light of others' candles so they cannot see your righteousness. Forgive us, God of Majesty and Power, blessing us with renewed strength and purpose. Amen.

ASSURANCE OF FORGIVENESS

In Jesus' name, disciples are forgiven and receive new breath and spirit. God accepts all who come in reverence and awe, believing. God delights in those who bring forth justice. Today our covenant with God is renewed and strengthened. Praise God for new life, for renewed opportunities.

COLLECT

Faithful God, whose Spirit descended as a dove on Jesus, we pray for spiritual baptism today. Confirm in us the gifts that enrich our knowledge and empower our speech. May your steadfast love and saving help equip this great congregation to witness more courageously and serve more fully. Amen.

OFFERTORY INVITATION

The wondrous works of God are more than we can number. God has blessed us far beyond our ability to name the gifts. In our baptism, God has called us to a life of witnessing. Let us glorify God through deeds of light and through words that bless and heal. May our offerings reach out around the world in Christ's name.

OFFERTORY PRAYER

Sovereign God, we have signed on to be your people, so we bring gifts that represent our best, that you might bless them and multiply their effectiveness among us and in global ministries in Christ's name. We thank you for times of renewal and blessing, which equip us to give ourselves more fully in the tasks you set before us. Amen.

COMMISSION AND BLESSING

God gives strength to all who are called to serve;
God has appointed us as agents of good news.
We are accepted by God, who shows no partiality.
We are chosen as witnesses to our forgiveness in Christ.
God sends us forth to declare a new day,
when eyes are opened and prisoners are freed.
We are ready to testify to the truth we find in Jesus.
We are prepared to share the love we have known.
God is pleased with our faithful service,
and equips us anew to do what is right.
May God give strength to the people!
May God bless all people with peace!
Amen. **Amen.**

(See hymn no. 18.)

Second Sunday After Epiphany

Lesson 1:   Isaiah 49:1–7
               Psalm 40:1–11
Lesson 2:   1 Corinthians 1:1–9
Gospel: John 1:29–34

CALL TO WORSHIP

People of God, called to be apostles of Jesus Christ:
gather in the grace and peace that God provides.
God puts a new song in our mouths;
we will sing of God's wondrous deeds.
Wait patiently for God, who hears our cries;
put your trust in God's steadfast love.
God's law is written in our hearts;
we will delight in doing God's will.
Receive God's saving help within your hearts;
acknowledge God's gifts in all you do.
God grants us spiritual gifts in abundance;
we will use them for the congregation of God's people.

INVOCATION

We listen once more for your call, O God, as your word summoned us from
our mothers' wombs and gave us life. You have been with us in times of joy
and triumph and in seasons of despair and desolation. When we labor in
vain, spending our strength without results, you preserve and encourage
us. When others despise and reject us, you do not give up on us. We rejoice
in your faithfulness through all our days. Amen.

CALL TO CONFESSION

Here is the Lamb of God who takes away the sin of the world. Meet Jesus
in those moments of self-examination and confession. Turn away from the
allure of false gods, the attraction of false security, the appeal of deceptive
ways. God is waiting to draw us up from the desolate pits into which we
have strayed.

PRAYER OF CONFESSION

God of Grace, we confess the uncertainty of our faith and the hesitancy of
our commitment. We have misused the gifts you have given us, spending
our strength for nothing but vanity. We have not trusted you or dared to
risk courageous witness to the truth we have known. We have ignored
your wondrous deeds and hidden the light you have asked us to carry
into the world. Draw us back with your forgiving love, lest we sink beyond
your reach. Amen.

ASSURANCE OF FORGIVENESS

Be glad in the deliverance God offers, taking your sins away in Christ Jesus, wiping out the burden of guilt we have carried. In faithfulness, God lifts us up, setting our feet on solid rock and making our steps secure. Rejoice in the saving help that calls and equips us to be saints and servants, glorifying our God and offering light to the nations.

COLLECT

God of our baptism, whose Holy Spirit empowers us day by day, reveal to us your affirmation and blessing. Enrich our speech and knowledge, confirming the testimony of Christ in our midst. Draw our attention to your word that we may encounter you with the enthusiasm of our ancestors in the faith and serve you with the daring courage they displayed. May we know and share the community you intend. Amen.

OFFERTORY INVITATION

God does not require sacrifices and burnt offerings, but in our delight to do the will of God we bring our best in thanksgiving and praise. We rejoice in the abundant gifts of God, which enable us to share. Let us generously support our mutual efforts to be faithful to the One who is faithful to us.

OFFERTORY PRAYER

We give you thanks, Faithful God, for the grace poured out on us in Jesus Christ. We are grateful for spiritual and material gifts that equip us to live abundantly. May we, through these offerings, share in your wondrous deeds and announce to the world your saving help. Amen.

COMMISSION AND BLESSING

God says to us, "You are my servants,"
and sends us out into the world as lights.
It is an awesome task to represent God,
to carry good news of steadfast love to our neighbors.
Sing songs of praise to the God of our salvation.
Tell of God's wondrous deeds by the way you live.
We call on God to help us live faithfully,
to mold us into a community of care-givers.
Grace to you and peace from God, our Mother and Father,
and from our Sovereign and Savior, Jesus Christ.
Empowered by our baptism, we will witness;
equipped by God's presence, we will serve.
Amen. **Amen.**

(See hymn no. 19.)

Third Sunday After Epiphany

Lesson 1:   Isaiah 9:1–4
              Psalm 27:1–6
Lesson 2:   1 Corinthians 1:10–17
Gospel: Matthew 4:12–23

CALL TO WORSHIP

Come, all who have walked without light;
come to the light that lives among us in Jesus Christ.
God is my light and salvation; whom shall I fear?
God is the stronghold of my life; I shall not be afraid.
Come, all who have quarreled or slandered another;
come to be united in one mind, one mission.
God invites us to find life's holy places;
we are welcomed to the joy and shelter of God's care.
Come, all who would heed the invitation of Jesus;
come together, to follow Jesus into the world.
God empowers us at the cross of Christ;
we are eager to receive good news to share.

INVOCATION

Out of the deep shadows of our suffering and our doubts, bring us to your
light, Gracious God. Out of our hiding places and fear-filled thoughts, deliver us. Shine into the gloom and anguish of the world, where people find
no reason to sing. Penetrate the chaos and confusion, the dissension and
strife, that keep your children from the unity you intend. Help us to discover anew the joy of participating in the good news of the gospel. Grant
us courage to follow where Jesus leads. Amen.

CALL TO CONFESSION

Have we said yes when Jesus invites, "Follow me"? Have we carried the
Christian name with confidence and joy? Why do we violate the best we
know or hide from God who shelters us? Why do we quarrel with one
another and focus on our differences? Who will save us from ourselves?

PRAYER OF CONFESSION

God, our light and our salvation, forgive our lack of faithfulness. Heal
the brokenness that separates us one from another and from our own
best selves. Rescue us from fears that immobilize and distort. Turn us
from quarrels that hurt and destroy. Grant us new depths of caring and
fuller encounters with the One who heals and sends us out to tell our joy.
Amen.

ASSURANCE OF FORGIVENESS

Light dawns, God reigns, evil is overcome. God lifts us up, allays our fears, and strengthens us to stand against enemies without and within. Let us claim the realm of heaven, offered to all who repent and follow where Christ leads.

COLLECT

God of triumphant light, shine on us in our everyday pursuits, that we might follow the way of Christ in faithful response to your call. Heal our infirmities and our divisions, that we may witness with joy to your saving power. Unite us in your service, that the dawning of your light may be known by all people everywhere. Amen.

OFFERTORY INVITATION

We will offer sacrifices in God's tent with shouts of joy, for light has come to us and oppressors have been defeated. The riches of God's bounty have been entrusted to us. Let our gifts and our lives answer the call of Christ.

OFFERTORY PRAYER

We invest our lives as disciples of Jesus. We give our offerings with thanksgiving and rejoicing. May we, with these gifts, share the beauty of God with all who walk in darkness. Unite us in faith and mission, in caring and service. Amen.

COMMISSION AND BLESSING

Walk in the light and salvation of God;
these are gifts to be shared.
> **We will not fear the world's darkness**
> **or be afraid of those who slander or oppress.**
God provides for us a dwelling place,
and shelters us in days of trouble.
> **We will sing and make melody to God,**
> **rejoicing in the abundance we have received.**
Listen each day for the call of Christ,
daring to follow, proclaiming good news.
> **We will invite others to unite with us**
> **in faithful service of the One who heals.**
Amen. **Amen.**

(See hymn no. 20.)

Fourth Sunday After Epiphany

Lesson 1:   Micah 6:1–8

                   Psalm 37:1–11

Lesson 2:   1 Corinthians 1:18–31

Gospel: Matthew 5:1–12

CALL TO WORSHIP

Be still before God, and wait patiently;
delight in God, who fulfills the desires of your heart.
With what shall we come before God?
Who is worthy to stand in God's presence?
Come, not in your wisdom, but in humility;
come, not to boast, but to learn.
We come without power or pretension;
we bring our weaknesses more than strength.
Consider your call, and commit your way to God;
trust in God to grant you light and new life.
God's blessing pours out on the crowds;
yet God's attention is focused on each one of us.

INVOCATION

O God, whose foolishness is wiser than our wisdom, and whose weakness is stronger than our strength, draw us to yourself. We delight in the abundance of prosperity with which you have blessed us. Even more, we delight in the gifts we have received in Christ Jesus. With glad rejoicing, we approach you to find those mountaintops from which to make sense of our lives. Bless us, we pray, in ways we least expect. Amen.

CALL TO CONFESSION

God asks us, "How have I wearied you?" What has God done to us that we have cut off communication, gone our own way, forgotten the source and sustainer of all life? Or is the fault with us, not God? Before the mountains of God's holiness, how shall we plead our case?

PRAYER OF CONFESSION

God of hills and valleys, of Jews and Greeks, of faithful ones and sinners, we bring our anger, our envy, our foolishness to your feet. We do not understand your ways, yet often we have not sought to understand. We do not believe that love works, that patience, meekness, and humility mark the way to fullness of life. So we have sought our own way of power and wisdom, wrath and warfare, impatience and evil devices. They have carried us to places where we do not wish to be. We turn to the folly of the cross, seeking the mystery of your grace. Will you forgive us once more? Amen.

ASSURANCE OF FORGIVENESS

God has redeemed many from their bondage. Shall we not trust that God will save us too? God vindicates us and offers us prosperity that is not based on worldly standards. God calls us to a new life of justice, kindness, and humility, of meekness, spiritual hunger, and mercy, of pure hearts and peacemaking. You are blessed; rejoice and be glad!

COLLECT

God of all who put their trust in you, speak once more to those who are reviled and persecuted for your sake. Comfort those who mourn. Satisfy all who hunger and thirst for righteousness. Source of all life, unite us in the community that you intend, that justice may be done and kindness lived out in loving ways each day. In humility, we seek to walk with you where Christ would lead us. Amen.

OFFERTORY INVITATION

What offering can we bring to God? All our wealth is not enough to express our praise. How shall we share in tasks beyond our ability to accomplish? Yet God chooses us and our gifts to make a difference in the world. God employs our weakness to shame the strong. God prospers our work and witness, transforming the world, beginning with us. Let us share in the joy of giving.

OFFERTORY PRAYER

Thank you, God, for hungers satisfied and dreams fulfilled. Thank you for the inheritance of faith, which blesses our life on earth. We trust you to accomplish good among us through the sharing of these gifts and the recommitment of our lives. Help us to do justice, love kindness, and walk humbly with you. Amen.

COMMISSION AND BLESSING

Trust in God, and do good.
Dwell with God, and enjoy security.
We have heard God's call and want to follow;
we have turned from our foolish ways to Christ's way.
God has shown you what is good;
God has laid before you all that is required.
We commit ourselves anew to do justice,
love kindness, and walk humbly with our God.
God is the source of your life in Christ Jesus;
rejoice and be glad, for heaven awaits you.
We have known the blessing of God in this place;
we go back to our daily rounds to share the blessing.
Amen. **Amen.**

(See hymns nos. 21, 22.)

Fifth Sunday After Epiphany

Lesson 1:   Isaiah 58:3–9a
               Psalm 112:4–9
Lesson 2:   1 Corinthians 2:1–11
Gospel: Matthew 5:13–16

CALL TO WORSHIP

God sends light to us this day
and invites us to meet one another in this light.
Light breaks forth like the dawn,
drawing us into relationship with one another.
Humble yourselves for the worship of God,
that you may be empowered to serve.
God calls us to trust with steady hearts
and to serve with righteous compassion.
Seek not for lofty words of wisdom,
but for powerful demonstrations of God's way.
God makes us to be the salt of the earth
and lights to show God's works to the world.

INVOCATION

Draw us, O God, into your secret and hidden wisdom that we may glimpse
your purposes for us. Calm our fears, and lead us to deeper trust. Steady
our hearts that we may not fear to undertake whatever mission you have
for us today. Grant us such compassion that we may open our hearts and
hands to others who need the help we can provide. Amen.

CALL TO CONFESSION

We have come to worship with varied needs and mixed motives. Some of
us have come for personal advantage, others from habit, some in desperate distress, others for momentary inspiration. Both within and outside the
church family, we have sometimes been quarrelsome and vindictive. Often we have failed to worship God in spirit and truth. Let us admit our
unfaithfulness.

PRAYER OF CONFESSION

Merciful One, hear our cries. Come to us in the midst of our distortions and
confusion to lead us to the good you have prepared for us. We confess that
we have put our own pleasure ahead of your purposes. We have preferred
our limited wisdom to your limitless revelation. We have been more ready
to fight with one another than to free the oppressed, more inclined to feed
our own egos than to give bread to the hungry. O God, we do not want to
continue our oppressive ways. Forgive us, and help us to change. Amen.

ASSURANCE OF FORGIVENESS

God, who knows our thoughts, answers our cries and rescues us from darkness. God, who understands our motives, reaches out to heal us and make us righteous. God, who is with us in our weakness, grants strength and power to live as salt and light. No eye has seen, nor ear heard, nor human heart conceived, what God has prepared for those who love God.

COLLECT

Gracious God, whose mercy embraces our hidden thoughts and whose light shines into the deepest shadows of our lives, let your Word meet us in our weakness. Illuminate our darkness and renew us as carriers of your light. Penetrate our doubts and fears so we may dare to let your light shine through us into other lives. Fill us with good works that glorify you. Amen.

OFFERTORY INVITATION

It is well with those who deal generously, the psalmist tells us. They have distributed freely, and have given to the poor. Bring your tithes and offerings to participate in the joy of our Creator. Let your light shine so others may see your good works and give glory to God.

OFFERTORY PRAYER

Use our offerings, O God of glory, to break yokes and free the oppressed. We give them that the hungry may be fed, the homeless find shelter, and the naked be covered. Along with our money, we give ourselves, trusting in you to empower our witness. We dedicate all that we have and are to your glory. Amen.

COMMISSION AND BLESSING

Walk in humility through another week;
walk with God in your work and worship.
Our faith is not in human wisdom, but in God's power.
We trust the Spirit to lead us through these days.
Go with hearts that are steady and unafraid.
Deal generously with both friends and foes.
God has given light to reassure and empower us.
Healing and wholeness are God's gifts to us.
God equips you to be the salt of the earth.
God sends you out as lights to the world.
God is gracious and merciful and righteous.
Our good works will give glory to God.
Amen. **Amen.**

(See hymns nos. 23, 24.)

Sixth Sunday After Epiphany

Lesson 1:   Deuteronomy 30:15–20
                 Psalm 119:1–8
Lesson 2:   1 Corinthians 3:1–9
Gospel: Matthew 5:17–26

CALL TO WORSHIP

Sisters and brothers, children in Christ:
gather that we may be fed by the One who gives life.
Blessed are those whose way is blameless,
who walk according to the law of God.
Love God, and obey the commandments God has given;
choose life, that you and your descendants may live.
Blessed are those who keep God's testimonies,
who seek God with their whole heart.
Let righteousness and faithfulness be your goals.
Let reconciliation be the mark of all your relationships.
We will praise God with upright hearts,
fixing our eyes on all God's commandments.

INVOCATION

God, whose ways reach beyond horizons we cannot see, and whose law plumbs the depths we only dimly discern, teach us today. We want to love you, but we do not know how to do that. We want to keep your commandments, but we find it hard to distinguish between eternal truths and human invention. We want to make the right choices in life, but often there are no clear directions through the clouds and shadows that beset us. Come among us, dwell within us, as we seek to worship you. Amen.

CALL TO CONFESSION

Hearts that have turned away are welcome to return. Footsteps that have gone astray can be turned around to follow God's ways. Intentions that have gone unrealized can find fulfillment. Seek God with all your hearts as we try to rid ourselves of all that stands in the way of true community with our Creator and with one another.

PRAYER OF CONFESSION

Sovereign God, we confess that we have chosen death and evil instead of life and good. That is not what we intended. We tried to listen to your voice. We tried to see the path where you wanted to lead us. We tried to breathe in your presence and let your love help us grow. But, instead, we relaxed some of your commandments and broke others, offended some of your children and hurt others. Forgive us, we pray, and go with us to bring reconciliation and healing in our relationships, Christ being our guide. Amen.

ASSURANCE OF FORGIVENESS

In Christ, we can put away the hostility and jealousy and strife that block our path toward fullness of life. When others seem against us, we can dare to walk with them. When we come to worship bearing grudges, God empowers us to seek reconciliation. If we have prayed with more than words, if our cry for help is sincere, God is even now forgiving us and granting new life.

COLLECT

God of the law and the prophets, whose commandments abide through all generations, open our minds and hearts to your Word. Fill us with understanding and fresh resolve to go where Christ leads. Grant that our faith may grow into wholehearted commitment to you and true reconciliation with all your children, that we may share your bounty and serve where you need us most. Amen.

OFFERTORY INVITATION

Unless we plant and water, how will God give the growth? If we do not share, how will others be fed? If we hoard God's love, how can new life burst forth into the world? Surely we are instruments of God, co-workers who can make a difference in the world. One way is through proportionate giving of our substance and ourselves.

OFFERTORY PRAYER

We have been blessed, most generous God, beyond our deserving. We have been fed in ways we have not acknowledged. We come to your altar in thanksgiving for all the blessings of life. We bring our offerings with full intent to love our neighbors as ourselves and to return the love you have so lavishly bestowed. Unite us with one another in your ministry of reconciliation. Amen.

COMMISSION AND BLESSING

Brothers and sisters, co-workers with God,
go out to feed others, hungry in body and spirit.
   We will go where God sends us,
   for we have been fed and equipped for service.
Love God and obey the commandments God has given;
point out the way of life you have discovered.
   We will lead others to seek God with their whole heart,
   for in our seeking, we are finding God's truth.
Serve with righteousness and faithfulness,
offering reconciliation in Christ to friend and foe.
   God blesses us on our way and does not forsake.
   God grants us length of days and dwells with us.
Amen. **Amen.**

(See hymns nos. 25, 26.)

Seventh Sunday After Epiphany

Lesson 1:   Isaiah 49:8–13
                 Psalm 62:5–12
Lesson 2:   1 Corinthians 3:10–11, 16–23
Gospel: Matthew 5:27–37

CALL TO WORSHIP

Sing for joy, all whom God has comforted;
listen to God who has saved and helped us.
God is our rock and our salvation;
we will pour our hearts before God our refuge.
Be responsive to the favors of God;
keep covenant with God, and let God speak through you.
God fills our hunger and thirst.
We will share food and living water with others.
Trust in God at all times, O people;
know that God's steadfast love upholds you.
God understands us and loves us beyond measure;
we will be still and wait for God in silence.

INVOCATION

Silent God, whose saving acts of deliverance speak louder than words, we
are here to listen to your rules of life and to respond to the ways you set
before us. We thank you for times of keen insight and spiritual discern-
ment. We are grateful for those high standards that shape fullness of life.
Be with us here in all your steadfast love and power. Help us to build on
the foundations Christ has laid among us. Amen.

CALL TO CONFESSION

Who are we whose eyes and hands and lips offend our sisters and brothers
and the Creator, who has made us all? How is it that we put our trust in
things we design rather than in God, by whose grace we have the capacity
to plan and build? Do you not know that our bodies are God's temple?
When will we say yes to God's covenant with us?

PRAYER OF CONFESSION

Have mercy on us, God of all wisdom, for we have defiled your temple
within us with our pretensions, falsehood, and unfaithfulness. We have
been so interested in riches that we tolerate robbery, so concerned with
comfort that we forgo community, so intent on our own hungers that
our hearts forget the vision you set before us. Look with compassion on
our misplaced trust and misdirected loyalties. Save us from ourselves.
Amen.

ASSURANCE OF FORGIVENESS

God, who knows our thoughts, claims us and calls us back into covenant. With steadfast love, God delivers us from the dungeons of our own devices to experience healing and help we do not deserve. Sing for joy, O heavens, for God answers us, provides for us, and grants us salvation.

COLLECT

Sovereign God, whose rule is over all you have made and whose grace allows us to be builders on the foundations Christ has laid, speak to us now. Fill our thoughts and empower our efforts that we may live faithfully and serve selflessly. We look to the day when all creation will follow your way and none shall hunger or thirst. Amen.

OFFERTORY INVITATION

God has favored us beyond our ability to appreciate and has fed us even when we knew no hunger. Our Creator has been our refuge amid dangers we did not discern and has saved us from the hell our poor choices have produced. How will we express our thanks?

OFFERTORY PRAYER

Expand our offerings of thanksgiving with wisdom to use well all you entrust to us, Generous God. Extend our ministry beyond what our eyes can see so the whole earth may be led to the mountaintop where good news is proclaimed. May Christ live once more within and among us as we give ourselves with our gifts. Amen.

COMMISSION AND BLESSING

According to the grace God has given,
build now on the foundation Christ has laid.
We are God's temple, still under construction;
God provides good material for our growth.
Rely not on your own wisdom but on God,
whose steadfast love is always available.
We seek to live by God's commands,
to say yes to God's high intentions for us.
This is the day of our salvation;
this is the day we are set free to become our best.
We will sing for joy and shout our praise,
for we have received God's comfort and compassion.
Amen. **Amen.**

(See hymns nos. 27, 28.)

Eighth Sunday After Epiphany

Lesson 1: Leviticus 19:1–2, 9–18
Psalm 119:33–40
Lesson 2: 1 Corinthians 4:1–5
Gospel: Matthew 5:38–48

CALL TO WORSHIP

Come apart for a while from popular viewpoints;
come looking for a better way to live.
Teach us your ways, Sovereign God;
turn our hearts toward your decrees.
As God is holy, we are called to be a holy people,
not aloof, but involved in problem-solving help.
Give us understanding, Holy God,
that we may observe your law in wholeness.
Come to the light of God's love,
that you may deal mercifully with yourselves.
Confirm in us your promises, Gracious God,
for we seek to be trustworthy stewards.

INVOCATION

Impartial and Loving God, we bow in awe before you. From our varied
concerns and competing views, we come seeking our common humanity
and the power to become uncommonly faithful. Open our hearts to receive
your teaching and our hands to do your work. Keep us from vengeance or
grudges as you help us to love our neighbors as ourselves. Amen.

CALL TO CONFESSION

How easily we become stumbling blocks when people want to grow in
the faith. We curse those who do not understand us and complain about
persons who do not see our point of view. Our feelings are easily hurt,
and our words and deeds injure others. Worst of all, we fail to work at
reconciliation. Let us confess to God, before one another, our guilt and our
need for newness of life.

PRAYER OF CONFESSION

O God, our actions have profaned your name and wounded your children.
We do not want to slander or deal falsely or oppress other people, but we
have done those things. We do not wish to be unjust in our judgments,
but we recognize our myopic outlook. We confess our complicity with evil
and our resistance to perspectives that differ from our own. We do not like
ourselves this way. We need your forgiveness and your transforming Spirit.
Hear our cries for help. Amen.

ASSURANCE OF FORGIVENESS

The glory of God, like a devouring fire, burns away bitterness and deceit. In holiness beyond our imagining, we are embraced by a God who affirms us all and links us once more to one another. God does not pronounce judgment on us here, but lifts us up to new possibilities. In the mysterious realm of God, we can reach out to affirm our enemies and pray for those who persecute us. Receive these gifts, that you may not succumb to the world's measurements or fail to share in the joy of forgiving love. We are pardoned and changed. Praise God!

COLLECT

God of all people, whose directives to us are not beyond our ability to carry out, reach into those inner recesses of our hurting lives to heal and challenge us. Keep us from being content to live by the lowest common denominator, for we want to reflect the values Christ has taught us. Teach us to love our enemies and pray for them, that we might learn to live and work together for the common good. Focus us beyond our misery on your mission, that all humanity might be lifted up to its fullest potential. Amen.

OFFERTORY INVITATION

The Mosaic law called on people richly blessed by good harvests to leave some grain in the fields to be reaped by those who had none. Vineyards were not to be stripped clean, because the poor and resident aliens needed to eat too. We have great needs, but we have also been richly blessed. When we are truly generous, the blessings seem to multiply. We are invited to trust God with our tithes and offerings.

OFFERTORY PRAYER

We rejoice in your generosity, O God. We are amazed at the bounty of your earth. May we be trustworthy stewards who use these gifts where they are most needed in the service of your realm, where enemies join hearts and reach out with willing hands. Amen.

COMMISSION AND BLESSING

Go forward, as forgiven and forgiving people,
rejoicing in the mercy of a loving God.
We are ready to go the second mile
that God, in us, may turn evil to good.
Diffuse anger with kindly, attentive listening.
Love your neighbor as God has loved you.
We reach toward the holiness of God,
in which we learn patience with one another.
God's promises are confirmed in you;
God's commendation lifts you up to be your best.
We receive and attune ourselves to God's promises.
We commit ourselves to care for God's children.
Amen. **Amen.**

(See hymn no. 29.)

Last Sunday After Epiphany *(Transfiguration)*

Lesson 1:   Exodus 24:12–18
               Psalm 2:6–11
Lesson 2:   2 Peter 1:16–21
Gospel: Matthew 17:1–9

CALL TO WORSHIP

Listen, God is calling us to worship;
come without fear into God's presence.
We will listen for God's voice
and be attentive to God's revelation.
Climb to the mountain where God reigns;
break through all that clouds your vision.
We will look around us to see God in others;
we will let God reach out to us through them.
Let yourselves be eyewitnesses of God's majesty;
enjoy the good earth God has created.
We will not turn from the dawn of a new day,
but will greet the morning star arising within.

INVOCATION

Surprising God, whose love leads us to new experiences, help us to be open
to your appearance among us and within. Let us sense your glory in the
sights and sounds of this day. Confront us with your law and the prophets'
word, that our lives may more fully reflect your purposes. May your Spirit
move us to speak of the light that you reveal. Amen.

CALL TO CONFESSION

What have we missed because we closed our eyes to what was happening
around us? Who has cried for our help and we have not heard? Where has
God sought to lead us, while we turned in another direction? When has
the vision been lost because we were preoccupied with our own agendas?
Let us examine ourselves and confess our waywardness.

PRAYER OF CONFESSION

We confess, Welcoming God, that we have cast you in our own image and
been impatient at your silence. We have missed the awe and mystery because we cannot be quiet long enough to encounter a transcendent vision.
We climb without pausing to appreciate the new vistas you reveal. We raise
the wrong questions and ask for things to benefit ourselves. Then we do
not wait for your answers, or resist them when they come. Forgive us, God,
and stir up a new responsiveness in us. Amen.

ASSURANCE OF FORGIVENESS

Rise and have no fear. We are beloved by God, who brings new dawns to our lives. Wait for God's word with expectancy. Listen once more for God's instructions. You will be empowered to respond to God's commands. Accept the forgiveness God offers. Participate in the light God sends.

COLLECT

God of mountaintops and valleys, ever present even when we shut you out of our lives, take us with you now to meet Christ. Allow us a vision of what life can be when we take our discipleship seriously. Let your Word be as a lamp shining in dark places to illuminate life's possibilities. Then send us out to witness to the nations the good news we have experienced. Amen.

OFFERTORY INVITATION

The ends of the earth are our possession for a time, as stewards of God's bounty. When we manage well the abundant resources of the earth, there is joy awaiting us. Enter into the joy of giving.

OFFERTORY PRAYER

O God, who has given us a vision of your purposes, help us to use the resources we dedicate here to accomplish the work you would have us do. With joy, we bring the fruit of our labor, the work of our hands, the days of our lives for your special blessing. Send your Spirit into our midst to consecrate us anew in your service. Amen.

COMMISSION AND BLESSING

God has set before us a vision for life,
and equipped us to be faithful to that vision.
We have seen and heard the works of God,
and have been prepared to serve in God's name.
God has planted in us a prophetic word,
and has given us uncommon wisdom.
We have listened quietly for God's revelation,
and are moved by the Holy Spirit to speak.
Go forth, unafraid, to witness to God's majesty,
for we are eyewitnesses to the light God grants.
God has affirmed us and empowers our service.
In awe and wonder, we dare to respond.
Amen. **Amen.**

(See hymn no. 30.)

THE LENTEN SEASON

Ash Wednesday

Lesson 1:   Joel 2:1–2, 12–17a
               Psalm 51:1–12
Lesson 2:   2 Corinthians 5:20b—6:10
Gospel: Matthew 6:1–6, 16–21

CALL TO WORSHIP

Once again, as the season of Lent begins,
we are summoned by a gracious and merciful God.
We respond to God's steadfast love,
calling us into solemn assembly.
Let all the people gather for self-examination;
let all bow in awe before the One Who Creates.
We approach God in reverence and wonder,
rejoicing in the invitation to holy places.
Walk humbly before God in secret disciplines,
in prayer and fasting and giving.
We seek the One who grants us life,
upholding us with a willing spirit.

INVOCATION

We, your people, come to claim your promise of salvation, O Reconciling
God. In your wholeness, we find healing. In your power, we gain strength.
In your love, we are thrust beyond our own concerns to embrace a hurting world. Blow the trumpet, that this solemn assembly may rejoice, that
remembrance can bring renewal, through Christ. Amen.

CALL TO CONFESSION

Sound an alarm amid the deep shadows of human conflict and sin: God
is not pleased with our hypocrisy. Return to God with all your heart, with
fasting and weeping and mourning. Seek those life-changing opportunities that move below the surface.

PRAYER OF CONFESSION

Spare us, Sovereign God, from the awful consequences of our wrongdoing.
We participate in a society that robs some people of their humanity and
treats others as slaves. We lay up treasures in the wrong places while in-
flicting hardships on people we don't even know. Have mercy on us to
blot out our transgressions, and wash away the stain of our sin. We want
to turn away from the evil we commit and allow others to commit. Create in us clean hearts, O God, and put a new and right spirit within us.
Amen.

ASSURANCE OF FORGIVENESS

Now is the day of salvation, a time for purity and kindness and love. God is creating a new wholeness within and among us, that we might serve truthfully and powerfully amid the afflictions and hardships of this world. Receive the joy that comes with the richness of God's grace. Accept your new life in Christ Jesus.

COLLECT

God of secret places, whose presence in our awareness is transforming and rewarding, meet us now in ways we do not expect. As we accept the inner disciplines of this season, we would also adopt those external practices that extend helping hands and healing hearts. May the whole world be drawn to you as we share the joy and gladness of reaching out in your name. Amen.

OFFERTORY INVITATION

We give in response to God's generosity. Whether we have much or little, our proportionate giving honors the God we worship. The size of our gifts is no cause for public acclaim. Give, and remember only the joy. Share with bold generosity.

OFFERTORY PRAYER

For blessing us with the opportunity to give, we pour out our thanks, O God of all nations. For your steadfast love and mercy, we are most grateful. For bridging the gap we have allowed to develop between ourselves and you, we bow in humble praise. Now we dedicate what we have given as an offering of gratitude, not to be seen by others, but to be used according to your purposes. Amen.

COMMISSION AND BLESSING

Go into this season with hearts attuned to God,
with time and treasure invested for God.
We can endure all things through Christ.
We will rejoice and express our gratitude.
Go out as bearers of truthful speech and love,
with purity, knowledge, forbearance, and kindness.
We go out as forgiven and empowered people,
to bring reconciliation and peace.
You can neither wander away from God's presence
nor be cut off from the Holy Spirit.
In the joy of salvation, we dare to witness;
in the assurance of belonging, we reach out to serve.
Amen. **Amen.**

(See hymn no. 31.)

First Sunday in Lent

Lesson 1:   Genesis 2:4b–9, 15–17, 25—3:7
               Psalm 130
Lesson 2:   Romans 5:12–19
Gospel: Matthew 4:1–11

CALL TO WORSHIP

The Creator has planted earth's garden for us;
God bids us to come and care for it.
In our worship and in our work,
we join with all creation to celebrate God's gifts.
Every morning we rise in God's steadfast love;
every evening that love sustains and protects us.
In times of triumph or of temptation
the grace and mercy of God is offered to us.
God spreads before us a spiritual banquet
and offers us life in all its intended wholeness.
We are here to receive once more from God's hand,
so we can be responsible care-givers each day.

INVOCATION

Continue your creation within and among us, Gracious God, as we gather
to worship you. Breathe into us the breath of life, so we may discover anew
your empowering gifts. We want to use well the talents and resources you
place in our hands, without coveting those beyond our reach. Open our
eyes, attune our ears, and increase our awareness of your presence with
us, so we may be equipped to face temptation and trial. Amen.

CALL TO CONFESSION

The temptation to sin is all around us — in beguiling whispers, in blatant
invitations, in fantasies of power, in avoidance of involvement. All that con-
tributes to our broken world and broken relationships keeps us from the
fulfillment God intends. We are not all we could be; we are not yet what
we will be when we confess our trespasses and experience God's grace.

PRAYER OF CONFESSION

Out of the depths, we cry out for your forgiveness, God of all hope. If you
kept account of all our iniquities, who could stand? We have strayed from
your ways and deserve your condemnation. We have fallen prey to temptation and have made decisions that hurt ourselves and others. We hide
from your judgment and cover ourselves in shame. (Be gone from us, Sa-
tan.) We want to live by God's law. O Loving God, hear us, forgive us, draw
us back to yourself. Amen.

ASSURANCE OF FORGIVENESS

In Jesus Christ there is poured out on us, in abundance, the free gift of God's grace. We are forgiven and set free from our addictions, our pretensions, our idolatry. We are released from self-centeredness, from playing to the crowds, from our preoccupation with things. Here is good news: In steadfast love, God redeems us. Live as those who have experienced God's glory and sensed God's healing in their lives. Amen.

COLLECT

Holy and Sovereign God, in whose providence we are provided with food for body and soul, be with us now that we may hear and understand your Word. Keep us from narrow and false interpretations that twist and distort your will. We seek to worship and serve with faithfulness, looking to that day when all will experience your grace abounding among us and overflowing the planet. Amen.

OFFERTORY INVITATION

We are stewards in God's garden, entrusted with the care of all the earth and of God's people, our sisters and brothers. Let us give account of our stewardship as we dedicate material offerings and as we rededicate ourselves to the tasks Christ sets before us.

OFFERTORY PRAYER

Thank you, God, for providing so bountifully for our needs and for equipping us to minister in your name. Above all, we are filled with gratitude that you sent Jesus to minister among us, accepting us where we are and leading us on grace-filled paths toward the way of righteousness you intend. We offer with our treasure our renewed obedience to your purposes. Amen.

COMMISSION AND BLESSING

We have been fed by God's Word;
let us share the Bread of Life with the world.
We are grateful for nourishment received
and eager to show others where to find food.
We have known the watchful care of God;
let us care for one another and the world.
We have found delight in God's love for us
and want to extend that love to all.
We have been privileged to worship our God;
let us serve in ways that invite others to worship.
We have been ministered to by word and deed,
and go out to live as ministers, by God's grace.
Amen. **Amen.**

(See hymns nos. 32, 33.)

Second Sunday in Lent

Lesson 1:   Genesis 12:1–8
               Psalm 33:18–22
Lesson 2:   Romans 4:1–17
Gospel: John 3:1–17 *or* Matthew 17:1–9

CALL TO WORSHIP

People of faith, listen for the wind;
children of God, dare to encounter the Spirit.
   Who will tell us what God wants us to do?
   How will we know that what we hear is of God?
Our ancestors in the faith dared to trust God;
they left all to follow a call and a promise.
   Where is it that God wants to lead us?
   How can we be born anew, born of the Spirit?
We have received the promise of steadfast love;
God has blessed us, and our hearts are glad.
   Will God listen to our doubts as well as our thanks?
   Does God have rebirth in mind for us?

INVOCATION

God of all generations, we come seeking truth we have not found in other
places. Sometimes we are not sure we can find it here. We wonder what
friends will think if we are too serious about matters of faith. We want to
feel the winds of your Spirit, but we don't want to be blown off our feet. O
God of Love, help us to trust you and dare to embrace your promises with
confidence and hope. Amen.

CALL TO CONFESSION

We who have been born of water have been invited to new life in the Spirit.
Yet we have insulated our lives against the wind and turned away from the
witness of those who speak knowingly of spiritual matters. Let us approach
God, who sent Jesus into the world for our salvation.

PRAYER OF CONFESSION

God of Abraham and Sarah, we confess that we have not listened with
all our being for your direction. We have not wanted to accept the cost of
following Jesus. We have not allowed the Spirit to engage us. We want life
on our terms. We want to play God. But the role is too big for us, God;
we confess it. We need you, God, especially when we fail to hear or refuse
to act. Forgive us, God, and strengthen us for right decisions and fruitful
actions. Amen.

ASSURANCE OF FORGIVENESS

God delivers us from the ways of death and shields us from the full consequences of our sin. We are forgiven, released from the burden of our guilt, restored to the inheritance God intends for us. By God's grace, we are granted new life, new opportunities. God has acted in Jesus to bring us to fullness of life. God is acting still to save us. Be glad in God.

COLLECT

God of Love, who sent Jesus among us for our salvation, grant rebirth to your people gathered here. Bestow on us a full measure of your Spirit that we may dare to act according to our faith. Lead us where you would have us go, to serve in ways that you intend. Our souls await your word, O God, our help and our shield. Amen.

OFFERTORY INVITATION

God has given us the gift of life and surrounded us with abundant resources. Again and again, we have been blessed beyond our deserving. God has bridged the gap between Creator and creatures in Jesus Christ, overcoming our unfaithfulness, overpowering death, and heralding the reign of love. Will we express our thanks in token offerings or in an outpouring of our best?

OFFERTORY PRAYER

Because you gave Jesus Christ as a gift to the world, we bring our gifts today. Because you have loved us, God, we renew our commitment to share love with your people. Because you are even now renewing our spirits and bringing us rebirth, we pour out our thanksgiving. The gifts we dedicate here have always belonged to you. The wealth we retain for our own use is yours as well. Use all that we have and all that we are to move your world from death to life. Amen.

COMMISSION AND BLESSING

You are loved toward wholeness;
let that love be good news to all you meet.
The winds of God have blown among us.
The power of God's Spirit rests upon us.
You are blessed with forgiveness and grace;
pass on the gifts you have received.
We have been born anew in God's love.
Our lives have changed and are changing.
You have inherited God's promises;
let them find fulfillment in and around you.
We will listen for the voice of God.
We will go to serve where God directs.
Amen. **Amen.**

(See hymn no. 34.)

Third Sunday in Lent

Lesson 1:   Exodus 17:3–7
               Psalm 95
Lesson 2:   Romans 5:1–11
Gospel: John 4:5–42

CALL TO WORSHIP

Come, let us worship and bow down;
let us kneel before God, our Maker!
God is creating the whole universe.
God rules the infinity of time and space.
Come to sing your thanksgiving to God;
make a joyful noise with songs of praise.
God has supplied us with food and water;
God feeds us and quenches our thirst.
Come to express your faith and hope;
then listen for the still, small voice of God.
God who is Spirit seeks us day by day;
God calls us to worship in spirit and truth.

INVOCATION

We hear you calling us, God. You are among us here and now. By your grace we have gathered for worship. With the assurance of your love, we dare to open our lives once more to your reconciling action. In you, we find the truth that reveals and transforms. In the sharing of songs and prayers, we find the courage to grow and change. Bless us, we pray, with gifts to empower our ministry. Amen.

CALL TO CONFESSION

What is it that cuts us off from God and separates us from sisters and brothers? How do we, in our narrow preoccupations, turn away from the life of love God offers? Why do we err in our hearts and ignore the revelation of God's higher purposes that surround us? God is ready to listen to our confession.

PRAYER OF CONFESSION

O God, when we sense who you are, we know our own sin. In our murmuring and fault-finding, we have forgotten your mercy. With hardened hearts, we have ignored your needy children. We have chosen to live in desert places rather than asking for a drink of living water. We have hoarded your blessings and forgotten they are for us to share. Our wealth has impoverished us, and our certainties have made us brittle. We are perishing! Please save us from ourselves, we pray through Christ. Amen.

ASSURANCE OF FORGIVENESS

It is God who disturbs our complacency, pricks our false certainties, and turns our complaints to constructive action. Even now, God is at work in our lives, turning us from self-destruction, prompting our desire for deeper knowledge, and leading us to more satisfying involvements. In Christ, we have been reconciled to this God who loves us and is ever ready to help us endure, grow in character, and live by hope. Make a joyful noise to the rock of our salvation!

COLLECT

Holy Spirit, you come to us in ordinary places with extraordinary truth. Quench our thirst, we pray, with living water. May words of long ago lead us to encounter the Word made flesh. Inspire us to live the good news of your loving provision for our lives. We would reach out in service to this world of yours, that all may come to know the peace of deeply grounded faith. Amen.

OFFERTORY INVITATION

Often we have come to the well of God's love, and there has been living water to quench our thirst. Sometimes we have needed others to draw the water for us. Sometimes it is we who offer it to them. The world is full of thirsty people. Through our offerings, we provide wells and water carriers and assurance of God's love in the place where we are and far beyond our own reach.

OFFERTORY PRAYER

What joy there can be, Loving God, in the giving and receiving of cool, refreshing water! Thank you for the living water we have received from Christ and are privileged to share. Bless the resources gathered today to sustain the programs and outreach of this church. May they and we give fitting expression to our thankfulness. Amen.

COMMISSION AND BLESSING

God, who creates and renews the universe,
has met us here and goes with us into each new day.
Christ, who spoke to the woman at the well,
offers us the same living water she received.
God, who sends us into the world as water carriers,
equips us with abilities to share good news.
When Christ comes to people in desert places,
complaints are stilled and hard hearts are melted.
God, who sent Jesus into the world for our sakes,
sends us out to be as Christ to our neighbors.
Where God sends, we will go, rejoicing,
for Christ dwells in us as listeners and care-givers.
Amen. **Amen.**

(See hymns nos. 35, 36, 37.)

Fourth Sunday in Lent

Lesson 1:   1 Samuel 16:1–13
               Psalm 23
Lesson 2:   Ephesians 5:8–14
Gospel: John 9

CALL TO WORSHIP

Draw near to the light of God's love;
flock to the One who leads us by still waters.
The Lord is our shepherd; we shall not want.
God is light for all who are stumbling in darkness.
Awake, all who are sleeping through God's wonders;
look around you and observe the light Christ gives.
We gather in the name of Jesus Christ,
who is the light of the world and our light.
The God revealed in Jesus Christ is our host.
we are guests of One who feeds and heals us.
We have come to worship the God of mercy.
we are here to be fed and enlightened.

INVOCATION

We are here, Sovereign God, because you have called us. Help us to be fully present to your gracious hospitality. There is much in our lives to distract us: the work we do, the difficulties we encounter, the losses we have sustained. Sometimes we are overwhelmed by all we must face. Yet in your house of prayer we sense your calming Spirit, the comfort of your care, the goodness and mercy you provide. In joyous anticipation, we come to worship. Amen.

CALL TO CONFESSION

We who are quick to identify wrongdoing in others are called to confess our own sin. We who are swayed by outward appearances are challenged to look into our own hearts. We who stumble in self-created shadows are invited into the light that reveals, in order to be restored to wholeness.

CONFESSION OF SIN

O God, our Shepherd, we have wandered far from your ways. We have pursued our own ideas as if they are were superior to your truth. We live with secrets which we fear to be known. We are afraid to face evil, to confront those we label enemies, to deal with issues of life and death. We are sometimes rigid and legalistic. We blame others for our own failures. Turn us around so we can accept your forgiveness, live more positively in the future, and truly rejoice in your good news. Amen.

ASSURANCE OF FORGIVENESS

God anoints us with forgiving love and reaches out to us with the healing touch of Christ. All who live in faith and trust are enabled to see and to serve. Rejoice at the wondrous works of God, giving thanks to the One who opens our eyes and helps us to see. Live your gratitude for opportunities to invite others to worship and discipleship.

COLLECT

Eye-opening God, whose compassion reaches out to all who walk in darkness, help us to recognize the blind spots in our lives. Keep us from aimless wandering, from narrow judgments, from unfruitful works and underhanded methods. We want to walk as children of light, to be instruments of healing, to recognize your activity among us. Illuminate and enlighten us now, that your church may express faith in Christ through all we say and do. Amen.

OFFERTORY INVITATION

We who have been anointed with God's love and set apart for discipleship are challenged to be the body of Christ in the world. We are privileged to share the resources entrusted to each of us, that together we may provide leadership and empowerment for the church's mission. Our offerings support the ministries we offer here and our outreach to many places where needs are greater than our own.

OFFERTORY PRAYER

For your goodness and mercy that overflow through our lives and equip us to share, we give thanks. No sacrifice can match your generosity; no offering is adequate to express our gratitude. We bring ourselves with our gifts, that all may be consecrated anew to your service. Amen.

COMMISSION AND BLESSING

Go forth into the world as children of light.
Go in Christ to do what is pleasing to God.
As light bearers, we have good news to share;
we carry Christ's healing presence wherever we go.
Have no fear of hostile persons or circumstances;
God's miracles of love flow in and through you.
We will expose and oppose evil in all its forms;
we will challenge the forces of darkness.
God chooses you for unexpected outpourings of grace;
God comforts and equips you with light and insight.
In hope and confidence, we face down life's enemies;
God's protection and care go with us always.
Amen. **Amen.**

(See hymn no. 38.)

Fifth Sunday in Lent

Lesson 1:   Ezekiel 37:1–14
               Psalm 116:1–9
Lesson 2:   Romans 8:6–11
Gospel: John 11:1–45

CALL TO WORSHIP

Return, people of God, for rest and renewal;
come to the source of life for new breath.
God has heard our voices and listened to us.
God's mercy saves and preserves us.
Celebrate this time of worship and remembrance.
Rejoice in the Spirit of God which dwells in you.
When the snares of death bring distress and anguish,
God keeps our feet from stumbling.
Give thanks to God, who is gracious and righteous;
walk before God in the land of the living.
We bring our doubts and fears, our work and worries,
To this time of reflection and refreshment.

INVOCATION

O God, we come to you from valleys where there are dry bones. Sometimes
we have passed them by. Sometimes they are in us. Sometimes we have
tried to breathe life into them apart from your Spirit's energizing power. Set
a vision before us today that the dry bones may hear your word, respond to
your breath, and live. Lead us, we pray, to that realm where people are no
longer bound but know the freedom of resurrection to new life in Christ.
Amen.

CALL TO CONFESSION

The hand of God has brought us together in this place, in this moment in
time. God invites us to look at ourselves and at our church. How consis-
tently have we opened ourselves to our Creator? How faithfully have we
loved God and neighbor? Confess with me the unfruitful wastelands of
your own experience of faith.

PRAYER OF CONFESSION

We confess, O God, that we have not been as open as you intend to the
winds of the Spirit. There are times when we merely exist, as if the tomb
had already closed us in. We have hoarded your bounty without thankfulness or generosity. We have set our minds on things of the flesh and
ignored your intentions for us. O God, forgive our foolish ways. Breathe
into us once more the breath of life, that we may walk before you in the
land of the living. Amen.

ASSURANCE OF FORGIVENESS

O dry bones, hear the word of God: I will put my Spirit within you, and you shall live. If the Spirit of the One who raised Jesus from the dead dwells in you, you will know life in all its abundance. Dare to believe that you are forgiven. In Christ, your sin has died, but you have been raised to new life. Praise God!

COLLECT

God of broken dreams and empty tombs, you meet us when we feel empty and without strength or purpose; you are present in the midst of our hopelessness and despair. You greet us in times of fulfillment and joy; you are with us when life is going well. As we hear stories of your people who have had experiences similar to our own, grant that we may know your transforming presence as they did. Bring new life to us that we may walk as your people, affirming your gifts and celebrating your love. Amen.

OFFERTORY INVITATION

There are many "stones" in our lives that must be rolled away if we are to break the bonds of death and enter fully into life. Sometimes our possessions are gigantic boulders. Sometimes our lack of basic necessities keeps us from focusing on anything but our own want. We need not be bound or feel locked away from life's new possibilities. God has granted us gifts to share, that all might know the abundant life in Christ Jesus.

OFFERTORY PRAYER

We worship you, God of Life, with all we place in these offering plates. Even more, we want to devote our time to you, and all the talents you have entrusted to us. Accept us as a congregation presented for your use on the altar of life. Let us be menders of broken relationships, bearers of your healing Spirit, proclaimers of your active and inclusive love. In Christ's name. Amen.

COMMISSION AND BLESSING

By the hand of God, we are sent into the world;
go out to testify to God's transforming Spirit.
Our bones were dried up and our hope was lost;
but God reconnected us when we felt cut off.
God has delivered and dealt bountifully with us;
God's Spirit is within us, empowering our lives.
God has heard our voices and our supplication;
our Creator has been merciful to preserve and save.
Jesus Christ is the resurrection and the life;
whoever trusts and follows Christ shall truly live.
As Christ has set us free from our bondage,
we go out to unbind those living in death.
Amen. **Amen.**

(See hymns nos. 39, 40.)

Sixth Sunday in Lent *(Passion Sunday)*

Lesson 1:   Isaiah 50:4–9a
                    Psalm 31:9–16
Lesson 2:   Philippians 2:5–11
Gospel: Matthew 26:14—27:66

CALL TO WORSHIP

Who will come this day to stand with Jesus?
Who is willing to face hostile detractors and accusers?
We are not sure we want to stand with Jesus.
We are not certain what or whom to believe.
The man of Nazareth comes once more to our cities.
Jesus calls for the reign of love among all people.
We doubt that love is a practical force for today.
We are skeptical of humility amid life's powerful ones.
Before our eyes, Jesus is whipped and spat upon.
Homeless and friendless, Jesus is abandoned even by us.
We have no confidence in our ability to intervene.
We hesitate to risk our own safety for another.

INVOCATION

Come, Jesus Christ, into this gathering of fearful, uncertain people. We want to believe, but we do not wish to suffer. We want to follow, but we do not wish to be deceived. We want to care, but we do not wish to be exploited. Be gracious to us, O God, for we are in distress. We like the routines of worship, but Jesus upsets them. We are not ready for brutal opposition to the reign of love, for we are just learning what it means to love. Help us, Holy One, to trust you in this fateful hour. Amen.

CALL TO CONFESSION

Come, all who have tried to play God, who have sought to do things your own way and to force others into your mold. Come in the spirit of one who did not count equality with God a thing to be grasped. Come, ready to empty yourselves of all that cuts you off from the discipleship to Jesus Christ.

PRAYER OF CONFESSION

Loving Parent, we bow down before you, recognizing our unworthiness to stand as your children. We have tried to use power and influence to our own advantage. When you call us to use our resources for the oppressed, we turn away as if we were powerless to help. When we are beaten down by grief and sorrow, we imagine that even you are against us. We struggle on alone, rather than reaching out to our sisters and brothers as a community of seekers. Deliver us, O God, from our enemies, those within and any who may oppose our walk with Christ through the shadows of these days. Amen.

ASSURANCE OF FORGIVENESS

God's help is always available. Forgiveness is offered to all who seek it. God delivers us from enemies within and around us. Jesus Christ has faced and conquered death itself, saving us with a steadfast love that will not let us go. Receive the mind of Christ, and let your tongues confess your faith and trust.

COLLECT

God of life's darkest hours, whose care for us continues through our times of limited awareness and fractured faith, speak to our deepest longing for a Savior not bound by cruelty and death. Teach us relationships unmarred by distortion and distrust. Lead us to discipleship freed from self-concern and debilitating doubt. We want to embody the love that Christ traveled all the way to a cross to express, for we too would sustain the weary, help the stricken, and give glory to your name. Amen.

OFFERTORY INVITATION

The Bearer of Sorrows gave life itself, in total dedication to God's way of love. We too have the privilege of investing our lives for others. The tithes and offerings we dedicate here are symbols of our willingness to answer God's call with all our time and talents.

OFFERTORY PRAYER

Your light shines through these gifts, gracious God. When we give that others may see and hear your good news, we bind ourselves more closely to them and to you. Multiply our generosity, expand the effectiveness of our giving, and strengthen all who are reached by our caring. Help us to be faithful to the tasks you set before us, through Christ. Amen.

COMMISSION AND BLESSING

Are you still sleeping and taking your rest?
The hour has come to go where Jesus leads.
   Our steps linger, but Christ gives us courage.
   We will let ourselves experience the agony Christ faced.
Turn away from the temptation to deny or betray.
Let love be shared with all persons you encounter.
   We will not be scattered by opposition or disagreement,
   for Christ calls us to unity that transcends differences.
God gives us a temple for our dwelling place,
A temple not made with hands, but eternal.
   Truly, Jesus Christ is God's chosen one.
   We will follow where Christ leads, with awe and joy.
Amen. **Amen.**

(See hymns nos. 41, 42.)

Sixth Sunday in Lent *(Palm Sunday)*

Lesson 1:   Isaiah 50:4–9a
                  Psalm 118:19–29
Lesson 2:   Philippians 2:5–11
Gospel: Matthew 21:1–11

CALL TO WORSHIP

Hosanna to the one who comes in God's name.
Shout your blessings! Sing your praises!
   Christ opens our eyes to better ways of living,
   not as haughty rulers, but as humble servants.
Have the mind of Christ among yourselves,
that you may be emptied of pretense and false pride.
   In Christ we are freed to be fully human,
   to celebrate and use our gifts to God's glory.
Give thanks to God, who has so richly blessed us;
Praise God, whose steadfast love endures forever.
   This is the day that God has made;
   We will rejoice and be glad in it.

INVOCATION

Awaken us, Loving God, to the possibilities this day may hold for us. Call us forth from our weary routines and meager faith. Stretch us beyond our limited understanding and cramped enthusiasm. Free us to sing "Hallelujah" and wave branches and spread your love among those who have not experienced its power. Come to us, Gracious God, that we may fully experience your presence. Amen.

CALL TO CONFESSION

Rebels and conformists, shouters and whisperers, awake or asleep, the hour has come to stand with Christ, and we are found wanting. Now is the time to identify with the mission of Jesus, and we are both exhilarated and afraid. Let us confess all that holds us back from full commitment and discipleship.

PRAYER OF CONFESSION

Wonderful God, we are not ready to celebrate. We know too much of sin and death. We feel the hunger and pain and loss that fill our world. We do not want to risk bringing more of it on ourselves. We do not want to take responsibility for its presence with our sisters and brothers. Can't you have a parade without us? We don't really want to be involved. And yet, O God, we feel lonely and cut off when we avoid the fullness of life you offer. Forgive our self-protective ways and free us to follow where Christ leads. Amen.

ASSURANCE OF FORGIVENESS

God lifts from us the burden of our guilt. God raises us to our feet and awakens in us the potential we did not know was there. By saving grace, we are made whole and confident in the face of evil. Let each one embrace the spirit of Christ and let the whole church embody Christ's presence, that God may be glorified within and among us, today and always.

COLLECT

Humble Savior, who did not regard equality with God as something to be exploited, appear among us as we remember your peaceful witness. Teach us once again that we may stand with you against unfairness and wrong. Equip us more fully to serve in your name among the weary and discouraged. Empower us to share good news, that all your children may celebrate your reign with hosannas of praise. Amen.

OFFERTORY INVITATION

What do we have to give? Time? Organizing skill? A listening ear? For what are we most thankful? Family? Friends? Education? Meaningful work and activities? The gift of life and breath? All good things we possess and all the time we enjoy on this earth are gifts from God. We are invited to a generous offering of thanksgiving.

OFFERTORY PRAYER

Use what we have to share, God of all people, so more of your children may know the good news of Christ. If we had a donkey, we would loan it. If we had branches, we would wave them. When we have extra garments, we would honor Christ by clothing our shivering sisters and brothers. We do have much to give, and we cherish the joy of giving. Bless these tokens of the fuller commitment they are meant to represent. Hallelujah! Amen.

COMMISSION AND BLESSING

Go out to tell your neighbors:
life is filled with the goodness of a loving God.
In humble thanks, we scatter with good news;
with genuine enthusiasm, we seek to share it.
Go out to live among friends and strangers;
carry the love of God in Christ into all relationships.
Among our closest loved ones and with strangers,
we will risk sharing who we are in Christ.
Go with the blessing of God, who expands our lives,
to see and hear and feel how valued we are.
We reach out as followers of Christ,
knowing we are loved, and chosen for service.
Amen. **Amen.**

(See hymns nos. 42, 43.)

Maundy Thursday

Lesson 1:   Exodus 12:1–14
                  Psalm 116:12–19
Lesson 2:   1 Corinthians 11:23–26
Gospel: John 13:1–15

CALL TO WORSHIP

One who loves us to the end has invited us here.
We are guests at the table of Jesus Christ.
We come to this memorial feast in gratitude;
we honor Christ's invitation above all others.
At this table, we know cleansing and forgiveness.
We are empowered here to live as Christ's disciples.
We are awed that our Savior has chosen us;
we are embarrassed that Christ would wash our feet.
Through the broken bread and the cup of blessing,
we participate in the new life Christ offers us.
We reach out for the gifts that Jesus offers;
we seek to pass them on in Jesus' name.

INVOCATION

We are your servants, God of all ages, meeting once more as disciples of Jesus, who revealed your love to us in ways we cannot forget. Your own beloved Child faced death that we might know the power of love beyond all other powers. Visit us here, in our acts of remembrance and rededication. Dwell within and among us as we seek to follow Jesus' example. Equip us with courage, lest the bitter herbs of life and the cup of suffering turn us from the paths where Christ leads. Amen.

CALL TO CONFESSION

Jesus said to the disciples, "Not all of you are clean." We know the stains we carry: the hurts we have inflicted on others by carelessness or intent, the good we have neglected in our busyness or inattention. We need not be paralyzed by the guilt we carry. When we face ourselves as we are and confess our sin, forgiveness is offered.

PRAYER OF CONFESSION

We call on your name, O God, out of our desperate need for healing and forgiveness. We have broken covenant, forgotten who we are, and lived by our own conceits. We act as if we have no need of you when things go well. When suffering and loss come to us, we complain. Forgive us, God, for wanting the whole world to revolve around us. Restore us to full membership and responsibility in your family, we pray. Amen.

ASSURANCE OF FORGIVENESS

God offers us the cup of salvation and the bread from heaven. We are precious in God's sight, worth saving from the judgment that we rightfully deserve. In Jesus Christ, we are loved into a new covenant with God and with one another. We are accepted, we are loved, we are forgiven. The Teacher washes our feet and sends us out as foot-washing representatives of God's truth. Praise God!

COLLECT

Loving Parent, whose care for us in Jesus Christ is deeper and wider than we can imagine, grant us now a sense of participation in the stories of Passover and the upper room. Meet us here as you met our ancestors in the faith, who testify to us still of your actions among them. May Christ's example inspire our renewed commitment and service. Amen.

OFFERTORY INVITATION

One way we can express our gratitude for life and for all God's bounty to us is to share the riches entrusted to us. We give through the church, believing that the witness of this faith community is a vital part of Christ's ministry in the world. We offer to God the sacrifice of our thanksgiving.

OFFERTORY PRAYER

For your sake, O God, we bear witness through this offering of love, returning a portion of all we have been given. For the sake of our sisters and brothers whose feet we cannot wash in person, we dedicate these gifts. For our own sake, needing to experience generosity and the sense that we have experienced something worth giving away, we consecrate this offering and ourselves. Amen.

COMMISSION AND BLESSING

We have remembered and celebrated together;
now we are sent out to serve in Christ's name.
   We have been washed and fed;
   now we go out to follow Christ's example of service.
Let your daily life express thanksgiving to God;
let your daily acts express God's love to others.
   We participate in a new covenant;
   remembrance of Christ inspires our caring.
Walk in confidence through Good Friday to Easter.
God's love sustains us through death to new life.
   God's steadfast love and faithfulness assure us.
   We dare to offer to others what we have experienced.
Amen. **Amen.**

(See hymns nos. 44, 45.)

Good Friday

Lesson 1:   Isaiah 52:13—53:12
               Psalm 22:1–18
Lesson 2:   Hebrews 4:14–16; 5:7–9
Gospel: John 18—19

CALL TO WORSHIP

Come to this place apart to pray;
God, who has given us life, meets us here.
Will God be revealed to us on this dark day?
Has not God turned away and forsaken us?
Come, all who are weary and discouraged,
God, whom you have trusted, has not deserted you.
Will God hear our cries and replenish our strength?
Who can believe in the midst of such sorrow?
Come, all who have laid loved ones to rest;
God, who grieves with us, watches with us now.
Will God's promise of new life be realized?
How shall we know truth, when Trust is crucified?

INVOCATION

On this darkest of days, we cry out against the contradictions we see and hear all around us. How, O God, can this day be called "good"? If you are Almighty, why do you not intervene against our inhumanity? We seek you night and day, without answer or rest. Our tears flow and our fears multiply. Why must suffering mark the road to salvation? Why is goodness crucified before our eyes? Hear our groaning, O God, and deliver us from the awful cruelty of Calvary. Amen.

CALL TO CONFESSION

Who is it who has heard the cock crow and remembered words of denial and acts of desertion? Who has shouted, "Crucify!" — if not with voice, with deeds that destroy God's Truth? Who has fled, in the face of ridicule or danger, from Christ's call to discipleship? Listen! God is calling us back. What can we say?

PRAYER OF CONFESSION

O God, we stumble back to your throne of grace. We have wanted to live life on our own terms. We have expected you to favor us and protect us from harm. We have relied on you to hold evil in check, even that which we cause. O God, we confess our halfhearted commitment and broken faithfulness. We are guilty of so much that separates us from the goodness you intend and from the people you have called us to love. Can you forgive us yet another time? Amen.

ASSURANCE OF FORGIVENESS

One has lived among us who bore our sin and sorrow, who even yet heals us and makes us whole. By the mercy and grace of God, we receive, through Christ, eternal salvation. We can trust once more, knowing God will not disappoint us and the purposes of God will prosper through us.

COLLECT

Patient God, watching in love even as we betray, deny, and desert, lead us once more into the presence of Jesus that we may walk with him through his humiliation and suffering. Remove from our discipleship the fickle self-concern that allows new Calvaries. Take away the fear and cowardice that thwart justice and truth. Strengthen our witness and service, that all people may come to know the love proclaimed on this day. Amen.

OFFERTORY INVITATION

In thanksgiving for the One who gave away everything for us, we bring our renewed commitment, our acts of kindness, our gifts of substance. No offering is sufficient response for all we have received. Yet God blesses and multiplies all that we share. Worship God in an outpouring of gratitude for Jesus Christ.

OFFERTORY PRAYER

We bring our gifts in grateful response for your saving gifts to us, Merciful God. They are expressions of love in answer to the love you have shown to us in so many ways. Thank you for the Savior who has borne our griefs and carried our sorrows. Receive us now as disciples of good news and bearers of your love. We dedicate ourselves and all we have to offer. Amen.

COMMISSION AND BLESSING

Who has believed what we have heard?
Who will go out to share the meaning of this day?
   Surely the One who was despised and rejected
   has borne our griefs and carried our sorrows.
Who has trusted God and felt God's sheltering arms?
Who has cried out and sensed God's rescuing presence?
   We who have drawn near to the throne of grace
   go out to help others in their time of need.
Who will boldly claim the role of disciple under fire?
You, who are claimed, trusted, and equipped for service.
   We follow, even to the cross of suffering,
   for we know death has no power over love and truth.
Amen. **Amen.**

(See hymns nos. 46, 47, 48.)

THE EASTER SEASON

Easter

Lesson 1:   Jeremiah 31:1–6 *or* Acts 10:34–43
               Psalm 118:14–24
Lesson 2:   Colossians 3:1–4 *or* Acts 10:34–43
Gospel: John 20:1–18 *or* Matthew 28:1–10

CALL TO WORSHIP

Come and see; come and rejoice.
God calls us together for a celebration.
We have come seeking Jesus of Nazareth.
We want to know the One who comforts and heals.
Enter into this time of worship with thanksgiving;
receive once more the good news of peace.
God is our strength and our song;
God has acted in Christ for our salvation.
The gates of righteousness have opened to you;
Jesus promises to meet you along life's way.
Christ is risen; what a joyous moment!
Christ is risen; we want to tell the world!

INVOCATION

Mighty God, the earth is shaken and nothing is the same. Defeat is turned to victory; death is overcome by life; the stone that the builders rejected has become the chief cornerstone. Meet us here, O God, amid events beyond our understanding. You appear to us from afar, yet touch us where we are. You love spans time and space, yet wraps itself around us here and now. Faithful God, we come seeking the things that are above. Amen.

CALL TO CONFESSION

All who are weeping and forlorn are welcome at the feet of Jesus. Listen, for you will hear your name. All who have survived the sword will know grace, even in the wilderness; watch for Christ's appearing. All who fear God, feel that presence which prompts our awe and wonder. Come to rid yourself of the burden of sin.

PRAYER OF CONFESSION

God of all people, be our God. We have forgotten who you are. We have turned away from what is right and good. We have participated in those actions which sent Jesus to the cross. We have rejected Christ as out of date and impractical. We set our minds on things of the earth rather than on your will. O God, we do not want to continue our destructive ways. Grant that we may see and believe the fullness of life you intend for us. Strengthen us to live as resurrection people. Amen.

ASSURANCE OF FORGIVENESS

Christ is life and has become our salvation. We shall not die, but shall live and recount the deeds of God. Do not fear, then, to follow where Christ leads, to feel the suffering of others and your own pain, to reach out in witness and service. We are acceptable to God, whose faithfulness continues and whose love never ends. Receive the healing Christ offers, and pass it on.

COLLECT

God of our Sabbath times and of all the days that follow, break through the defenses we have erected to shut you out. Meet us among the tombs we visit in our despair, and call our names once more. At the feet of Jesus we would now worship and learn, so our discipleship may be reclaimed and strengthened. We want to tell the world the incredible story that love is alive and can make all the difference. Amen.

OFFERTORY INVITATION

Our generous offerings are but one response to the good news of Easter. They are appropriate expressions of thanks to God. They bear witness to the degree of our commitment. But no offering is a substitute for personal faithfulness to God, who calls us to be healers, witnesses, and lovers of the world's people, whom Christ came to save.

OFFERTORY PRAYER

No gift we bring is adequate to return the love you have given us, O God, in the Christ-event. Anoint these expressions of our thanksgiving with power to accomplish your will among our neighbors and in your world. In response to your grace, we rededicate ourselves to serve in faithfulness wherever you may lead. Thanks be to you, O God, for the new life you have granted. Amen.

COMMISSION AND BLESSING

Darkness has lifted, and light has come to us;
God is building us into a faithful community.
   God's mighty deeds have caught our attention;
   our minds have been turned to what is important.
We have experienced anew faith's transforming power;
now God sends us out as witnesses to resurrection.
   We are alive to recount the deeds of God;
   we will sing again the songs of our salvation.
Go quickly and tell what you have encountered:
goodness reigns, and tombs have no power to destroy.
   We depart from worship with glad anticipation;
   we take up our service to the risen Christ with joy.
Amen. **Amen.**

(See hymns nos. 49, 50, 51.)

Easter Evening

Lesson 1:   Daniel 12:1–3 *or* Acts 5:29–32
                 Psalm 150
Lesson 2:   1 Corinthians 5:6–8 *or* Acts 5:29–32
Gospel: Luke 24:13–49

CALL TO WORSHIP
Celebrate with sincerity and truth;
Christ is alive and offers new life to us.
We want to celebrate the good news,
but the world does not believe our story.
God's promises come in the midst of our doubts;
God's assurances are real amid our troubles.
We want to claim the light of the stars,
but often we sleep the sleep of the dead.
God calls us now to this time of worship;
Praise God, praise Christ, in the sanctuary.
We marvel at God's exceeding greatness;
let everything that breathes praise God.

INVOCATION
We have come together to be clothed with power from on high. Meet us here with truth we can wear with confidence and joy we can share with sincerity. Stay with us to extend this day which is far spent into many days to come. Awaken us to life in all its fullness here and now, and prepare us for everlasting life with Christ, in whose name we worship. Amen.

CALL TO CONFESSION
Christ is alive; we need not live in our shame. Christ is alive; our boasting has no place, for we are called to a new righteousness. Christ is alive; evil is overcome and malice is subdued. Let us seek to reform our lives to God's design.

PRAYER OF CONFESSION
Patient God, we are ashamed. We have listened to siren voices from the world rather than obeying your word. We have boasted in our own accomplishments rather than recognizing your grace. We have treated others with contempt while promoting our own interests. We have been slow of heart, unready to believe and accept your better way. Forgive, and help us to change. Amen.

ASSURANCE OF FORGIVENESS

The promises of God are upon us. All who truly repent will realize forgiveness. They will glow with the brightness of the sky; their righteousness will shine like the stars. Praise God with trumpets and cymbals and dance. Praise God with lute and harp and timbrel and strings. We are forgiven! We are witnesses to all God has done in Christ.

COLLECT

God of amazing good news, who exalted Jesus as Leader and Savior, open to us the scriptures. Talk to us along life's way, meet us as we break bread together in our homes, and move us in worship to claim your promises. Open our eyes and quicken our hearts, that we may be about your mission of sharing the good news with both disciples and strangers. May our witness lead others to obedience. Amen.

OFFERTORY INVITATION

How shall we praise God for the sacrifice of Jesus Christ? How will we respond when our hearts burn within us? What gifts will show our thanks for all we receive day by day? Will we arise to give ourselves in proclamation and service? Will we share our substance for the work of ministry?

OFFERTORY PRAYER

For the goodness you bestow, for the truth you reveal, for the acceptance you offer, we give thanks. All that is ours is yours. Help us to live that truth. All whom we meet are yours. Equip us to treat them as honored guests. Accept our offering as our expression of renewed commitment. Amen.

COMMISSION AND BLESSING

The Christ whom we meet here goes with us;
walk life's roads with confident trust.
> **We will praise God in our daily walk.**
> **with every step, we remember God's goodness.**

The God whose promises are upon us
clothes us with vision and power.
> **We will praise God who empowers our service.**
> **We receive from God all that we need.**

The Holy Spirit is given to us as a gift;
live in obedience, praising God with every breath.
> **We will praise God's exceeding greatness.**
> **We celebrate the festival of Easter joy.**

Amen. **Amen.**

(See hymns nos. 52, 53.)

Second Sunday of Easter

Lesson 1:   Acts 2:14a, 22–32
               Psalm 16:5–11
Lesson 2:   1 Peter 1:3–9
Gospel: John 20:19–31

CALL TO WORSHIP

We have entered this place in confident expectation.
Let us be open to the One who greets us here.
    God, who is everywhere, welcomes us here;
    Our hearts are filled with joyous anticipation.
This is a special place of meeting and inspiration.
We are glad for one another in God's awesome presence.
    God tests our faith and examines our community;
    Our Creator gives us counsel and instructs us.
Let us praise our God, revealed to us in Jesus Christ.
Glory and honor to the One whose Spirit we receive.
    In Christ, we are born anew to a living hope.
    In the Spirit's blessing, we know true peace.

INVOCATION

You are always before us, O God, even in the midst of grievous trials. We are tested in the fires of loss and grief. We are swayed by out doubts and fears. Assure us once more that we are not alone, that you do not abandon us. Help us in our time together to focus on the pleasant places where you have led us and on the goodly heritage that is ours. We dwell secure in your caring presence. Amen.

CALL TO CONFESSION

We turn to God once more to confess our sin, not so much because we are weighed down by guilt as because we do not often pause to consider God's will for us. We forget to think about the Source of life. We fail to contemplate the claims of Christ. We resist the prompting of the Holy Spirit. The apostle Peter calls us lawless people, responsible for the crucifixion. Let us pray together.

PRAYER OF CONFESSION

God of Mercy, we find it hard to accept blame for Jesus' death, yet we know in our hearts that we often turn away from our Savior's teaching. We fail to live as resurrection people, finding joy in each day. We pursue proofs as skeptics rather than affirming the values Christ proclaimed. Forgive our indifference and our narrow views of faithfulness. Lead us to the fullness of joy that you intend for all your children. Amen.

ASSURANCE OF FORGIVENESS

As God raised Jesus, we too are lifted up from death to experience new life. Let hearts be glad and tongues rejoice, for God's mercy abounds, and our salvation is already assured. We are a forgiven people, called to forgive others. It is our inheritance to live together in hope.

COLLECT

O Risen Christ, whose presence was real to your first disciples, come among us in spite of the barriers we erect. Breathe on us that we too might receive the Holy Spirit. Lead us to stronger faith, evoke in us a forgiving spirit, and open our eyes to see the signs and wonders of God in our midst, that our service may be empowered. Amen.

OFFERTORY INVITATION

How amazing are the works of God! By God's mercy, we are alive; in God's presence, we are filled with hope. One way to pass on the gift is to share our material wealth, which God entrusts to us. As we offer our substance to be blessed in service to the risen Christ, let us rededicate ourselves as well.

OFFERTORY PRAYER

O God, by whose example giving is a blessed way of life, fill us now with the exultant joy of your love, which is more precious than gold. May we be bold to proclaim the glorious good news of salvation, with glad hearts and with deep and genuine trust. Grant us the opportunity, through these gifts and in our daily living, to lead others to a life-affirming faith, in Christ's name. Amen.

COMMISSION AND BLESSING

Peace be with you as you depart to serve.
Christ sends you out as witnesses to the world.
We have experienced God's signs and wonders.
We have known the peace Christ brings.
Christ breathes a blessing on you;
the Holy Spirit fills you with hope and joy.
We are equipped to share new life in Christ.
We rejoice with unutterable and exalted joy.
Wherever you go, God is beside you.
God is a present help in all you do.
We are witnesses to resurrection power;
in thanks and praise, we proclaim salvation.
Amen. **Amen.**

(See hymns nos. 54, 55.)

Third Sunday of Easter

Lesson 1:   Acts 2:14a, 36–41
              Psalm 116:12–19
Lesson 2:   1 Peter 1:17–23
Gospel: Luke 24:13–35

CALL TO WORSHIP

What shall we render in thanks to God?
How shall we show gratitude to our Creator?
We will gather with God's people for worship;
we will renew our vows to our Maker.
How shall we respond to the Power who frees us,
who rescues us from our futile ways?
We will offer the sacrifice of our thanksgiving,
and enlist once more as servants of the Most High.
Who will open our eyes to Christ's presence with us?
Shall our hearts burn with the joy of recognition?
We will stop to listen and to offer hospitality.
We will break bread with others in remembrance.

INVOCATION

We call on your name, O God, for you have offered us the cup of salvation and welcomed us into your family. How can we thank you for the love you have shown us in Jesus Christ? Meet us again in this hour, that we may grow in faith and be responsive to your truth. Fill us with hope, renewing our confidence to face life in faithful trust and obedience. Amen.

CALL TO CONFESSION

Let us remember our baptism and repent of all the ways we have violated our covenant with God. Let us remember our baptism and confess all our subtle accommodation to a corrupt generation. Let us remember our baptism and reclaim our new life in Christ.

PRAYER OF CONFESSION

When we consider who you are, O God, we are ashamed. When we ponder all we have neglected, we fall on our faces in horror before you. When we look once more into the face of Christ, we sense the judgment that is our rightful due. Forgive us, God, for forgetting that we are disciples, not spectators. Forgive our silence when you call us as ambassadors of good news. Forgive our neglect of your children who need the promises you have given. Forgive us, through Christ. Amen.

ASSURANCE OF FORGIVENESS

God meets us where we are, to turn our lives around. God raised Jesus to assure us of new life. God's promises are for us and for our children, for those who are near to us and for all who are far away. God calls us into relationships that build up, not destroy. We are forgiven. Praise God!

COLLECT

Revealing God, you walk among us unseen: open our eyes. Calling, inviting God, you speak to us in myriad unheard ways: open our ears. Stretching, challenging God, you push us to widen our circle of responsibility: touch the depths of our caring. Use our eyes and ears and emotions to provide a welcome at your table for people who usually receive no invitation. We need their presence among us to be fully human, to be your family. Amen.

OFFERTORY INVITATION

Our stewardship of God's gifts to us can provide a place at the table for some who are hungry, and shelter for some who have no place to lay their heads. But most of all, our offerings express thanks to God for the bounty we enjoy and the loving acceptance we have known through Christ.

OFFERTORY PRAYER

For all your saints, O God, who have guided our lives, for all the ways you have saved us from ourselves, for all the times your love has been poured out on us, we give thanks. You have taught us to offer hospitality and to share what you have given. This we do, with joy and gratitude. Receive these tokens of our renewed dedication. Amen.

COMMISSION AND BLESSING

Christ has sat among us and walks with us;
we are assured that God's presence goes with us.
> **We face the world with renewed faith and hope;**
> **God's word endures and abides with us.**

Let your hearts burn within you as you dare to trust;
Embrace God's promises as you believe and care.
> **We will speak of what we have seen and heard;**
> **God's love is real and alive in us.**

Live in gratitude each and every day;
Love one another earnestly from the heart.
> **We seek to act in obedience to God's truth;**
> **We will love sincerely and live confidently.**

Amen. **Amen.**

(See hymns nos. 53, 56, 57.)

Fourth Sunday of Easter

Lesson 1:   Acts 2:42–47
                Psalm 23
Lesson 2:   1 Peter 2:19–25
Gospel: John 10:11–10

CALL TO WORSHIP

The doors are open; the good shepherd calls.
Come in to find a place of comfort and safety.
We turn away from our weariness and fear;
We leave behind our anxiety and cares.
There is bread here to feed our every need;
there are still waters to refresh our souls.
We would devote ourselves to learning and praying.
We seek to live in genuine community.
There are tasks for all of glad and generous heart.
Find strength in this hour to follow Jesus' steps.
Praise God for this time apart;
praise God for refreshment and renewal.

INVOCATION

God of signs and wonders, open our eyes to the marvelous evidence of your care for us. Open our ears to hear the voice of the Good Shepherd calling us by name. Link us with one another in a true community of caring, in which the needs of each are the concern of all. Shower your goodness and mercy on all who gather here, that we may be equipped to share your blessing now and in days to come. Amen.

CALL TO CONFESSION

We have been given the model of Jesus Christ, who came that we might have life, and have it abundantly. Though reviled, Christ did not revile in return. While suffering, Christ did not threaten. As we think about our own ways of meeting criticism, rejection, and opposition, let us consider whether we are following Christ.

PRAYER OF CONFESSION

O God, it is so easy to stray from the best we know. Before we realize it, we are lost in our fears, dominated by life's shadows, preoccupied with our own suffering. We complain of our lot, even though our cups overflow with your goodness and mercy. We are reluctant givers and ineffective followers. Turn us around, God, for we want to be disciples. Amen.

ASSURANCE OF FORGIVENESS

With steady rod and staff, God comforts and leads. The table of forgiveness and blessing is spread before us. Christ bore our sins that we might die to sin and live in righteousness. In ways we cannot fathom, Christ's wounds have extended healing to us. Let us live as whole people, forgiven and forgiving.

COLLECT

Good Shepherd, who calls us by name and leads us in the way you would have us go, grant the wisdom, devotion, and courage to follow you. We would dare to be disciples who are learning patience and generosity, that we might share with others the abundant life you are revealing to us. Add to our number daily those who are being saved. Amen.

OFFERTORY INVITATION

We partake daily of God's abundance. Sometimes we appear to be thieves and robbers, diverting to our own use what God entrusts to us for the benefit of all. We are stewards of riches we do not own. We are managers of talents we did not create. We are gifted with time to invest for our Creator. Let us offer our best, our all, in renewed dedication.

OFFERTORY PRAYER

O Guardian of our souls, we give thanks for your watchful care. We are grateful for the many ways you offer healing and renewal. We are delighted with the opportunity to return, with glad and generous hearts, the love you have given us. We praise you with our offerings and by rededicating our time, talents, and treasure to the ministry of healing your broken, troubled world. Amen.

COMMISSION AND BLESSING

Go out into God's pastures; they are everywhere;
there is food enough for all to share.
A table is prepared for us and all people;
we will invite others to God's feast.
Let the still waters run deep within you.
God has promised an abiding presence.
We will listen for the Shepherd's voice.
We will trust God to guide us.
Go out to live courageously and give abundantly;
Christ's life and love empower you.
Surely goodness and mercy will follow us;
we will dwell with God and serve humanity.
Amen. **Amen.**

(See hymn no. 58.)

Fifth Sunday of Easter

Lesson 1:   Acts 7:55–60 *or* Acts 17:1–12
                  Psalm 31:1–8
Lesson 2:   1 Peter 2:2–10
Gospel: John 14:1–14

CALL TO WORSHIP

Look up and see the heavens open to us;
sense the mystery of God's presence with us.
It is our custom to gather, that God may uplift us;
God is our refuge, in whom we trust.
Do not let your hearts be troubled or afraid;
Celebrate the good news: Christ is risen.
We will not fear losses or suffering;
We are raised with Christ to new life.
Come to Christ, the living stone, rejected by many.
Come to Christ, chosen by God, and precious to us.
We rejoice in God's steadfast love.
We are glad for God's faithfulness that redeems us.

INVOCATION

Incline your ear to us, Steadfast God; hear our cries. Open to us once more
the place of refuge you provide. In the safety of this community, minister
to our hurts and strengthen us to face affliction and adversity. We long for
the spiritual milk you alone can provide; feed our hungry souls. Set our
feet in a broad place that we may walk with Christ, the way, the truth, and
the life. Amen.

CALL TO CONFESSION

In this place we are reminded that our best intentions so often go astray. We
join the gangs in the marketplace, instead of standing with the believers.
We take up stones and throw them, instead of raising our voices in defense
of what is right and true. What do we need to confess this day?

PRAYER OF CONFESSION

God of all people, we have cared more for our safety and popularity than
for the needs of those without power or defense. We have stopped our ears
to the cries of sisters and brothers. We have closed our eyes when there is
wrongdoing. Sometimes our jealousies and skepticism prevail when you
are calling us to new ways of responding. Save us, O God; in your righteousness deliver us, for we cannot save ourselves. Amen.

ASSURANCE OF FORGIVENESS

God does not hold our sin against us or put us to shame. We have already
received the mercy of God, which we earnestly and honestly seek. God

is faithful in equipping us to grow into salvation. Our Creator sees our affliction and delivers us from our enemies. We are God's people, and God is ever our rock and our fortress.

COLLECT

Faithful God, eager to reveal to us your marvelous light, explain to us now what it is necessary for us to know. Show us the way you would have us go, that your will may be accomplished among us. As we examine the scriptures, we would receive your word with eagerness. May it equip us to do the greater work to which you call us, that the world may see you and believe. Amen.

OFFERTORY INVITATION

The truth for which Stephen gave his life has been passed on to us as a gift. The Christ, whom Paul proclaimed against fearful odds, has become our Savior because many before us have kept the faith and shared it. The spiritual sacrifices of many have contributed to our legacy of faith. It is our privilege to pass on these gifts through our tithes and offerings, through our giving of self.

OFFERTORY PRAYER

We dedicate these gifts and ourselves to you, Generous God, for we want to accomplish the greater works to which Christ calls us. Increase our generosity that we may learn to give in proportion to the mercy we have received. Ready us for the sacrifices that may be required of all who seek to live in faithful response to the way, the truth, and the life. May the programs supported by our offerings turn us and many others from our vain idols and distracting pursuits. Amen.

COMMISSION AND BLESSING

God has prepared a place for you;
go out to live as citizens of God's realm.
   Into God's hands, we commit our spirits;
   in God's work, we would spend our days.
You are a chosen people, gifted by God's grace;
through you, the family of faith may grow.
   We are believers, and thus priests of God;
   others will know they are God's own through us.
Be empowered as you examine the scriptures;
declare the wonderful deeds of God in your life.
   We are ready to turn the world upside down;
   we will share the steadfast love we have received.
Amen. **Amen.**

(See hymns nos. 59, 60.)

Sixth Sunday of Easter

Lesson 1:   Acts 17:22–31
               Psalm 66:8–20
Lesson 2:   1 Peter 3:13–22
Gospel: John 14:15–21

CALL TO WORSHIP

Come and hear, all you who fear God.
Listen to one another as you tell what God has done.
God has listened to our prayers in steadfast love;
God has tested us, but has not rejected us.
Have no fear, and do not be troubled;
the Spirit of truth dwells in you.
God is never far from us, even though unknown;
the Spirit gives us breath and keeps us alive.
Bless God, all nations; let praise be heard.
God has brought us to this time and place.
In Christ we live and move and have our being.
We are made righteous and restored to wholeness.

INVOCATION

Elusive God, we seek to feel your presence and to experience the reality of
your promises. We want to keep your commandments and to do what is
right, but we wish that were not so costly. We long for your love to reign
in the world, yet we want to confine you to the shrines we have made.
Come dwell in us, we pray, that we may break out of the narrowness of
our limited vision. Go with us through fire and water to sustain us in life's
troubles. Be known to us now, through Christ. Amen.

CALL TO CONFESSION

Before the judgment of our Creator, our best intentions and highest accomplishments seem so feeble. We do not want to admit our paltry efforts
or glaring omissions. We would rather avoid looking at hurts we have inflicted on others. But Christ invites us to full confession, that we may be
freed for new life.

PRAYER OF CONFESSION

Forgive us, God, for religion without passion and relationships that lack
compassion. Take away the divisive attitudes that separate us from individuals and groups who are different from us. Release us from jealousy
and iniquity and self-serving comparisons. Help us to see ourselves as you
intend us to be, through Christ. Amen.

ASSURANCE OF FORGIVENESS

In Christ, God assures us, "I will not leave you orphaned; I am coming to you." God loves us and hears our prayers. God is waiting to flood our lives with healing and hope. We are reconciled to one another and to our own best selves. Live in gentleness and reverence, as a people released from guilt and shame.

COLLECT

Speak to us, Holy Counselor, and empower us to live by eternal values. Dwell in us, Spirit of Truth, to fill us with love that surpasses knowledge. Manifest your presence in us, to link us with all who seek your will and long to unite as your people. Make us channels of hope to more of your children. Amen.

OFFERTORY INVITATION

Praise God with sacrificial offerings. Return thanks to the Creator, who gives us life and breath. Manifest God's love for the world through your sharing. Reaffirm your baptism as you dedicate your time and talents with the material gifts God has loaned to you.

OFFERTORY PRAYER

We give that others may live. We give to praise you for life and love. We give to share with the world the presence and promise of the God unknown to them, in whom we live and move and have our being. May these tokens of your abundant mercy give counsel and hope to your children near and far. Amen.

COMMISSION AND BLESSING

God, made known to us here, goes with us;
God's love will be manifest through us.
   God's promises are faithful and true.
   we will dare to do what is right and good.
God, who raised Jesus, has lifted us up;
we have been granted new life in Christ.
   In Christ, we are alive to life's possibilities;
   we will celebrate life in ourselves and others.
The Spirit of truth dwells in us;
we will live in the Spirit day by day.
   We will listen to the Counselor within.
   we will give heed to Reality beyond us.
Amen. **Amen.**

(See hymn no. 61.)

Ascension *(or Seventh Sunday of Easter)*

Lesson 1:   Acts 1:1–11
                    Psalm 47
Lesson 2:   Ephesians 1:15–23
Gospel: Luke 24:46–53 *or* Mark 16:9–16, 19–20

CALL TO WORSHIP
Why do we stand looking up to heaven?
The signs of God are all around us.
We are here to remember and rejoice.
We pray God will enlighten our eyes.
Why do we live as if nothing has happened?
Jesus Christ has been seen alive among us.
We have come to challenge our unbelief.
We have gathered to share in the story.
When will we witness to all Jesus taught and did?
We have been commissioned to share the joy.
We want to sing and pray and clap our hands.
We profess Jesus Christ as head of the church.

INVOCATION
Ruler of earth and heaven, we do not know your times and seasons, but we wait for your promise to be fulfilled. Reveal to us here enough of your wisdom and purpose for us to act today as your people. Confirm in us the good news that releases shouts of joy and the clapping of hands. May we know the hope of your reign, not just in future fulfillment but in present glimpses of life at its best! Amen.

CALL TO CONFESSION
Who has not doubted the joyful message and discounted the messenger? Have we set ourselves up as judge and jury of what is true? Have we proclaimed ourselves rulers of the earth? Do we not need to confess our pretensions?

PRAYER OF CONFESSION
God of all worlds, we admit our desire, at times, to cut off the earth from any rule but our own. We revere our nation before all others; we elevate our perceptions as the norm for all. We want to control time and circumstances to our own advantage. Faith is too vague to be real, and love too fleeting to trust. We shrink from the risks of living by the Spirit's leading. Turn us around, we pray, before it is too late. Amen.

ASSURANCE OF FORGIVENESS
Jesus upbraided the disciples for their stubbornness, but they were forgiven. God comes to us in our unbelief, not to condemn, but to correct.

Our eyes are being enlightened. Our ears are retuned to good news. Our tongues are loosened to utter praises welling up within us. We are a forgiven and forgiving people.

COLLECT

Reigning God, whose appearances among us came in many forms, grant that we may be alert and responsive to your presence. When our limited expectations cut us off from you, open our senses to new experiences, not just for ourselves but that the world may believe. May that relationship of trust open up vistas of service that link all humankind in caring community. Amen.

OFFERTORY INVITATION

Our lives have been so richly blessed that we often take our heritage for granted. We look up to heaven, expecting increases as our due. How much more should our hearts be raised in thanksgiving and our hands outstretched, not to receive, but to share! What a privilege and joy it is to return a portion of all we have received.

OFFERTORY PRAYER

With these offerings, we proclaim the good news we believe. With these gifts, we go into all the world with the joy of the gospel. Through our giving, we preach to the whole creation that promises and power of God that we have experienced. Thank you, God, for faith and love, for knowledge and wisdom, for all the seasons of life that present us with opportunities for growth and fulfillment. Receive our gifts and our renewed commitment. Amen.

COMMISSION AND BLESSING

The gifts of heaven have come to us;
the signs of God are everywhere in the world.
We rejoice in all God reveals to us daily;
we give thanks for eyes to see God's world.
God has come to us here; our world is changed.
The risen Christ has appeared, even to us.
Faith keeps emerging from our unbelief.
Our stories are linked with the biblical story.
Go and tell; clap hands and shout for joy:
Jesus Christ is alive and empowers our lives.
We return to our homes with great joy.
The head of the church, Jesus Christ, goes with us.
Amen. **Amen.**

(See hymns nos. 62, 63.)

Seventh Sunday of Easter

Lesson 1:   Acts 1:6–14
                Psalm 68:1–10
Lesson 2:   1 Peter 4:12–14; 5:6–11
Gospel: John 17:1–11

CALL TO WORSHIP

Let the righteous be joyful and exult before God!
Sing to God, sing praises to God's name.
The Spirit of God rests upon us;
the glory of Christ has been revealed to us!
God has granted us homes in which to dwell.
God draws us into a spiritual community.
God's goodness provides for the needy;
God's power equips us to witness.
Come now, that we may pray together.
Let us lift up songs to One who rides on the clouds.
We come to the source of life for new strength.
We seek unity within and among us.

INVOCATION

We have come together, O God, longing for a glimpse of heaven. Out of the clamor and fiery ordeal of the world, we bring our anxieties and suffering to this place of meeting. Here we find others who share our quest for meaning and purpose. Here we can reflect on your generosity, and take time to pray. Reveal yourself to us here, so we may recognize your presence with us in other times and places. Amen.

CALL TO CONFESSION

When we look up in awe to know our Creator, how dare we stand? When the glory of Christ is revealed, who among the disciples can claim to be faithful? Here we are in the presence of Truth. Let us truthfully acknowledge our need for restoration and empowerment.

PRAYER OF CONFESSION

Receive us, God, a fearful and broken people. Receive us in all our false pride and shattered humanity. Embrace us in our bewilderment and anxiety. Save us from the wrong we do and the evil we allow. Tame our rebellion, strengthen our faith, and establish your reign among us. Grant us courage to live more fully as your people. Amen.

ASSURANCE OF FORGIVENESS

God is present to assure us of unfailing love. The Spirit of God rests upon us with healing power. God restores, establishes, and strengthens us. Surely we have been forgiven. Surely we are blessed. Rejoice and be glad. Sing praises to God's name.

COLLECT

God of Glory, in whose service we sense the eternal amid the everyday, we would be your witnesses. May we see through your eyes, that our thoughts may be your thoughts and our words be those you would have us speak. May our actions glorify your name and our prayers unite us with all your children in seeking that better world you intend. Keep us in your name, and make us one. Amen.

OFFERTORY INVITATION

The rains of God come in abundance. God provides daily for our needs. How shall we show our gratitude? Giving is not a dutiful obligation so much as a delightful opportunity. What a joy to give thanks! What a blessing to be able to share!

OFFERTORY PRAYER

All we have is from you, O God. All that we enjoy is the rich bounty of your love poured out on us. In Christ, we have witnessed your care; in Christ, we have learned to share. In joy, we worship you with our gifts and present ourselves for your blessing. Send your Spirit once more to empower our service, in Christ's name. Amen.

COMMISSION AND BLESSING

Look up, and look around you.
God blesses you with companions for life's journey.
Let God rise up, let God's enemies be scattered;
let all who live in hate flee before God!
God empowers us as messengers of good news;
God equips us to face our adversaries.
Let Christ live once more in our witness;
let good be accomplished through our suffering.
Live as a prayerful and giving people;
the God of grace will be with you.
Let us praise God in the wilderness.
Let us celebrate God's presence everywhere.
Amen. **Amen.**

(See hymns nos. 64, 65.)

PENTECOST AND AFTER

Pentecost

Lesson 1:   Acts 2:1–21 *or* Isaiah 44:1–8
               Psalm 104:24–34
Lesson 2:   1 Corinthians 12:3b–13 *or* Acts 2:1–21
Gospel: John 20:19–23 *or* John 7:37–39

CALL TO WORSHIP

The day has come, and we are together;
let us face bravely into the winds of God.
We are listening for the sounds from heaven;
we hear the rush of a violent wind.
Surely God is in this place!
How manifold are the works of God!
The Spirit of God fills us with amazement.
God sets us afire with wonder and awe.
We will sing to God as long as we live;
we will celebrate the gifts of God.
Together we are members of one body;
all have been baptized by the Spirit.

INVOCATION

In joyous expectation, we celebrate the birthday of your church. Pour out your Spirit on all flesh, that our sons and daughters may prophesy, the young see visions and the old dream dreams. Re-create us as daring people, open to the new possibilities you offer. Calm our fears, lest they block us from receiving your power. Refashion our doubts, that they may lead to bold inquiry rather than cautious retreat. Come, Holy Spirit, to reform your church. Amen.

CALL TO CONFESSION

Before the wonders of God, we live too often as bored and skeptical people. We doubt what we cannot see and resist what we do not understand. We hide behind closed doors while a needy world awaits our witness. The God who created us calls us back into a relationship of trust and obedience.

PRAYER OF CONFESSION

God of Majesty and Power, we tremble when we become aware of who you are. All worlds are in your hands. Who are we that you should visit us or expect something from us? We confess our preference for the predictable. We admit our resistance to the Spirit. We acknowledge our misuse of gifts you grant to us. We prefer our divisions to your unity. Forgive us, God of hosts, that we may forgive. Draw us back into a right relationship with you, so that we may remember to share your forgiveness with the world. Amen.

ASSURANCE OF FORGIVENESS

God has reached out to us once again, offering salvation, making us whole, drawing us into the body of Christ, where life is integrated and meaningful. The Spirit comes to us, making holy the commonplace. In a cup of water, in the touch of a hand, in a breath, God blesses and equips us. We are pardoned that we might share God's wonders.

COLLECT

God of all nations, who sent Jesus among us as a messenger of peace, grant living water to quench our thirst. Speak your word to nurture our faith. Send your Spirit to empower our service. Awaken in us the gifts you have granted us, that your vision for the world may become our vision. Amen.

OFFERTORY INVITATION

God has fed us, and we have not noticed. God fills our lives with good things, and we take the credit. God's gifts are so numerous we cannot count them. Now is the time to declare by our giving that we are grateful. Now is the time to claim the mission God entrusts to us as we express our thanks.

OFFERTORY PRAYER

O God, we have thirsted and you provided water. We have been hungry and you have fed us. We have been torn and bewildered and you gave us your peace. We rejoice and give thanks for all your gifts. May our offerings and our lives witness to rebirth and renewal. Send us into your world strengthened and freed by the Holy Spirit to respond to people and circumstances as Christ's disciples. Amen.

COMMISSION AND BLESSING

The wisdom of God has been shared with us;
re-creation and renewal have been offered us.
   O God, how manifold are your works!
   In wisdom you have made them all.
In Christ, we are one body, united and uniting.
Varied gifts are preparing us for service.
   The waters of baptism have drawn us together;
   the Spirit is given to each for the common good.
The Spirit has visited us and prepared us to dream;
wind and fire have equipped us to witness.
   We have been filled with the Holy Spirit;
   let us dare to speak and act as inspired people.
Amen. **Amen.**

(See hymns nos. 66, 67, 68.)

Trinity Sunday *(First Sunday After Pentecost)*

Lesson 1:   Deuteronomy 4:32–40
                    Psalm 33:1–12
Lesson 2:   2 Corinthians 13:5–14
Gospel: Matthew 28:16–20

CALL TO WORSHIP

God, who is always with us, is present here;
rejoice in God, all you righteous ones.
   Play skillfully on harp and lyre and strings;
   praise God with a new song.
God, who has displayed terrifying power, welcomes us;
the earth is full of the steadfast love of God.
   The work of God is done in faithfulness;
   God loves righteousness and justice.
Stand in awe before the counsel of God;
there is one God who speaks and disciplines.
   God has chosen us as a heritage;
   we will proclaim God's statutes and commandments.

INVOCATION

Amazing God, Creator and Confronter, open our hearts to hear your voice
in unexpected times and places. Appear to us in forms we cannot deny.
Challenge us in ways we cannot avoid. Lead us in paths from which we
cannot turn back. Discipline us, that our self-discipline may be better in-
formed and more consistent. Test us that we may test ourselves by the
model of Christ, in whose name we pray. Amen.

CALL TO CONFESSION

In these moments, we are invited to examine ourselves to see whether we
are holding to our faith. Do others see Jesus Christ through us? Do we build
up rather than tear down? Do we devote ourselves to the teachings and
commandments that are our spiritual heritage? Let our personal reflections
and corporate prayer deal honestly with these questions.

PRAYER OF CONFESSION

Ever-present God, we have ignored your presence and denied your power.
We have doubted rather than trusting you. We have complained when we
should have celebrated. We have pursued private agendas while you summon us to community concern. We have kept our faith to ourselves when
you call us to share good news. Forgive our unfaithfulness, O God, and
enable us to mend our ways. Amen.

ASSURANCE OF FORGIVENESS

Rejoice in the mighty acts of God among our ancestors in the faith. Give thanks that God's wonders and signs continue. God still speaks and acts. We are richly blessed by our Creator, who loves, forgives, and promises to be with us. The counsel of God stands forever. Greet one another, therefore, as forgiven people whose lives are renewed by God's grace.

COLLECT

Sovereign God, by whose grace we have been commissioned as disciples of Jesus Christ, turn our doubts to gladness for your truth. Open us to the authority of Jesus Christ, in whose name we were baptized. Teach us, so we can teach. Enrich our lives to such attractiveness that others around us will be drawn to Christ and want to become disciples. Amen.

OFFERTORY INVITATION

The God who brought Israel out of Egypt still calls nations and peoples out of bondage. This is the work of the church, to which we are committed. Wherever truth and freedom are suppressed, we are called to proclaim God's will for self-giving love and genuine peace. Our offerings help to make this possible.

OFFERTORY PRAYER

May our offering, O God, be a fitting response to your manifold gifts. May it help to communicate the wonders of your mighty hand and outstretched arm, by which we are protected and blessed. May it send others to give counsel in nations where we cannot go, while equipping us here for the witness we are called to make. Keep us humbly aware that we have much to learn from your children in other times, places, and circumstances. Link us in discipleship. Amen.

COMMISSION AND BLESSING

Go and make disciples of all nations.
Teach them to obey everything that Christ has commanded.
Christ is alive in us, perfecting God's truth among us.
We greet one another as saints in Christ Jesus.
Agree with one another and live in peace;
the God of love and peace will be with you.
We will keep God's statutes and commandments;
we will discipline ourselves for the ministry we share.
The grace of Jesus Christ, and the love of God,
and the communion of the Holy Spirit be with you all.
In steadfast love, God upholds and strengthens us.
In faithfulness, God blesses and equips us to serve.
Amen. **Amen.**

(See hymns nos. 69, 70.)

Pentecost 2 – Sunday Between May 29 and June 4
(if after Trinity Sunday)

Lesson 1:   Genesis 12:1–9
                    Psalm 33:12–22
Lesson 2:   Romans 3:21–28
Gospel: Matthew 7:21–29

CALL TO WORSHIP

Happy are all whom God has chosen as a heritage;
come to God, who welcomes all humankind.
God fashions our hearts and observes our deeds;
all who express awe before God will be blessed.
God's eye is on all who hope in God's steadfast love.
God's grace abides in all who live by faith.
We wait in silent expectation for God's revelation.
Our hearts are glad, for we trust in God's holy name.
In our moments together, God shows us a new way.
God blesses us, that we may be a blessing to others.
We have come to know God more fully.
We are here to join our voices in worship and praise.

INVOCATION

Let your steadfast love, O God, be upon us, even as we hope in you. Deliver us from the death of selfish ambition and self-centered pursuits. Keep us from misplaced trust in weapons and defenses. Draw us away from pretense and boasting. Lead us to know ourselves truly, as we bow before your majesty. We are your children, knowing the benefits of your love and the responsibilities that come with the gift of life. Amen.

CALL TO CONFESSION

The apostle Paul said it simply and pointedly: "All have sinned and fall short of the glory of God." The measure of our faithfulness is not our goodness in comparison to others, but the ways our lives reflect divine radiance. Do we walk humbly with our God moment by moment, day by day?

PRAYER OF CONFESSION

God, you have forgiven us many times. Still we wander away from you, living as if we need not account to anyone for our words or deeds. We depend on our own cunning rather than on your direction. We flex our muscles instead of relying on your mercy. We build our lives on other foundations than the one you have given us in Jesus Christ. We boast of our accomplishments rather than your generous provision for us. Merciful God, we need your forgiveness again. Amen.

ASSURANCE OF FORGIVENESS

We are justified by God's grace as a gift. The good works we do are not to earn God's favor, but become our joyful response to God's righteousness and mercy. God has passed over our former sins. God welcomes the renewal of our faith. We rejoice in God's welcome to all who repent and are truly sorry for past mistakes and broken promises. God restores us to full relationship with the Eternal.

COLLECT

Sovereign Parent, whose word we have heard again and again, show us your will for us once more. Open our ears to hear your word in fresh ways. Open our wills to respond with renewed purpose. Open our lips to share the good news with the gentle authority of Christ, not so that we may be justified, but that others may be blessed and your name glorified in all the earth. Amen.

OFFERTORY INVITATION

How can we make sure that others will hear the good news that has meant so much to us? How will they learn to build their houses on rock, not on sand? Who will be present to help when the rains fall and the winds blow and people feel beaten and alone? The church is present as a visible embodiment of God's care. It is our thankful support that continues to make this possible.

OFFERTORY PRAYER

We dedicate all we have to your will and way. We set aside these tokens for our common ministry in Christ's name. May this church teach with the authority of Christ. May we venture into new territory with the courage of Abraham. May we serve with the conviction of Paul. May we do all to the glory of your holy name. Amen.

COMMISSION AND BLESSING

Not everyone who speaks of God will be blessed.
Seek, rather, to live by the faith that is ours.
   May our words be expressions of humble trust.
   May our deeds be full of thanksgiving.
God's blessing is given neither for words nor for deeds;
God's steadfast love is a gift, freely given.
   Praise God for generous promises and unexpected gifts;
   thank God for a heritage of love and hope.
Let us live with thanksgiving and with hope.
Let us build on the foundation of Jesus Christ.
   We will pass on what we have received;
   we will help each other build on solid ground.
Amen. **Amen.**

(See hymn no. 71.)

Pentecost 3 – Sunday Between June 5 and June 11
(if after Trinity Sunday)

Lesson 1:   Genesis 22:1–18
               Psalm 13
Lesson 2:   Romans 4:13–18
Gospel: Matthew 9:9–13

CALL TO WORSHIP

Come, all people: righteous and sinners,
rejoice together in the salvation God offers.
How long will you forget us, O God?
How long will you hide your face from us?
We may forget the Creator, source of our lives,
but God does not forget us in our need.
How shall we trust when our lives are shaken?
How can we worship when we are afraid?
God calls to us to assure and comfort us;
the promises of God give us hope.
Will God ease the sorrow of our hearts?
Dare we look to God to heal the pain of our souls?

INVOCATION

Consider and answer us, O Sovereign God. Lighten our eyes lest we become the walking dead, numb and unfeeling. Save us from those who seek our harm, and from our own fears and doubts. Grant us faith that moves beyond adherence to the law. Help us to trust enough to climb mountains when the tops are not visible, when answers to our questions elude us. Let us hear your voice to give us direction. Let us know your purposes, that we may obey. Amen.

CALL TO CONFESSION

We are together as a seeking people who often misunderstand God's intention for us. It is often hard to make sense of life or faith. When we give up the search for meaning, the emptiness grows, and we feel cut off from the One who seeks to bless us.

PRAYER OF CONFESSION

God of our Ancestors, we confess that we have denied you by our neglect of true worship and our lack of faithful response to your direction. When you have invited us to follow Christ, we have often pretended not to hear, or have turned away to pursue other interests. We have substituted ritual for commitment and pious words for caring deeds. Forgive our lack of faith, O God, and restore to us knowledge that your promises are for us. Amen.

ASSURANCE OF FORGIVENESS

The promises of God rest on grace, not on our deserving. God is willing, at any time, to restore us to a right relationship with our Maker, with other persons, and with our own best selves. God will provide for us when we ask and will bless us when we are merciful. Live by faith and by the best you know. The Eternal One is with us in all circumstances.

COLLECT

Great Teacher and Physician, whose love embraces saints and sinners, call us through your word to new places and experiences. Join us at our tables and in all our ventures. Grant us faith to hear and understand what you want us to learn. Hear the pain and sorrow that keep us from fullness of life, in the footsteps of Christ. Amen.

OFFERTORY INVITATION

In gratitude and devotion, we approach this time of giving. What are we willing to sacrifice for the sake of the gospel? God has provided for us in unexpected ways. Let us worship with joy through our offerings.

OFFERTORY PRAYER

We remember and give thanks, O God, as you provide for all our needs. Your love has kept us from foolish mistakes and selfish ambition. Your bounty enables our giving of self and substance. Lead us now that we may be generous and inspire generosity in others. We would withhold nothing from you; employ us and our gifts for your purposes. Amen.

COMMISSION AND BLESSING

Lift up your eyes to see where God sends you.
Let your worship continue as you serve.
May God enlighten our eyes and hearts;
we seek to meet God in daily prayer.
God will provide on mountaintops and in the valleys.
As we seek to obey God's will, we are blessed.
God's mercy and grace fill us with hope.
God's promises summon us to fuller life.
Follow Christ, who calls us as disciples.
Follow Christ to minister to all who need healing.
With joy, we claim our role as disciples.
With trust, we dare to go where Christ sends us.
Amen. **Amen.**

(See hymn no. 72.)

Pentecost 4 – Sunday Between June 12 and June 18
(if after Trinity Sunday)

Lesson 1:   Genesis 25:19–34
              Psalm 46
Lesson 2:   Romans 5:6–11
Gospel: Matthew 9:35–10:8

CALL TO WORSHIP

Come to enjoy the mighty works of God.
Be still, and know that God is God.
God is our refuge and strength,
a very present help in trouble.
In the midst of turmoil, confusion and change,
God is with us to support and uphold.
We rejoice in God, who answers prayer,
who is with us in our suffering and grief.
We have been reconciled to God through Christ.
Rejoice this day in the love of God.
We marvel that God knows us and cares for us.
We come in awe that God calls us together.

INVOCATION

From the trembling foundations of the earth, we come to worship. From
the changing scenes of nations and peoples, we assemble to ponder your
word and remember your works. From the fears that overwhelm us, we
flee to your presence, asking you to speak once more, Mighty God. Come
within us to bring strength, overcoming our weakness. Come among us to
build community, turning our differences into creative energy. Receive us
now as your seeking children. Amen.

CALL TO CONFESSION

Who among us has realized the fullness of life God intends for us? Have we
not settled for immediate gratification rather than long-term good? Were
there not times when we compromised our values for personal gain? Like
Esau and Jacob, we have lived as rivals, not as brothers and sisters. Dare
now to seek a better way.

PRAYER OF CONFESSION

God of all people, we confess to you our rivalries and deceit. We have not
lived by the best that we know. We have identified as enemies persons who
are different from us, while you call us to be family. We have closed our
eyes to needs around us, afraid of what we might lose if we respond. We
have received in abundance and made skimpy return. You have given us
life, and we have hoarded it as our own. O God, move us out of our tiny

orbits of self-interest that we may dare to enlist as laborers in your harvest. Amen.

ASSURANCE OF FORGIVENESS

The God of hosts has shown love for all people, even when we have acted as enemies of one another and of our Creator. While we still were sinners, Christ died for us. While we were rebelling, Christ was reconciling. While we were focusing on fragments, Christ was making whole. Rejoice in all the gifts we receive from God's hand, for we are a forgiven and forgiving people. Amen.

COLLECT

God of the harvest, whose all-seeing eye and all-inclusive love embrace many we choose not to see, equip us for our labors. Grant us eyes and ears attuned to your compassion and to your children's needs. May we discern in the harassed and helpless an opportunity for discipleship. Keep us alert to the commission you are giving us today. Amen.

OFFERTORY INVITATION

The Good Shepherd bids us to send laborers into the harvest. Who will go, proclaiming God's realm? Who will support those who preach and teach and heal in Christ's name? As you received without paying, give without expectation of further reward.

OFFERTORY PRAYER

As we bring our offerings, we pray, O God, that you will send laborers among all your children to preach good news, to bring healing, to feed the hungry. We would support them with our gifts. And if there are tasks for us to do, help us to respond with our lives, not with our leftovers. Amen.

COMMISSION AND BLESSING

God, who has been present here, goes with us.
God will continue to work within and among us.
   The Good Shepherd has met us here;
   we are no longer harassed and helpless.
God, whose strength we celebrate, empowers us.
God sends us as laborers into the harvest.
   God has claimed our energies once more;
   we have been equipped for service.
Go forth in the love of God, reconciled and blessed;
as you have been healed, bring healing to others.
   The Spirit empowers our ministry and mission.
   We claim the values that transcend our differences.
Amen. **Amen.**

(See hymns nos. 73, 74.)

Pentecost 5 – Sunday Between June 19 and June 25
(if after Trinity Sunday)

Lesson 1:   Genesis 28:10–17
                  Psalm 91:1–10
Lesson 2:   Romans 5:12–19
Gospel: Matthew 10:24–33

CALL TO WORSHIP

Come, dwell in the shelter of the Most High;
abide in the shadow of the Almighty.
    God is our refuge and our fortress;
    in God we trust.
God will deliver you from the terrors of night;
in this place, you will find the shelter of God's wings.
    God is with us as we gather;
    God will keep us wherever we go.
Pause to experience the grace of God;
know that God values you, individually and together.
    How awesome is this place!
    This is the house of God and the gate of heaven.

INVOCATION

God of our dreams and of our waking hours, we give you thanks for all your promises to us. You have said you will accept us and keep us wherever we go. You have set aside resources for our use. How awesome are your blessings in all the earth. Open our spirits to receive the gifts of your grace. Open our lives to receive and fulfill the assignments you would give us. May we worship with true devotion. Amen.

CALL TO CONFESSION

Sometimes when darkness descends on our broken promises and dishonest dealings, we must wrestle in our dreams with the God who calls us to greater faithfulness. If we are truly to worship God, we need to confess all that cuts us off from God and bars for us the gate of heaven.

PRAYER OF CONFESSION

Loving God, you know our hidden thoughts and deeds. You judge us in our disobedience and lack of faith. We aspire to honors we do not deserve and to places of privilege you do not intend. Our sins not only injure ourselves but also hurt other people. O God, deliver us from ourselves, that we may learn from our teacher, Jesus Christ. Turn us away from unworthy aspirations, that we may identify fully with those whom we seek to serve. Unite us all as your children, learning and serving together. Amen.

ASSURANCE OF FORGIVENESS

Forgiveness is God's free gift to us, needing only to be received with penitent hearts. By the grace of God, we are made righteous in Jesus Christ. We need not fear, because we are of unlimited value to God, who loves us. Our Sovereign, who led our ancestors in faith, will also lead us where we need to go. God will bless the earth's people, even through us.

COLLECT

God of Revelation, whose will is our fullest joy, call us now into the light where we may learn and teach as humble disciples. Keep the souls of your servants pure, that our highest intent may be to do your will. May all who deny you be turned around to join with all humanity in praising you. Amen.

OFFERTORY INVITATION

God has entrusted the earth to our stewardship. Once again, we give account of our management as we return a fair portion to do the work of the church. How can we give thanks for the free gift of God's forgiving grace? How shall we honor the One who numbers the hairs on our heads and weeps for those persons unvalued and forgotten in our midst?

OFFERTORY PRAYER

We worship you with our offerings, Great God of all people. With these tokens, we remember all your kindness to us. We would live gratefully day by day, appreciating the wondrous gift of life, caring for the bodies you have given us, and disciplining ourselves as your servants. Inspire us to do our part, that our lives may teach your truth. Amen.

COMMISSION AND BLESSING

Go forth as disciples of Jesus Christ;
find ways to serve as Christ served.
   In confidence, we go to make our witness;
   in humility, we dare to represent our Savior.
God has blessed you with an abundance of grace;
God has claimed you in Jesus Christ.
   We will proclaim God's faithfulness;
   we will share our experience and learn from others.
God goes with you wherever you dwell;
God blesses you, and others through you.
   We will abide in the shadow of the Almighty;
   how awesome is the presence of God in all places!
Amen. **Amen.**

(See hymn no. 75.)

Pentecost 6
Sunday Between June 26 and July 2

Lesson 1:   Genesis 32:22–32
               Psalm 17:1–7, 15
Lesson 2:   Romans 6:3–11
Gospel: Matthew 10:34–42

CALL TO WORSHIP

The God of steadfast love calls us together.
We are gifted by God's promised presence.
God names us and gathers us as one body;
God inclines an ear to us and hears our prayers.
When we meet God, there is refuge for us;
when we meet God, there is also struggle and pain.
God leads us to face ourselves and our potential;
God prompts us to wrestle with our fears.
God calls us to daring commitment and service.
In Christ, we take the risks of faithful discipleship.
We come to hear God's promises once more;
we dare to seek the new life Christ offers.

INVOCATION

In awe and wonder, we meet you here, O God of the prophets and our God. We have struggled with you in lonely places and praised you in the company of your people. We have cried out to you, and you have shown your steadfast love. We have resisted you, and you have drawn us back into the circle of Christ's disciples. Pour out your blessing on each one, we pray. Hear our prayers, and renew our spirits. Amen.

CALL TO CONFESSION

We are sometimes people of unrealized vision and unfulfilled dreams. Our wrestling with forces within and beyond us exhausts rather than empowers. We have missed the mark so often that we sometimes feel enslaved to sin. Yet God visits us at night and accompanies us by day, seeking to welcome and bless. Let us be open to God's transforming spirit.

PRAYER OF CONFESSION

God of the prophets, hear our cries. We do not intend to deceive or to utter lies. We seek to avoid violence and divisions. We want to live peaceably among all people. Yet we find ourselves violating the best we know and shrinking from situations that call for courageous witness. We are far from realizing the full life you intend for us. Hear us. Forgive us. Bless us, we pray, through Christ. Amen.

ASSURANCE OF FORGIVENESS

God meets us face to face and listens to our every longing. In Christ, we are given a refuge and are saved from our deceits. We are freed to give up our old ways and to walk in newness of life. Let us live, then, as people who are dead to sin and alive to God in Christ Jesus. Amen.

COLLECT

God of abundant mercy, we turn to you for water for all your thirsting children. We come seeking your hospitality, that we may be equipped to welcome others. We reach for those high standards of commitment which you call forth, that our loyalties may not be misplaced. Keep us from easy assurances that would lure us from the challenges of faithful living. Amen.

OFFERTORY INVITATION

We have been blessed with gifts we have not sought. We have received strength amid our struggles. We have been raised from death to new life. Even our wounds remind us of a God who cares for us and counts us worthy to bear the name of Christ. Let us give thanks, and our full commitment, as we dedicate our offerings.

OFFERTORY PRAYER

For your abounding grace, we give thanks, O God. For your steadfast love, we pour out our gratitude. May our gifts provide for those who seek refuge from doubt, from oppression, from ignorance, from calamity. Through giving in Christ's name, we seek to grow in the Spirit of One who gave life itself for us. Amen.

COMMISSION AND BLESSING

God has named us anew and commissions us to serve.
Go forth to fulfill your baptism as Christ's disciples.
Our steps will hold fast to paths where God directs;
our lips will proclaim God's steadfast love.
Live as people freed from bondage to sin;
celebrate the gift of new life in Christ Jesus.
We will dare to say the unsayable, in love,
and do the unpopular when that is necessary.
Welcome all who take up their cross to follow Christ;
minister to the needs of all God's children.
We will cherish the prophet's word and the child's faith.
We will seek first the will of our Creator.
Amen. **Amen.**

(See hymns nos. 76, 77.)

Pentecost 7
Sunday Between July 3 and July 9

Lesson 1:   Exodus 1:6–2:10*
              Psalm 124
Lesson 2:   Romans 7:14–25a
Gospel: Matthew 11:25–30

CALL TO WORSHIP

Come to Christ, all who are weary.
Gather together, all who carry heavy burdens.
Our help is in the name of God,
who made heaven and earth.
Bless God, who is revealed more clearly to infants
than to those considered intelligent and wise.
Thanks be to God through Jesus Christ,
who rescues us from sin and death.
Seek the renewal of your spirits;
delight in God's law in your inmost selves.
Praise God for all who live in awe,
for all who seek to do God's will.

INVOCATION

Visit us, O God, with your protection and guidance. Save us from the wrong we do not intend, and rescue us from the poor choices we sometimes make. Draw us out of the raging waters of our narrow conceits to the wider vision you have for us. Be a midwife to us as we seek new life in Christ. May we find delight in your law and gain wisdom in your service. Amen.

CALL TO CONFESSION

God is on our side, yet how easily we move away from God's side. God is eager to walk with us through the turmoil and troubles of life, yet we hide from God and flee from the only relationship that can fulfill us. God offers us rest and renewal, but we often refuse to turn away from our busy schedules to receive God's gift. Who will rescue us from this body of death?

PRAYER OF CONFESSION

O God, who rescued our spiritual ancestors from their bondage to slavery, deliver us from the sins we confess and the unknown evil we have allowed. How wretched we are, knowing what is right and good, yet failing to do it. How miserable we feel, trying to avoid wrong, yet finding ourselves in the middle of it. How deep is our desolation when we reach for spiritual

---

* *Common Lectionary* reading amplified to include women.

heights yet live in slavery to passions of the flesh. Break these patterns, we pray, to allow our growth in gentle and humble service. Amen.

ASSURANCE OF FORGIVENESS

The Creator of heaven and earth is our helper and will deliver us from the ways of death. We are not destined to live in bondage to our worst selves, but are freed to grow in faith and trust. God promises acceptance and forgiveness through Jesus Christ. The yoke of Christ is easy and the burdens light for those who live their thanks and seek God's will. Thanks be to God!

COLLECT

God of heaven and earth, by whose gracious will we have been privileged to know you through Jesus Christ, reveal yourself once more through ancient word and present action. Lift the heavy burdens we cannot carry alone and the sin that clings so closely, that we may be freed to worship and serve you. As we welcome the yoke of Christ, we seek the gentleness and humility that empower us for the tasks you give us. May we share with all the rest Christ offers the weary.

OFFERTORY INVITATION

In thanks for all we have received, and for the privilege of sharing, we gratefully bring our tithes and offerings.

OFFERTORY PRAYER

We give thanks for all whose courage has passed life and faith to us. We lift up all who trust you, O God, in spite of ruthless oppression. We offer ourselves with our gifts, that right and truth may prevail throughout your world. Amen.

COMMISSION AND BLESSING

Greet the world with refreshed spirits;
go to lift burdens, as yours have been lifted.
God has quieted the wars within us;
God unites us with one another in service.
God dwells with you and strengthens you;
God multiplies your energy and influence.
God has delivered us from slavery to sin;
we receive Christ's easy yoke and light burden.
Go out to listen and to testify.
Open yourself to the wisdom of children.
God is being revealed in all our meetings;
God will be praised in all we say and do.
Amen. **Amen.**

(See hymns nos. 78, 79.)

Pentecost 8
Sunday Between July 10 and July 16

Lesson 1:   Exodus 2:11–22
               Psalm 69:6–15
Lesson 2:   Romans 8:9–17
Gospel: Matthew 13:1–9, 18–23

CALL TO WORSHIP

The Word of God awaits us here; come to worship.
The Holy Spirit welcomes us; gather to pray.
From the routines and struggles of our lives, we come.
Amid the stresses and worries of every day, we gather.
Come to be renewed in the Spirit of Christ;
God is waiting to offer us a new life of freedom.
In hope, we seek God's caring presence;
in faith, we dare to trust God's steadfast love.
Plunge into soul-refreshing waters that invigorate;
offer to one another the bread of life.
We are resident aliens in a foreign land;
God's realm is the true home we are seeking.

INVOCATION

God of hosts, renew in us the hope that survives disappointment and the faith that rises above ridicule. Help us to stand for what is right and to champion the cause of those who have no voice or power of their own. You, O God, are the source of life, our true Parent. By your Spirit, we are your daughters and sons and are sisters and brothers to one another. Equip us to live as members of your family, uniting in your worship and praise. Amen.

CALL TO CONFESSION

Like our spiritual ancestor Moses, we may try to bury our sins, hoping no one will ever know what we have done. Yet we cannot hide our guilt from ourselves, and most certainly we cannot hide our wrongdoing from God. Neither can we run away from ourselves, or from God. We are invited to let go of all that isolates us from God and from our own true selves.

PRAYER OF CONFESSION

Rescue us, O God, from sinking in the mire of pretension and guilt. Save us from the deadly grasp of unacknowledged sin. Keep us from presuming to judge others when we ourselves need even more to be corrected. We confess now, in silence, the offenses we recall. . . . Forgive, we pray, our sins of the flesh, which keep us from life in your Spirit. Amen.

ASSURANCE OF FORGIVENESS

This is God's acceptable time of forgiveness and healing. Even before we sinned, God provided for us a way of restoration and renewal. We are debtors, called to live by the Spirit as heirs with Christ of all God's promises. Live, then, as a free people who celebrate God's mercy and reach out to others in Christ's name. Amen.

COLLECT

Sower of good seed, by whose word we are equipped for fruitful living, we long to be good soil in which your truth can take root. May we hear your word and understand it, not just for ourselves, but for the sake of sisters and brothers who need our faithful witness. Amen.

OFFERTORY INVITATION

Because we care, we give: to lift burdens, to provide fresh water, to share bread, to build self-esteem, to make disciples. Most of all, we give in thankfulness to God, who has multiplied in us great blessings.

OFFERTORY PRAYER

For all who have made life more pleasant for us, we give you thanks, O God. For the abundance of your steadfast love, which rescues and enlivens us, we are most grateful. We present here practical expressions of thanksgiving, to extend your purposes in the world. May this offering scatter seeds of love in life-changing ways. May we learn from all we help, that all of us may grow toward discipleship. Amen.

COMMISSION AND BLESSING

As carriers of the word, your worship continues;
God is worshiped through our daily service.
May our routines be transformed by new awareness,
and our worries be an avenue to true devotion.
Go out from this place, renewed by the Spirit.
God has freed us to pursue life at its fullest.
God's care goes with us into daily life and work.
God's steadfast love is ours to pass on to others.
You are heirs of God's promise, with Christ.
You are God's adopted and beloved children.
We seek to grow in Christlikeness.
We aspire to bear fruit in caring service.
Amen. **Amen.**

(See hymn no. 80.)

Pentecost 9
Sunday Between July 17 and July 23

Lesson 1:   Exodus 3:1–12
                Psalm 103:1–13
Lesson 2:   Romans 8:18–25
Gospel: Matthew 13:24–43*

CALL TO WORSHIP

God's steadfast love extends beyond the farthest star,
yet that love is also present among us.
   Bless the Lord, O my soul,
   and all that is within me, bless God's holy name.
God's saving acts were experienced by our ancestors,
and God continues to act in our own day.
   Bless the Lord, O my soul,
   and do not forget all God's benefits.
God's concern is for all creation, for all worlds,
yet that care draws us close in these moments.
   The whole creation is filled with eager longing;
   bless the Lord, all who live in hope.

INVOCATION

God of awesome moments and fearful challenges, grant us eyes to see and ears to hear your revelation in our midst today. We have turned aside from our daily routines to encounter your mystery. We have dared to step out of our safe places to hear the cries of your people and observe their affliction. We tremble at the thought of what you may require of us, yet we are eager for your presence and open to your call. Amen.

CALL TO CONFESSION

With the apostle Paul we long to be set free, with all creation, from our bondage to decay. By our own actions, the flame of God's Spirit is so often dimmed within us that others cannot discern it. Yet God is always willing to re-create and renew us as we confess our neglect, wrongdoing, and need.

PRAYER OF CONFESSION

O God, we have pursued futile plans, without seeking your guidance. We have resisted the way you would have us go. We demand proofs before we will believe, yet close our eyes to your wonders on every hand. We do not seek the leaven of your word and Spirit to expand our lives and make them attractive and useful. O Holy One, we need a new vision and the self-discipline to embrace your realm here and now. Help us! Amen.

---

* *Common Lectionary* reading expanded.

ASSURANCE OF FORGIVENESS

As parents long to extend forgiveness and offer a more abundant life to their children, so God has pity on us when we realize our offenses. When we come before God in awe and amazement, we find God to be merciful and gracious, slow to anger, and abounding in steadfast love. God redeems us from the depths to which we have sunk and removes our transgressions from us. Our lives are made new in the realm of God.

COLLECT

O Great Storyteller, whose life of loving compassion fulfilled all God's intentions for humanity, help us to see the potential greatness in the tiniest of seeds and the quiet influence of a bit of yeast. Grant that we may burst out of our shells to make growth possible. Let us be leaven in your world, not for our glory, but that your realm may expand. May there be an abundant harvest of good among all your children. Amen.

OFFERTORY INVITATION

Who will lead God's children to their promised land? Surely it will be those who have begun to live in the realm of God, who know God's mercy and remember God's benefits. To the extent that our offerings are generous, the church can be the yeast of God in a needy world.

OFFERTORY PRAYER

We bless you, O God, and remember your steadfast love and mercy. We have heard your challenge to us on behalf of our sisters and brothers who are oppressed. With these resources, we would minister to people who suffer in cruel surroundings. With our personal efforts, we would make way for your glorious reign among us. Bless our offerings of self and substance to the glory of your holy name. Amen.

COMMISSION AND BLESSING

The place where you are standing is holy ground.
Where you live and work and play are holy too.
God's steadfast love is with us wherever we go.
We will bless God's holy name every day.
The God our ancestors trusted has a mission for us.
God sees the misery of many in the midst of abundance.
God sends us to our sisters and brothers in need.
We are here to respond to one another's cries.
Wait patiently for what God is yet to reveal.
Live daily in God's realm, with confidence and hope.
We long to be good seeds toward a good harvest;
we mean to live as children of the heavenly realm.
Amen. **Amen.**

(See hymns nos. 82, 83.)

Pentecost 10
Sunday Between July 24 and July 30

Lesson 1:   Exodus 3:13–20
                  Psalm 105:1–11
Lesson 2:   Romans 8:26–30
Gospel: Matthew 13:44–52

CALL TO WORSHIP
O give thanks to God; call on God's name.
Make known God's deeds among the nations.
Sing to God, sing praises to God;
tell of all God's wonderful works.
Glory in God's holy name;
let the hearts of those who seek God rejoice!
Seek God and the strength God provides;
seek God's presence continually.
Remember the wonderful works that God has done,
the miracles, and the judgments God uttered.
God made a covenant with our ancestors;
God keeps covenant with us forever.

INVOCATION
We give you thanks, Holy God, for promises kept and blessings bestowed. Your saving acts introduce us to the realm of heaven we only dimly perceive. Your Spirit reaches out to us with strength and power beyond our understanding. Your glory surrounds us in love too deep for words. Your wonders embrace us on every hand. In these moments we would remember who you are and remind ourselves that we are nothing apart from you. You have made us for life in your realm. Teach us now how to live as you intend. Amen.

CALL TO CONFESSION
God's judgments are in all the earth. God's intentions for human life are clear. We violate God's purposes at our peril, cutting ourselves off from the realm of heaven. We are invited in this time of self-searching and prayer to renew an active relationship with our Creator.

PRAYER OF CONFESSION
We do not know how to pray, Sovereign God. We have doubted you in the face of affliction and ignored you when things go well for us. We have not pursued your realm as the only treasure worth claiming. We have feared to trust your assurance and guidance or to lead the search for your saving purposes. We ask your forgiveness, and seek the renewal of our covenant with you and with one another. Amen.

ASSURANCE OF FORGIVENESS

The Spirit helps us in our weakness, interceding for us and for all God's saints. God points us to the way of forgiveness and freedom. In everything, God works for good with all who love God and are called according to God's purposes. Before we even were, God planned for us to share the image of Christ, to live as believers, to share in the covenant. Praise God!

COLLECT

God of Glory, whose wondrous works are ever before us, open to us the hidden treasure in your Word. With great joy, we would discover anew the riches of heaven. Equip us to be both learners and teachers in your realm, which is being revealed to us in this community of faith. Let all hearts rejoice as we share gladly what we are discovering. Amen.

OFFERTORY INVITATION

Jesus invites us to put the claims of God's realm before all else in our lives, to sacrifice all we have in order to obtain it. God's rule is not only a future promise; it is a present reality, waiting to be accepted by individuals and shared in community. Our offerings and the work we do together are meant to announce and demonstrate the realm of heaven.

OFFERTORY PRAYER

Thanks be to you, O God, for drawing us into covenant and providing for us day by day. Our abilities, and life itself, are gifts from your hand. Because you have promised to work for good with those who love you, we dedicate our offerings to your service. Reveal to us the work of your realm that you intend for us to do. Amen.

COMMISSION AND BLESSING

We know that in everything God works for good.
Look around you this week for the good God is doing.
We will seek to find good in the worst around us,
and we will celebrate the good we find in all places.
You are called, according to God's purposes.
Listen for the ways God wants you to go.
The image of God dwells within us;
the treasures of God's realm are available to us.
God sends you on life's journey with a promise:
God will bring you out of your misery to freedom.
We enter this week with confident enthusiasm;
there is treasure to be found where God rules.
Amen. **Amen.**

(See hymns nos. 84, 85.)

Pentecost 11
Sunday Between July 31 and August 6

Lesson 1:   Exodus 12:1–14
              Psalm 143:1–10
Lesson 2:   Romans 8:31–39
Gospel: Matthew 14:13–21

CALL TO WORSHIP

This is the appointed time of memorial and celebration.
We gather in the festival of worship to honor God.
We stretch out our hands to the living God;
our souls thirst for God like a parched land.
Nothing can separate us from the love of God.
In life and death, in the heights and depths, God is with us.
Our spirits faint within us; our courage fails.
Doubts overwhelm us, and hope is crushed.
Hear once again the promises of God.
Out of nothing, God creates abundance for all our needs.
Let your Spirit, O God, lead us on a level path.
We lift up our souls that you may teach us.

INVOCATION

Hear our prayers, O God, and give ear to our supplications. When life
seems full of enemies and our spirits are crushed, it is hard to believe you
are present. In the darkness of our despair, we know not where to find
you. Let us hear once more of your steadfast love and feel once again the
assurance of One we can trust. Stand with us against rulers and powers,
to deliver us from our fears of things present and things to come, through
Jesus Christ. Amen.

CALL TO CONFESSION

Sin is not just the horrendous acts of a few, but the habitual neglect of all
of us. It is found not only in the things that become our idols, but in the
narrowness of our vision. Sin lurks not so much in our doubts as in our
dogmatic certainties. All that separates us from the living God, who is more
than we can ever imagine, is sin that needs to be confessed.

PRAYER OF CONFESSION

Righteous God, we admit our preoccupation with small concerns and personal problems. The circle of our caring is too often bounded on all sides
by ourselves. When our compassion reaches out to others, it is usually to
those we know well. The embrace of our concern leaves out many we
call enemies, and others unlike ourselves. We find ourselves demanding
much and giving little in return. Yet there are also times when we do not

value ourselves as we should. Do not condemn us, O God. Forgive our distorted ways of thinking and living, that we may be freed to live in true faith. Amen.

ASSURANCE OF FORGIVENESS

God did not spare Jesus from cruelty and death. Yet, in Christ, love triumphed and life for us all was renewed and made whole. It is God who justifies; who is to condemn? Christ is with us; Christ intercedes for us; in Christ, we are raised from the bonds of sin to newness of life. Rejoice, and give thanks.

COLLECT

God of Compassion, whose provision for us is marvelous beyond all expectation, feed us now. When our resources seem as nothing, multiply among us a generous expectancy that makes it possible to share the little we have. Direct our vision beyond ourselves, that we may be participants in your work of feeding all humankind. Amen.

OFFERTORY INVITATION

Our spiritual ancestors followed specific instructions for their offerings. A tithe belonged to God, and sacrifices were expected. Perhaps it is our casual commitment that creates doubts and desperation within and among us. What would happen if all of us were to give in proportion to what we have received, with joy and deepest gratitude?

OFFERTORY PRAYER

O God, we will continue to ask for your healing presence, for we are needy people. We will continue to request blessings from your hand, to call forth the resources you given us. But we will also increase our thanksgiving and our grateful sharing. You have made us more than conquerors through Christ who loved us. Nothing will separate us from that love as we seek to live it every day. Amen.

COMMISSION AND BLESSING

Jesus blessed and broke the food of sharing,
and there was enough for all. Give what you can.
We will not fear famine or thirst;
we will not be bowed down by any lack.
Christ gave life itself on our behalf.
That love sustains us today. Share what you receive.
Distress or peril or sword will not destroy us.
Nothing in all creation can keep us from God's love.
Go forward in confidence and trust;
God's Spirit goes with you to teach and lead.
God's steadfast love renews us each morning.
God's presence is sure in all times and places.
Amen. **Amen.**

(See hymn no. 86.)

Pentecost 12
Sunday Between August 7 and August 13

Lesson 1:   Exodus 14:19–31
               Psalm 106:4–12
Lesson 2:   Romans 9:1–5
Gospel: Matthew 14:22–33

CALL TO WORSHIP
Consider the wonderful works of God;
remember the abundance of God's steadfast love.
> **We have been blessed in ways we have not realized;**
> **we have received more than we could ever deserve.**
See the prosperity and abundance around you;
remember the heritage of a nation richly blessed.
> **How merciful is the God of our ancestors!**
> **How gloriously our nation has prospered!**
We have gathered because we believe God's word;
we are together to sing praise to our Deliverer.
> **We are here to be claimed again by our God.**
> **We have assembled to express our gratitude.**

INVOCATION
Move before us, O God, as we worship and seek your blessing in this hour.
Be to us a light in our darkness to lead the way. Be as a cloud to protect
us from all that would distract us from your truth. Keep us moving toward
the goals you intend and the mission on which you send us. Teach us again
to pray with Christ, that we may have courage to follow without losing
heart. Strengthen our faith as we prepare for life in the world that forgets
or ignores you, and invites us to do the same. Amen.

CALL TO CONFESSION
We have been guided through the rough seas of life by a Presence we have
often ignored. We have survived many perils by the mercy of an unseen
hand. Yet how often have we considered the wonderful works of God or
given thanks to the Source of Life? Let us confess our sin and rebellion.

PRAYER OF CONFESSION
Gracious God, we confess that we have been ungrateful and insensitive,
cutting ourselves off from you and from other people. We do not see our
own iniquity. We do not sense any wickedness in our own ways. We seek
to measure life by our own standards, not yours. We do not recognize our
own lies or the oppression we inflict on people by whose labors we benefit.
Awaken our consciences, we pray, that we may receive pardon and new
life. Amen.

ASSURANCE OF FORGIVENESS

The abundance of God's steadfast love is always available to those ready to receive it. The God of covenant claims us as beloved children, redeemed and forgiven. Rejoice in the gladness of God's people, for God is ready to accomplish great things through us. Live in humble trust, willing to try new ventures. Be alert to opportunities to share what God entrusts to your use.

COLLECT

Sovereign God, whose ways are not our ways, summon us from our safe places to hear your challenge and respond to your invitation. Lead us through our fears to deeper trust. Lift us from our doubts to more winsome faith. Work your miracles in us so we may witness to your mighty power, for the sake of all your children. Amen.

OFFERTORY INVITATION

What is our response to God, who has acted mightily on our behalf, who has blessed us with abundance and prosperity? How will we show our thanks to One who saves us from foes within and beyond us? May our offerings be expressions of gratitude.

OFFERTORY PRAYER

Thank you, God, for guiding us through life. Thank you for the abundance we have enjoyed. Thank you for prospering our efforts and blessing us far beyond our own work. We are grateful for all we have learned when we dared to trust you in difficult times. Use these experiences to your glory. Use our offerings to prosper your mission among us and beyond us. Use our lives to communicate your salvation to all who long for the fullness of life you intend. Amen.

COMMISSION AND BLESSING

Take heart; have no fear; live by faith.
Dare to respond to the invitation of Jesus Christ.
We believe God remembers us and saves us.
We want to follow where Jesus leads.
There are signs of God's presence on every hand;
there is evidence of God's favor all around us.
God is with us at the morning watch;
God is present in the darkest night.
Live with gladness in a nation richly blessed.
Live with generosity for the sake of all people.
We will remember the abundance of God's love.
We will share the heritage we have received.
Amen. **Amen.**

(See hymns nos. 87, 88.)

Pentecost 13
Sunday Between August 14 and August 20

Lesson 1:   Exodus 16:2–15
               Psalm 78:1–3, 10–20
Lesson 2:   Romans 11:13–16, 29–32
Gospel: Matthew 15:21–28

CALL TO WORSHIP

Our faith draws us together this day.
Let us trust enough to open our ears and hearts.
We have heard of God's miracles in other times;
our ancestors have kept the story alive for us.
Give ear, all people, to God's word for today.
Taste the bounty of God's blessing here and now.
We long for a faith that makes sense today.
We want to keep the story alive for new generations.
God's revelation is for all people, near and far.
God is waiting to communicate with you and me.
May God have mercy on us and all people.
Surely God's will shall be made known to us.

INVOCATION

Where are you, O God, when our prayers go unanswered? When our hopes are fulfilled, how will we know it is you who has acted on our behalf? Why do some prayers seem never to be heard? Speak to us, God, for we need yet more proof of your caring presence. There is much we do not understand. Some of what seems clear to us we do not like. Break through our resistance, to meet us here, we pray. Amen.

CALL TO CONFESSION

What attention have we given this week to our covenant with God? Do we recognize God's law, and walk in it? Have we remembered the ways God has led us and provided for us? Or are our lives full of other concerns, so that forgetfulness and rebellion break our relationship with the Eternal?

PRAYER OF CONFESSION

O God, our thoughts are not full of your love. We forget to listen for your guidance. When we speak to you, it is often to beg or complain, not to give thanks. Our greed outruns our gratitude. We live fearfully rather than faithfully. When you assure and bless us, we are not satisfied. O God, we cannot turn ourselves around. Help us to change. Amen.

ASSURANCE OF FORGIVENESS

God's mercy comes to us in our disobedience. God's gracious favor answers our cry for help. God hears our complaining and provides for us in unexpected ways in the desert places of our lives. Come to the saving waters. Taste the bread God gives us to eat. We are a people forgiven and blessed.

COLLECT

God of all people, whose healing grace answers our cries of faith, open our eyes to see your wonders, our hearts to experience your love, our lips to share our faith. Move us from self-concern to inclusive actions, that all your children may be encouraged to explore a vital relationship with you that has a positive impact on your world. Amen.

OFFERTORY INVITATION

Have you not received bountifully from God's hand? Give generously in response. Have you not prayed for the hungry and homeless? Give caringly that they may be helped. Have you not been taught and reminded and comforted by the church? Give to sustain the community of faith in this place.

OFFERTORY PRAYER

For all your gifts — those we remember and all we have not recognized — we give thanks, Loving God. We are grateful for the privilege of giving from the abundance you provide. We are thankful for the influence of this congregation in our lives and in our community. Help us together to use what we have shared to fulfill your purposes. Amen.

COMMISSION AND BLESSING

Go out to gather and share what God provides.
There is work to do; there are people to help.
God rains on us daily the bread of heaven;
it is ours to receive and share.
Be aware in new ways of God's presence.
Be open to God's gifts and God's call.
We will dare to ask questions and risk a response.
We will seek to notice and appreciate God's gifts.
Every morning you will see the glory of God;
every evening you will know God's mercy.
Holiness and mercy are all around us.
On every hand, there are resources to strengthen us.
Amen. **Amen.**

(See hymn no. 89.)

Pentecost 14
Sunday Between August 21 and August 27

Lesson 1:   Exodus 17:1–7
               Psalm 95
Lesson 2:   Romans 11:33–36
Gospel: Matthew 16:13–20

CALL TO WORSHIP

Come, let us sing to our Creator;
make a joyful noise to the rock of our salvation.
We come into God's presence with thanksgiving;
let us make a joyful noise with songs of praise!
Come, let us worship and bow down;
let us kneel before God, our Maker!
This is our God, and we are God's people.
We are like sheep, with God as our shepherd.
O the depth of the wisdom and knowledge of God!
Who can begin to know the mind of God?
How unsearchable are God's judgments;
how inscrutable are God's ways!

INVOCATION

O God, all things come from you, and you are in all things. Yet you are not confined to what we can see or imagine. You are beyond our highest and deepest thoughts of you. The tallest mountains and deepest seas are as nothing before you. The vast reaches of time and space are your design. Sovereign Ruler, how dare we harden our hearts against you? Speak to us here to remind us of your glory and of our need for you. Amen.

CALL TO CONFESSION

Like the Hebrews of old, we find ourselves in the Wilderness of Sin — dry and empty, discouraged and angry, doubting and demanding. We wander in and out of the desert, sometimes staying so long that we are hollow corpses. Wherever we, personally, are today, we know that some of us need desperately to find a way out of the wilderness.

PRAYER OF CONFESSION

Abiding and Eternal God, we confess our desperation. We need water, but our own wells are dry. We are fearful of coming to the living waters, lest they be a mirage. We are afraid to drink deeply from your hand, lest more be asked of us than we are ready to give. We are content so often to go through the motions of religion rather than confess a faith that may be challenged. God, help us. Amen.

ASSURANCE OF FORGIVENESS

God, whatever name we use, is among us. There is a creative, loving Power in the universe on whom we can depend. God smiles on us, even when we test and demand proof. And all around us are the miracles of every day, speaking of a Reality that is so much more than we can know or think. O that today we would listen to the voice of God — the God who refreshes and renews and forgives!

COLLECT

Unknowable God, whom we have glimpsed in Jesus of Nazareth, we await your voice. Speak to us through the Bible, in our inmost thoughts, in our quiet conversations, through those who teach and preach, through all who humbly serve. Bring us to a confession of a faith strong enough to sustain your servant church in a needy world. Amen.

OFFERTORY INVITATION

Who has given a gift to God to receive a gift in return? Who has complained when the faithful fare no better than others? Have we forgotten that the riches of God are far deeper than surface appearances? Have we lost the joy of giving for the sheer exhilaration of celebrating the wonders of life?

OFFERTORY PRAYER

Our offerings are an expression of our faith, O God. They tell of our thankfulness; they speak of blessings received and cheerfully shared. What a privilege is ours, what riches we possess, to be able to give with joy for the work of your church! We worship you with these tokens and the rededication of our lives and work to your will. Amen.

COMMISSION AND BLESSING

God sends us out to bind and to set free.
We have a faith to share in our everyday world.
The Christ we have met here shows us the way.
May our actions reflect the faith we confess.
God bids us drink deeply of life's possibilities;
the fountain of God's love never runs dry.
In the heights and depths we will praise God.
We are, like Peter, rocks from the rock of salvation.
God entrusts to our use the riches of this planet.
We are given knowledge and wisdom to use them well.
Everything comes from God and belongs to God.
To God be the glory forever and ever. Amen.
Amen. **Amen.**

(See hymn no. 90.)

Pentecost 15
Sunday Between August 28 and September 3

Lesson 1:   Exodus 19:1–9
                  Psalm 114
Lesson 2:   Romans 12:1–13
Gospel: Matthew 16:21–28

CALL TO WORSHIP

Tremble, O earth, at the presence of God!
Obey God's voice, and keep covenant with God.
Day by day, we are lifted up on eagles' wings.
Today we have been led to this place of worship.
I appeal to you, sisters and brothers:
remember the mercies of God, and seek God's will.
We bring ourselves as living sacrifices,
that we may be transformed, and our minds renewed.
Seek here what is good and acceptable and perfect.
Recognize once more the gifts God has given you.
We are here to recognize ourselves as one body.
In Christ, we are empowered to be the church.

INVOCATION

In this sanctuary set aside for your worship, we pause to contemplate your greatness, O God. Out of the thick clouds that limit our vision, we hear you whisper our names and call us into community. The mountains and the seas tremble before you; all living things announce your presence. You claim us as your own and equip us to be a holy people. Help us to accept that role without misusing it, that your name may be honored in all we do, and your way be lifted up among all people. Amen.

CALL TO CONFESSION

In what do we take pride? To whose standards do we conform? Is our faith all that God intends? Are we functioning effectively as members of one body? Are we using the gifts God has given for the benefit of all of God's creation? As we examine ourselves before the wonder of God, let us confess all that falls short of God's plan for us.

PRAYER OF CONFESSION

We tremble before you, O God, when we consider our broken and damaged relationships. You have made us for community, but we act as isolates. You seek our transformation and renewal, but we tend rather to conform to the world's agenda. You call us to love that is genuine, and to affectionate devotion, but we have put self-interest first. You have called us to be zealous for the good, but we have become complacent about evil. You have given us gifts to use for the common good, but we have hoarded them for our advantage. Save us from our self-destructive ways. Amen.

ASSURANCE OF FORGIVENESS

Of what advantage will it be to gain the whole world and forfeit our lives? God has entrusted us with the gift of life and challenged us to spend it as followers of Jesus. In Christ, we find our true identity and experience the forgiveness and wholeness God intends for us. God claims us, grants us gifts, and equips us for our service in the world.

COLLECT

God of power and glory, whose ways are not our ways, recall us again to selfless devotion to your will, to what is good and acceptable and perfect. Grant us the courage to follow the way of love in the face of all that would deny it. Speak to us, that we may hear and do what you intend. May we take up the cross, not as a burden, but as a sign of hope. May our cheerful zeal provide a contagious witness for the cause of Christ. Amen.

OFFERTORY INVITATION

The God who bears us up on eagles' wings invites us to participate in the transformation of the world. The church at its best is devoted to nothing less than changing peoples' thoughts and actions to a more loving way. Contribute in liberality; give aid with zeal; serve with caring devotion. Our offerings symbolize our commitment.

OFFERTORY PRAYER

We give our best, Gracious God, lest in gaining the whole world we lose life itself. As a covenant people, we seek to do our part to witness to your will and way. As we give, help us to perceive more clearly what you would have us do with the wealth entrusted to our management. As we contribute to the needs of the saints, we present ourselves as living sacrifices. Direct us according to your will. Amen.

COMMISSION AND BLESSING

Address the world in genuine love and affection.
Hate what is evil; hold fast to what is good.
All that God has spoken, we will do;
we will keep covenant with our Creator.
Walk with Christ in self-giving service;
live in genuine affection as one body in Christ.
We will use our differing gifts faithfully;
we will give our best for the sake of all.
Christ has promised to come to us again.
In Christ, death itself is emptied of its power.
We enter a new week aglow with the Spirit.
we pray that God's will may be done through us.
Amen. **Amen.**

(See hymns nos. 91, 92.)

Pentecost 16
Sunday Between September 4 and September 10

Lesson 1:   Exodus 19:16–24
               Psalm 115:1–11
Lesson 2:   Romans 13:1–10
Gospel: Matthew 18:15–20

CALL TO WORSHIP

God is here to meet us: glorify God's name.
God welcomes us: put your trust in God.
We are here to celebrate God's presence.
We honor God's steadfast love and faithfulness.
God reveals to us the idols that limit us;
God's governance is our help and our shield.
We give thanks for God's saving work.
We rejoice in authorities who seek our highest good.
Our Creator seeks to establish community among us.
God calls us to be a reconciling people.
Where two or three gather in Christ's name,
God is present to strengthen and uphold.

INVOCATION

Your trumpets summon us, O God, to this time of remembering and renewal. We have sensed your presence through fire and storm, when we felt threatened and afraid. We have known you in and through other people. Now, in these moments, we seek to bring the wholeness of our being into deep relationship with you. Touch our spirits, fill us with your love, equip us for our life in the world. Amen.

CALL TO CONFESSION

We who so often seek glory for ourselves rather than glorify God are invited to examine ourselves before the Eternal One. We who are far more likely to judge others than to look at our own shortcomings are summoned to honest self-appraisal. For in confronting our sin and seeking forgiveness, we can be freed from its deadly grasp.

PRAYER OF CONFESSION

Steadfast God, we have doubted your presence and involvement in our lives. We have focused on immediate concerns rather than eternal values. We worship the idols we have made, the things we have accumulated, the successes we have enjoyed, the activities that give us pleasure. We rebel against any authority that challenges our self-interest or bids us be neighbors to all. We find it hard to believe that your ways are better than our ways. Turn us around, God, for we do not want to be lifeless and unfeeling. Amen.

ASSURANCE OF FORGIVENESS

God loves us, even when we do not return that love. God's forgiveness is always available to anyone who is truly sorry for all the wrong that has broken trust with God and fractured community with neighbors. God is our help and shield when we put our trust in God. Live as forgiven people, gathering in Christ's name, consecrated and committed to a new way of life.

COLLECT

God, whose forgiveness we have known, teach us to be forgiving people. Heal our relationships within the church, that we may become a reconciling force in the world. Gathering in Christ's name, we open our ears and minds to your word and ways. Instruct and equip us for service that we may be instruments for reshaping the earth as your realm. Amen.

OFFERTORY INVITATION

We would not steal for ourselves what God has entrusted to us for the benefit of our world neighbors. We would not claim as our own what God has loaned to us for our management in this lifetime. Therefore, we bring our offerings in joyful trust and obedient service.

OFFERTORY PRAYER

We dedicate this money as one evidence of our stewardship, Loving God. Our silver and gold have no value except as they are invested according to your purposes. Our lives gain value as we give our time and talents in loving service. Use all that we have and give to build the community you intend, through Christ. Amen.

COMMISSION AND BLESSING

We are children of God and neighbors to one another;
therefore, let us live as God's family.
We are subject to God's authority;
therefore, we seek to be listeners and reconcilers.
We are the church, the body of Christ;
therefore, we bind and loose in Christ's name.
We are a people of prayer and action.
therefore, we dare to trust God to lead us.
God will be our help and our shield;
God's steadfast love will sharpen our senses.
We will listen and speak as God empowers;
our hands and feet are in God's employ.
Amen. **Amen.**

(See hymn no. 93.)

Pentecost 17
Sunday Between September 11 and September 17

Lesson 1:   Exodus 20:1–20
               Psalm 19:7–14
Lesson 2:   Romans 14:5–12
Gospel: Matthew 18:21–35

CALL TO WORSHIP
God is waiting to speak with all of us;
do not fear to listen for God's word.
We are waiting and listening for wisdom from God;
the law of God is not a threat, but a guide.
God is here to embrace and enlist us;
do not be afraid to respond to God's love.
Our hearts rejoice in God's acceptance of us;
God's mercy inspires us to be merciful.
God is welcoming us into the realm of heaven;
do not hesitate to enter this time of praise.
We are here to be enlightened and empowered;
may our thoughts and words honor the Christ.

INVOCATION
We observe this day to honor you, Awesome God, to bow before you in
fear and praise. You have shown your steadfast love even when we betray it. You have been with us amid the thunder and lightning. You have
been our rock and redeemer. Yet you also judge us and allow us to reap the
consequences of our broken covenants. Make your presence and purposes
known to us here, that we may delight in your law and experience your
grace, through Christ. Amen.

CALL TO CONFESSION
The law of God is perfect, reviving the soul; the testimony of God is
sure, making wise the simple; the precepts of God are right, rejoicing
the heart; the commandment of God is pure, enlightening the eyes; the
fear of God is clear, enduring forever; the ordinances of God are true,
and righteous altogether. Have we not doubted and denied the ways of
God?

PRAYER OF CONFESSION
O God, whose ways are not our ways, we confess that we have discounted
or ignored your commandments. We have chosen our own standards instead of seeking ultimate good. We have substituted our illusions for your
truth. Our words and actions have hurt others and diminished us. We have
become so comfortable with our own sin that we find it hard to recognize.

We have been so unforgiving of others' sin that they cannot discern the Christ in us. Please, God, will you forgive us again? Amen.

ASSURANCE OF FORGIVENESS

If you forgive others from your heart, you are open to receive God's forgiveness of you. If you cannot forgive those from whom you are estranged, even God cannot mend all the brokenness. Let us rejoice that the worst we have done does not cut us off from God's love. God's forgiveness is real to us when we forgive. Let us live as a forgiven and forgiving people.

COLLECT

God of law and grace, you have called us to be a caring and forgiving people. We would praise you in the way we treat others. Grant us patience with our sisters and brothers, lest we demand of them what we ourselves cannot deliver, or expect of them what they are not yet able to do. Help us as we seek to strengthen our relationship with you, that we may also live in community with one another and grow into the fullness of Christ. Amen.

OFFERTORY INVITATION

Through our offerings, we are invited to put God first in our lives, to show our gratitude and our commitment. We owe everything to God: our lives, our health, people who love us, meaningful work and activities. Let us respond in proportion to our gratitude.

OFFERTORY PRAYER

God of our Ancestors, whose laws are timeless and whose ways empower the church, we bring to you the results of our labors. We would recognize all our moments and days as precious gifts from you. We dedicate ourselves anew to fulfilling your purposes through all you entrust to us, not just through the portion we here return. Bless all that the church seeks to accomplish in Christ's name. Amen.

COMMISSION AND BLESSING

We have remembered together that today is holy;
observe every day as a way to honor God.
We will honor God's name in awe and wonder;
we will answer God's love with loyal devotion.
We have examined ourselves in light of God's commands;
seek to live by God's design day by day.
We will affirm life and loyalty and honesty;
the well-being of others is our continuing concern.
We have offered our praise and thanksgiving;
meditate daily on God's word, and speak God's truth.
Our souls are revived and our eyes enlightened;
God is our rock and our redeemer.
Amen. **Amen.**

(See hymns nos. 94, 95.)

Pentecost 18
Sunday Between September 18 and September 24

Lesson 1:   Exodus 32:1–14
              Psalm 106:7–8, 19–23
Lesson 2:   Philippians 1:21–27
Gospel: Matthew 20:1–16

CALL TO WORSHIP

Remember again the wonderful works of God;
rejoice in the abundance of God's steadfast love.
God has blessed us beyond all deserving;
how wonderful it is to recognize God's presence!
Examine before God the quality of your commitment;
come to worship the one true God.
God promises to dwell with us;
how easily we forget to look for God's signs.
The glory of God fills the place where we are;
respond together to God's mighty power.
God, who dwelt with our ancestors, meets us now;
we will feast on God's presence together.

INVOCATION

The gospel of Christ has drawn us once more to seek the realm of heaven. Your ways, O God, surprise us, for your standards are not our own. We want quick results, while you work patiently for steady transformation. We seek to comprehend within narrow limits, but you come to us to broaden our horizons. We dare to worship what we cannot see because Christ has demonstrated that your love is real. Love us now into becoming all we are meant to be. Amen.

CALL TO CONFESSION

The people of Israel thought they needed gods they could see, so they fashioned their own idols of gold. Their sin is not foreign to us. The things we accumulate to fill our lives can easily preoccupy us. Do our possessions rule us and become as gods?

PRAYER OF CONFESSION

We confess, Mighty God, that worshiping you is not the center of our lives. We prefer busyness to quiet contemplation. We reach for artificial excitement instead of the steady pace of faithful service. We are a stiff-necked people who embrace individuality at the expense of community, yet insist on conformity in preference to originality. Forgive us, God, for insisting on our own way. Amen.

ASSURANCE OF FORGIVENESS

The wrath of God against our sin does not destroy the mercy of God toward all who seek a better way. We are saved for the sake of God's name, in order to make known God's mighty power. Seek to grow in faith, that your manner of life may be worthy of the gospel.

COLLECT

Unpredictable God, whose generosity exceeds our imagination, grant us the opportunity to work in your vineyard. We seek to be involved in your purposes, not for recognition and prestige, but because we want your ways to prevail. Grant that more people may join in your service and find the rewards and fulfillment we discover when we are faithful. Amen.

OFFERTORY INVITATION

The wonderful works of God surround us. How will we show our gratitude? The generosity of God exceeds all our limits. How will our manner of life reflect the abundance of God's mercy? Surely our offerings are one measure of our response.

OFFERTORY PRAYER

All the world is your vineyard, O God, and we are laborers therein. The fruits of our labors are yours, but you allow us to manage them for you. Most we use for our own benefit, but today we bring a portion to help others, as you have commanded. We do so joyfully, asking you to bless the work of your church here and everywhere. Help us to be more faithful stewards. Amen.

COMMISSION AND BLESSING

God's wonderful works have drawn us together;
look now for the marvels of God as we depart.
God's steadfast love is all around us;
we will not forget the great things God is doing.
The gospel of Christ is ours for sharing;
walk in the Spirit, that you may lead a worthy life.
The Spirit strengthens us and fills us with joy;
we seek to grow in faith and help others to grow.
God's harvest needs the labor of our hands.
God's love evokes the generosity of our hearts.
May our labors bear fruit for Christ.
May our manner of life be worthy of the gospel.
Amen. **Amen.**

(See hymn no. 96.)

Pentecost 19
Sunday Between September 25 and October 1

Lesson 1:   Exodus 33:12–23
               Psalm 99
Lesson 2:   Philippians 2:1–13
Gospel: Matthew 21:28–32

CALL TO WORSHIP

Enter with conscious intent into the presence of God;
the Almighty looks on us with compassion and favor.
Let all the people tremble before the Holy One;
let the earth quake before God, who reigns over all.
The glory of God surrounds us day by day;
our Creator is gracious and merciful.
Let us praise God's great and terrible name!
Let us proclaim God's justice and equity.
God is at work in us and in all people;
the Sovereign One has gifted us with Jesus Christ.
Let our minds be shaped by the mind of Christ.
Let our service follow the patterns Jesus taught.

INVOCATION

O God, how shall we know you? How can we experience your presence
with us? Do you really know our names and care about each one of us? If
we have found favor in your sight, how will that be known? We cannot see
you with our eyes or hear your voice with our ears. Speak to us in language
our souls can receive. Enlighten our inner being, that joy may radiate in our
actions. Work in and among us, that we may glimpse your pleasure for all
humanity. Amen.

CALL TO CONFESSION

We are summoned to work out our own salvation with fear and trembling.
The saving work of Christ is incomplete without our acceptance for ourselves of all Jesus lived and taught. So we view ourselves today in the
mirror of Christ, seeking a clearer image of the person God intends us
to be.

PRAYER OF CONFESSION

Holy God, we have heard you call us, and we have answered yes. Yet,
we have gone our own way, ignoring the paths you bid us travel and the
work you would have us do. We have considered ourselves to be good
people, deserving special favor, yet we have not put you first in our lives.
We have been conceited and selfish in our relationship with others. Seeing
ourselves in the mirror of Christ, we begin to realize that we deserve your

wrath, not your forgiveness. We are not worthy of the love you offer and the acceptance you extend. Help us, Gracious God. Amen.

ASSURANCE OF FORGIVENESS

The realm of God is available to all who repent and believe. God is at work in you, enabling you both to will and to work for God's good pleasure. Have the mind of Christ among yourselves, looking always for the interests of all humanity, not just your own well-being. In obedience to Christ, we will find our true identity.

COLLECT

Ruling God, whose purposes are often clearer to us than we admit, show us once more the way you would have us live and the work you would have us do. Send your Spirit to enliven our participation in this faith community, increase our sympathy and affection for all your children, and empower our obedient service. May your name be glorified and your reign acknowledged, through our faithful efforts. Amen.

OFFERTORY INVITATION

Each of us is to look not only to personal interests but also the interests of others. We come together as the church of Jesus Christ to do this. We are devoted to a mission whose benefits are not for us alone. This is our opportunity to share in important work in this community and around the world.

OFFERTORY PRAYER

Thank you, God, for the generosity that enables us to share. We are rich in so many ways. Help us to empty ourselves of pretense, even as we pour out gifts of gratitude. We dedicate our offerings and ourselves to shaping that community you intend, in the spirit of Christ. Amen.

COMMISSION AND BLESSING

Depart to serve, in obedience and faith;
there is work for us all in God's vineyard.
We dare to respond as disciples of Jesus;
we believe that God will bless our labors.
Share affection and sympathy, inspired by love;
there are many who need our encouragement.
We seek the mind of Christ in all encounters;
we trust God to supply the courage we lack.
A gracious and merciful God goes with us;
the glory of God will be revealed among us.
We commit ourselves anew to daily prayer;
surely God is at work in our midst.
Amen. **Amen.**

(See hymns nos. 97, 98.)

Pentecost 20
Sunday Between October 2 and October 8

Lesson 1:   Numbers 27:12–23
                 Psalm 81:1–10
Lesson 2:   Philippians 3:12–21
Gospel: Matthew 21:33–43

CALL TO WORSHIP

Come away to the mountaintop for a while;
stand apart from your daily pace to know God.
   Life's blessings are more than we can count;
   the commonwealth of heaven is beyond our imagining.
Sing aloud to God, our strength and defender;
shout for joy to the one who listens and hears.
   God has given us an example to follow;
   in Christ, we are enabled to live at our best.
Hear God's word for us and do it;
give to God your loyalty and your labor.
   We are eager to respond to God's direction;
   we are ready to sing as God gives us voice.

INVOCATION

All-powerful God, you have placed us in the vineyard of your world to
tend and care for all your creation here. You have called us to be a fruitful
people. Send among us the leadership we need to do as you intend. Grant
that we may hear your voice and obey your commands. Set before us goals
we can attain and prizes to claim. Surely our highest aim and purpose is to
live as your people. We praise you for that opportunity. Amen.

CALL TO CONFESSION

What difference has it made in our lives to have hands laid on us in baptism
and confirmation, to have been entrusted with good news to share? Are we
moving from rebellion to obedience, from strife to unity in Christ? Are we
growing beyond the things of this earth to embrace the realm of heaven?
Let us seek God's mercy.

PRAYER OF CONFESSION

Merciful God, we have forgotten our commission and denied your authority in our lives. You have given us the care of your vineyard, and we have
tried to claim it as our own. You have entrusted us with management responsibilities, yet our destructive ways have produced no fruit. Our strife
and rebellion deny the message and mission of Christ. We have rejected
the cornerstone of faith. Save us from ourselves. Amen.

ASSURANCE OF FORGIVENESS

When we call on God in our distress, we are heard. When we confess our self-centered rebellion, God delivers us. Surely our Creator will lead us to that realm where we are known and welcomed as forgiven sinners. Live no longer as enemies of the cross, but as friends of Christ.

COLLECT

Creator of all things, in whose realm we are called to faithful service, help us to recognize one another as sisters and brothers. Take from us the jealousy and possessiveness that erect barriers among us. Keep us from destroying one another, and turn us away from the cruel acts that led to Jesus' crucifixion. We want to be fruitful laborers in your vineyard. May our work attract others to your realm. Amen.

OFFERTORY INVITATION

We bring the fruit of our labors to be blessed by God, reminding ourselves that earthly things are temporary. Yet the commonwealth of heaven can be glimpsed and shared as we pursue the heavenly call of God in Jesus Christ. How much of ourselves will we invest, with our offerings, that others may hear the truth of God?

OFFERTORY PRAYER

For the land you have given us, for the rich abundance that surrounds us, for all who lead us toward the life you intend for us, we give thanks. May generosity divert us from the pursuit of things that do not satisfy. In our giving, keep us from too easy satisfaction with what we have already accomplished. Set our minds on the possibilities before us, that we may live as citizens of heaven while coping with the controversies of our times. Bless and use our offerings of self and substance. Amen.

COMMISSION AND BLESSING

God sends us out into the vineyards of life;
let us seek to imitate the best we know.
   The encouragement of Christ sustains us;
   the Spirit evokes our affection and sympathy.
God calls us to maturity of outlook and purpose;
let us live by values for which we would even die.
   We seek to move beyond selfishness and conceit;
   the interests of others are as important as our own.
God meets us when we gather to worship;
God goes with us as we depart to serve.
   We would empty ourselves to become servants;
   in obedience, we will work for God's good pleasure.
Amen. **Amen.**

(See hymn no. 99.)

Pentecost 21
Sunday Between October 9 and October 15

Lesson 1:   Deuteronomy 34:1–12
               Psalm 135:1–14
Lesson 2:   Philippians 4:1–9
Gospel: Matthew 22:1–14

CALL TO WORSHIP

Climb the heights to view the promises of God;
stand in the house of God to give praise.
Praise God; praise the name of God.
Sing to God, who is great and good and gracious.
God has chosen us, and claims our loyalty;
God opens our eyes to see life's possibilities.
Praise God for all the wonders of creation;
praise God for saving acts of mercy.
Rejoice in the God of peace who welcomes us here;
God is listening to our words and to our hearts.
We will not turn away from God's invitation;
we are here to celebrate with our host.

INVOCATION

Enter our hearts, Gracious God, to quiet the clamor of our busy days and fill
the emptiness of aching hearts. Help us to put aside our work, our worries,
and all distractions to focus on you. Bring eternal values to the center of
our attention. May this hour be filled with all that is true, honorable, just,
pure, pleasing, commendable, and excellent. We are ready to learn what
you wish to teach us. Amen.

CALL TO CONFESSION

The mercy and goodness of God are but dimly realized apart from encounter with God's judgment. Our Creator has high expectations of us.
When we violate those intentions, someone suffers. When we seek to live
apart from God and the faith community, our alienation has consequences
for ourselves and others. Pray with me for release from our bondage to sin.

PRAYER OF CONFESSION

O God, your repeated invitations to us have fallen on deaf ears. Your promises are revealed before unseeing eyes. We have resisted your companionship and failed to grasp the peace you offer. We are anxious about many
things, and we allow our differences to divide us. Have compassion on us,
Amazing God, and vindicate us. Center us once again on Jesus Christ and
on the peace you are eager to give us. Amen.

ASSURANCE OF FORGIVENESS

God has laid hands on us and blesses us. The wonders of God are all around us, assuring us of forgiveness and welcome. God hears our requests and answers when we call. God invites us to the feast of life in all its fullness, opening to us here and now the very realm of heaven. The peace of God which surpasses all understanding, is ours to receive and enjoy.

COLLECT

God of hospitality and bountiful provisions, whose generous invitation we have often ignored and whose expectations we have defiled, help us now in these moments to hear your word for us, to see the possibilities you place before us, and to respond with joy. We long to be true and honorable and just, in the Spirit of Christ. We would ponder what is pure and pleasing and commendable, not alone for our enrichment, but that we might be equipped to serve with excellence and to be channels of your peace in the world. Amen.

OFFERTORY INVITATION

We are called to companionship with all who labor side by side with us in the gospel of Jesus Christ. We have been blessed with resources we are privileged to share. From our rich heritage, we reach out to invite the world to God's banquet. What a joy it is to give!

OFFERTORY PRAYER

Thank you, God, for choosing us to receive your generous mercies and to pass them on. May our gifts and our way of life provide an open invitation and attractive summons to your table for all whom we meet. Bless and expand our sharing. Amen.

COMMISSION AND BLESSING

We have been honored by God's presence with us;
we have been strengthened by being together.
We have experienced God's truth;
we have been united in praise.
Now we are sent out to gather others for God;
we are commissioned to do what we have learned.
Equipped by God's promises, we go out to serve.
Answering God's call, we reach out to others.
The peace of God, which surpasses all understanding,
Will guard your hearts and minds in Christ Jesus.
The peace of God goes with us;
we will praise God in all we do.
Amen. **Amen.**

(See hymns nos. 100, 101.)

Pentecost 22
Sunday Between October 16 and October 22

Lesson 1:   Ruth 1:1–19a
               Psalm 146
Lesson 2:   1 Thessalonians 1
Gospel: Matthew 22:15–22

CALL TO WORSHIP

Praise the Lord; praise God, O my soul!
Let us praise God as long as we live.
God alone is worthy of our devotion;
we will sing praise to God all our life long.
Happy are those whose hope is in God,
who labor in steadfast faith and love.
God lifts up those who are bowed down;
prisoners are freed, and the blind see.
Grace to you and peace, from God whose care we know.
Worship now, giving to God all that belongs to God.
We bring all that we are to this time of worship.
Praise God for the joy inspired by the Holy Spirit.

INVOCATION

We gather in faith and hope to worship and praise you, God of all people. You have fed us in ways we did not know and have supported us when we had no strength of our own. You turn us from the idols we continue to create. You bring us together to remember the good news of your healing love and to experience the joy of your Spirit moving among us. Thanks be to you, O God, for all your gifts to us. Amen.

CALL TO CONFESSION

If others were to imitate us, would the world be a better place? If they were to know all our thoughts and actions, would God be praised thereby? Is our first loyalty to our Creator? Before God, whose reign is forever, we bow down to confess our narrow vision, our limited response, our self-serving plans.

PRAYER OF CONFESSION

We confess, O God, that we have not fulfilled the tasks for which you have chosen us. We have failed to share the joy of faith. We have neglected to learn and pray and witness to your living presence among us. You have not received our full loyalty and devotion. We have found idols to occupy the time you have given us. O God, help us to refocus our energies and reclaim the mission you set before us. Amen.

ASSURANCE OF FORGIVENESS

By God's grace, we are empowered to recognize and live by new priorities. We can set aside the distractions that rob life of its true purpose. God lifts up those who are bowed down and redirects those who have followed destructive paths. Receive God's forgiveness, and rejoice in God's love. Amen.

COLLECT

Ruler of all, whose ways are just and whose life-giving Spirit raises us up from the ways of death, clarify for us what is right and true, that we may give loyal devotion where you intend. Strengthen our relationships with those who are closest to us and widen our concern for the sojourners we will never meet, that all who are afflicted in any way may know the embrace of your love. Amen.

OFFERTORY INVITATION

In the best of circumstances, we can delight in the blessing of unrestrained giving. In the worst of conditions, there is yet much to share. So we come today, rich and poor, fulfilled and bereft, forever on a journey that calls for our generosity. God will bless all our efforts.

OFFERTORY PRAYER

We give thanks that the gospel finds voice through us and our gifts, sounding forth against the rival claims of today's Caesars. We dance for joy, knowing that hungry people will be fed and the oppressed will find freedom. Surely you provide a homeland for us all where we are accepted and loved and given a ministry. Multiply, we pray, the work of our hands. Amen.

COMMISSION AND BLESSING

Until our breath departs and we return to the ground,
let us trust in God and sing praises to the Almighty.
   Where Christ leads, we will follow;
   where God sends us, we will go.
God watches over all of us, life's sojourners,
upholding all in need and helping all who call.
   God's people are our next of kin;
   all who suffer are our sisters and brothers.
Throughout all generations, God reigns;
Wherever we go, we are God's representatives.
   Through our lives, we will express our faith;
   in all we say and do, may God be praised.
Amen. **Amen.**

(See hymns nos. 102, 103, 104.)

Pentecost 23
Sunday Between October 23 and October 29

Lesson 1:   Ruth 2:1–13
               Psalm 128
Lesson 2:   1 Thessalonians 2:1–8
Gospel: Matthew 22:34–46

CALL TO WORSHIP

Blessed are those who stand in awe before God;
happy are all who walk in God's ways.
   The true and living God turns us from our idols.
   The Spirit directs us in the way we should go.
Link your hearts with one another in God's presence;
know that you are a part of God's family.
   The love of God chooses and unites us;
   that love causes us to value ourselves and others.
Open yourselves to God's testing and God's demands;
receive God's gentle care and warm embrace.
   God is our judge and our inspiration;
   God is our comfort and our refuge.

INVOCATION

We bow down before you, Sovereign God, for your power fills all the universe, and your ways are beyond our knowing. We, who so often feel like strangers to you and to one another, want to understand more fully what it means to live in your realm and be guided by your Spirit. Meet us where we are. Speak to us in accents our hearts can understand. Move us to fuller communion with you and with all your children. Amen.

CALL TO CONFESSION

How often have we been unwitting opponents of the gospel, denying good news by the way we work and relate? How much do we rely on human wisdom, rather than thirsting for the pure waters of eternal reality? Who do we seek most to please, God or influential persons? Let us confess our unfaithfulness and the limits of our trust.

PRAYER OF CONFESSION

We confess, O God, that we have not held the gospel in trust nor been diligent to share the good news. We have substituted empty words of flattery for gentle messages of truth. We have nursed our grievances rather than the people who need our care. We have been more concerned with honor than with service. Our greed outruns our generosity. Perhaps we have not loved others because we have not fully claimed our own worth as your beloved children. Grant us the will and the courage to change. Amen.

ASSURANCE OF FORGIVENESS

Peace be with you. Walk without fear. Toil with renewed hope. You are not foreigners to God, but brothers and sisters of Jesus Christ, in whose name you are accepted and forgiven. Surely the fruit of your labor will be blessed, and even in times of trial you will do well. So be ready to share yourselves, that you may live fully while God gives you breath.

COLLECT

Eternal God, whose love for us is boundless and whose mercy extends to all your children, help us to love you with our whole being, that we may live confidently, growing in our relationship with you and with one another until the whole world shares in the experience of your loving care. May the great commandments of Christ, summing up all the law and the prophets, motivate and empower the whole family of humankind. Amen.

OFFERTORY INVITATION

We have been issued the invitation and the means to be generous, whether in material things or in the capacity to care. All of us have received, and all of us have something to give. Our offerings are a symbol of our intent to please God and to realize in and through the church the community God intends.

OFFERTORY PRAYER

Giver of all gifts, we seek to share as you have shared with us. We want to serve in the spirit of Christ. Therefore, we rededicate ourselves with this offering. As we seek your blessing, we ask no more for this faith community than we would ask for all people everywhere. May we love you and one another as we learn to love ourselves aright. Amen.

COMMISSION AND BLESSING

God has given us commandments by which to live.
God has embraced us with love that inspires our love.
We will love God with heart and soul and mind;
we will love ourselves and our neighbors.
Carry with you the lingering sense of God's presence;
hold in your prayers your brothers and sisters.
Surely God goes with us wherever we go;
we will meet God in others, and they, in us.
Blessed are those who daily worship the living God;
happy are all who share the gospel in word and deed.
May God be praised in our speech and our work;
may we be gentle apostles and faithful disciples.
Amen. **Amen.**

(See hymns nos. 105, 106.)

Pentecost 24
Sunday Between October 30 and November 5

Lesson 1:   Ruth 4:7–17
              Psalm 127
Lesson 2:   1 Thessalonians 2:9–13, 17–20
Gospel: Matthew 23:1–12

✃CALL TO WORSHIP

Blessed be God, who restores and nourishes us.
Surely it is God who grants us rest and food.
We have been claimed by God's love;
Christ welcomes us as next of kin.
Come away from self-serving pretense;
let not honors or fame be your motive.
We are assured by Christ's teaching;
we are encouraged to lead worthy lives.
Gather in confidence and hope to receive God's word;
worship with thanksgiving and praise.
God's word is at work in us day by day;
God's revelation is available to us here and now.

INVOCATION

God of Glory, we gather here from our anxious toil and lonely hopes for
a quiet time of restoration and renewal. We bring the burdens we carry,
knowing that your love makes them seem lighter. We bring our pretenses,
seeking to lay them aside in honest humility. We long to lead lives worthy
of the best we know. Speak your word to us once more, to sharpen our
hearing and guide our actions. Amen.

CALL TO CONFESSION

Jesus, who had compassion for those who suffered, expressed contempt
for others who pretended to be more than they were. He identified as sin
the self-centered desire for honor and the best seats in the synagogue. We
are invited to look at our inner motives, to turn from all that separates us
from others and from true communion with God.

PRAYER OF CONFESSION

Humble us, O God, when our pretense gets in the way of right relations
with you and with other people. Lift us up when we belittle ourselves
and fail to live as your children. We confess our fascination with pastimes
that have no substance and pursuits that have no merit. We seek honors and recognition more than faithfulness to your word. We need your
forgiveness. Amen.

ASSURANCE OF FORGIVENESS

God, who has nourished our lives from their beginning, seeks to build with us and bless us. God heals us from self-seeking, that our relationships may be honest and fulfilling. Surely the word of God is at work in us now, restoring and making whole. Live with joy the abundant life God intends for us.

COLLECT

We turn to you, Father and Mother of the whole human family, for you have much to teach us. In the spirit of Christ, we would turn away from honor and privilege to identify with our burdened sisters and brothers. Grant us the humility and courage to practice what we preach, that the best interests of all humankind may be served and all your children find joy in one another. Amen.

OFFERTORY INVITATION

The work of the church goes on night and day. Around the world, our partners in ministry labor and toil for the cause of Christ. In every land, the word of God is at work in believers who share good news through speaking and doing. We join them through our tithes and offerings and in our own efforts where we live. Let us dedicate all to God.

OFFERTORY PRAYER

May our offerings give support to building the world as you intend. May we turn from anxious toil to effective service. We commit ourselves once again to lead lives worthy of you, O God. We bear witness to the world through all we gladly give, not to call attention to ourselves, but to bless your name. Prosper our efforts as we find joy in the ministries you entrust to us. Amen.

COMMISSION AND BLESSING

God sends us out, with encouragement and challenge:
lead lives worthy of God's realm and glory.
   We are eager to live as God intends;
   we are happy to serve where God sends us.
Give nourishment to those who hunger;
restore life to all weighed down with burdens.
   We will reach out to help our brothers and sisters;
   we will witness to the best we know.
God watches over us night and day;
God continues to bless our lives with good things.
   We rejoice in the gift of life and hope;
   we will work and rest in God's care.
Amen. **Amen.**

(See hymns nos. 107, 108.)

Pentecost 25
Sunday Between November 6 and November 12

Lesson 1:   Amos 5:18–24
                Psalm 50:7–15
Lesson 2:   1 Thessalonians 4:13–18
Gospel: Matthew 25:1–13

CALL TO WORSHIP

Gather in sacred and solemn assembly;
break out in loud and joyous celebration.
God is not pleased with empty rituals;
our songs of praise must be genuine.
Hear God's word of invitation;
listen also to God's word of judgment.
Worship prepares us for deeds of mercy;
God calls us to work for justice for all.
Offer to God a sacrifice of thanksgiving,
and pay your vows to the Most High.
In gratitude for the earth's abundance, we come;
in thanks for the privilege of sharing, we give.

INVOCATION

Meet us here, Gracious God, for we need your reassurance. Amid our griefs
and empty toil, comfort and redirect us. From our fears, deliver us. In our
confusion, lend your light to guide us. Gather us in watchful anticipation,
lest we miss the signs of your presence and fail to hear your summons to
ministry. Amen.

CALL TO CONFESSION

Have we slept through the cries of hunger and pain that are all around
us? Have we used the resources God entrusts to us without providing for
the ministries to which God calls us? Has our worship served our own ends
rather than equipped us to act for justice? Surely we have much to confess.

PRAYER OF CONFESSION

Before your light, O God, we become aware of the shadows in which we
live. In the midst of your abundant gifts, we sense the poverty of our
response. Daring to identify with the plight of sisters and brothers who
hunger and mourn and suffer oppression, we realize how little we have
done to ease their pain. Forgive us, God, for focusing on our narrow concerns and complaints. Open us to sacrifices of thanksgiving. Amen.

ASSURANCE OF FORGIVENESS

God's word of assurance comes, even in the midst of reproof and correction: "Call on me in the day of trouble; I will deliver you." Live always with resurrection hope, preparing for God's presence and reign. Give thanks in this day and hour for what is and what shall be.

COLLECT

Eternal God, whose rule extends through all times and places, nudge us to remain alert and watchful and ready for each moment's possibilities. Keep us from weariness, lest we miss Christ's presence and the opportunity to bear witness to the Spirit's movement among us. May our prayers and praise and service glorify you today and always. Amen.

OFFERTORY INVITATION

The world and all that is in it belongs to God. The Creator has blessed us with material resources and human companionship. Let us return to God the sacrifices of our thanksgiving.

OFFERTORY PRAYER

You have trusted us with abundance, Gracious Provider, and we are grateful. You have comforted and delivered us in times of trouble, and for this we pour out our thanks. When our lamps have gone out, you have not condemned us but have sent fresh vision and energy. We bring ourselves with our gifts, asking you to help us use all we have in the best possible ways. Amen.

COMMISSION AND BLESSING

The world seeks light amid all its shadows;
let your lamps burn brightly with good news.
> **We have received the light of God's love;**
> **we want that light to shine through us.**
The world needs to hear authentic songs;
let your melodies proclaim a joyful faith.
> **We embrace the joy of festive times;**
> **we celebrate righteousness and deliverance.**
God meets you in your need, to strengthen you;
God blesses the world through you.
> **We will be watchful and alert;**
> **we will live with thanksgiving and anticipation.**
Amen. **Amen.**

(See hymns nos. 109, 110.)

Pentecost 26
Sunday Between November 13 and November 19

Lesson 1:   Zephaniah 1:7, 12–18
                Psalm 76
Lesson 2:   1 Thessalonians 5:1–11
Gospel: Matthew 25:14–30

CALL TO WORSHIP

The day of the Lord is at hand;
be silent before our God.
God brings judgment against oppressors;
against all who misuse earth's resources.
The great day of God is near;
it brings distress to those alienated from God.
God breaks the weapons of war,
and strips away the advantages of the comfortable.
God has not destined us for wrath,
but for salvation through our Lord Jesus Christ.
We gather in faith and hope and love,
to encourage one another and build new life.

INVOCATION

God of judgment, the whole earth bows in fear before you. Who will deliver us from your wrath? Before your majesty, the mountains quake; before your anger, we are filled with terror. We, who have taken your love for granted, are stunned by the judgment that calls us to account. We are shaken, yet strangely reassured by a God who wants only the best for us. Meet us here to turn us from our sinful ways. Amen.

CALL TO CONFESSION

The great day of God is near, near and hastening fast. Because we have sinned against God, this is a bitter prospect. Surely we will reap the distress and anguish we deserve, the ruin and devastation that follow on unfaithfulness. How can we stand before an angry God who judges our stewardship?

PRAYER OF CONFESSION

Ruler of all time and space, we are afraid. We have hidden the gifts you entrust to us. We have wasted the resources of the earth for our self-indulgence. We live in darkness rather than in the light, ignoring your purposes and your needy people. O God, save us from our blind pursuit of the wrong goals and our careless disregard of your guidance. Bring us to the day of salvation, that we might live by the encouragement of Christ. Amen.

ASSURANCE OF FORGIVENESS

God has not destined us for wrath, but to obtain salvation through Jesus Christ, who died for us. Whether we wake or sleep, it is God's will for us that we find life in Jesus Christ, that we encourage one another and build one another up. Invest well the talents God has entrusted to you. By God's grace, live as children of the day, who make your vows to God and perform them. Surely God will bless your caring ministries with the affirmation, "Well done, good and trustworthy servant!"

COLLECT

Giver of good gifts, in whose service our talents are multiplied and our lives fulfilled, grant us now the capacity to hear both your commendation and your word of judgment. As we see, on every hand, the terrible consequences of unfaithfulness, help us to discern your saving grace and to join with others to claim it in our lives. May we do this, not just for ourselves, but that good news may be shared with many who have not heard or experienced it. Amen.

OFFERTORY INVITATION

Bring now a portion of the abundance God has committed to your care as an offering of thanksgiving. God rewards our faithfulness with further opportunities and responsibilities, with deeper fulfillment and joy. Let all around bring gifts to God, who is to be feared and honored.

OFFERTORY PRAYER

Accept our sacrifices, O God, for we bring them with joy. Receive our thanks for all the mercies granted us by your divine majesty. May you be glorified by these gifts, even as they encourage us in our work together. May the ministries they enable carry good news to many we will never know. Amen.

COMMISSION AND BLESSING

Go forward on your journey through life;
God entrusts much to your careful management.
Let us keep awake and be sober,
equipping ourselves with faith and love.
Talents multiply when they are invested;
faith grows as it is shared with others.
The hope of salvation is a gift we would share;
the promise of wholeness inspires our service.
Find times to be silent before God;
find occasions to encourage one another.
We will listen for God's word in quiet praise.
We will build up our sisters and brothers.
Amen. **Amen.**

(See hymns nos. 111, 112.)

Pentecost 27
Sunday Between November 20 and November 26

Lesson 1:   Ezekiel 34:11–16, 20–24
               Psalm 23
Lesson 2:   1 Corinthians 15:20–28
Gospel: Matthew 25:31–46

CALL TO WORSHIP

God comes searching for us, seeking our response;
like a shepherd, God watches over us.
God provides for us all that we need;
by still waters, God leads us to green pastures.
God gathers us from many backgrounds and traditions.
God rescues us from the shadows of our scattered places.
The worship of God restores our souls;
the righteousness of God calms our fears.
God lifts us up to the mountain heights;
here we are strengthened for life in the valley.
Evil and death hold no terror for us;
surely God's goodness and mercy will follow us.

INVOCATION

Waken us from our sleep to sense your nearness, O God. Save your flock from enemies within and without, from temptation and division, from self-concern and lack of compassion. We gather to remember all you have done for us and to make our response. We come to find rest amid our weariness and grief. We come to be fed, for we hunger after the bread of life only you can provide. Meet us here to make us whole. Amen.

CALL TO CONFESSION

Are you among the lost or strayed whom God seeks? Most of us do not see ourselves that way most of the time. Yet our priorities are confused as we live without a clear sense of direction. The world's values prey on us. Self-interest limits our vision and outreach. Prayers of confession offer positive avenues of growth.

PRAYER OF CONFESSION

We confess, O God, that we have failed to see Jesus in the strangers around us. We have been doubtful that prisoners are worthy of our help. We blame the sick and hungry and homeless for their condition. Yet we too have been needy and weak and afraid. We walk through the same valley of the shadow of death. O God, forgive our self-concern that shuts out others and cuts us off from you. Amen.

ASSURANCE OF FORGIVENESS

As all die in Adam, so all will be made alive in Christ. As we focus only on our own interests, our lives are diminished, but when the Spirit of Christ reigns in us, life becomes fulfilling and purposeful. We are God's flock. We have known God's care. Our cups overflow. Let us give thanks for the goodness and mercy God has given.

COLLECT

Ruler of all time and space, whose eternal realm is prepared for all who accept your rule, help us to see riches even in our poverty, to sense your wholeness even when we are sick, to embrace your freedom in the midst of oppression, to hear your voice amid the clamor and the silence of our days. We seek these gifts that we might share them generously and abundantly with all your children. Amen.

OFFERTORY INVITATION

We know about the hungry, homeless, and lost of our world. We have seen those who walk long miles for water in a parched land, who languish as prisoners of conscience amid oppressors, who live in lonely old age. Christ dwells in them, and among them is where we will know God. Our offerings mark us as faithful servants who intend to help one another.

OFFERTORY PRAYER

For drawing us to the mountain heights, O God, we give thanks. For feeding and strengthening us, even as you watch over us, we give you our praise. For health and warmth and guidance, we pour out our gratitude. Because you have invited us into your presence, we would share the joy, in person and through our resources. Amen.

COMMISSION AND BLESSING

As we go our separate ways, God contrives to unite us;
as we scatter, God plans, through us, to gather others.
We will seek the lost and bring back the strayed;
we will assist the crippled and strengthen the weak.
Surely God leads us in paths of righteousness;
goodness and mercy follow us all our days.
We will join God's work for justice;
We will share God's compassion for all.
God sends us to all who need our help;
Christ meets us, in them, as gifts are shared.
As we reach out to the least of God's people,
we know them to be our sisters and brothers.
Amen. **Amen.**

(See hymns nos. 113, 114, 115.)

SPECIAL DAYS

All Saints – November 1

(or first Sunday in November)

Lesson 1: Revelation 7:9–17
Psalm 34:1–10
Lesson 2: 1 John 3:1–3
Gospel: Matthew 5:1–12

CALL TO WORSHIP

We are here to serve God through our worship;
blessing and glory and wisdom be to our God.
We will bless God at all times;
God's praise shall continually be in our mouths.
We are here to be purified and equipped for our tasks;
thanksgiving and honor be to our God forever.
O magnify our God with me,
and let us exalt God's name together.
We are here to be guided toward all who need us;
power and might be to our God forever and ever.
O taste and see that God is good;
happy are those who take refuge in God!

INVOCATION

Meet us here, Saving God, for we hunger and thirst for solid food and
springs of living water. Feed us as only you can do. Teach us from wisdom that breaks the bonds of earth. Wash us once more in the waters of
our baptism, that we may celebrate the good news of salvation. Fill us with
that radiant joy that comes with the experience of your presence and help.
Claim us again as your children, blessed by hope. Amen.

CALL TO CONFESSION

We who make boastful claims for ourselves are humbled before the majesty
of God. We who have relied on our own wisdom, as if it originated with
us, are brought low before the eternal knowledge of our Creator. As God
takes our measure, let us confess our stunted growth.

PRAYER OF CONFESSION

Loving God, Parent of all life, we confess that we have not lived as your
children. We have shut you out of our lives and cut ourselves off from sisters and brothers. Anger and deceit, false pride and arrogance, scattered
attention and limited vision have denied our links with you and with our
neighbors. Give attention to our tears, O God. Forgive our rebellion and
our apathy. Teach us how to live. Amen.

ASSURANCE OF FORGIVENESS

Those who seek God lack no good thing. The gifts of God are already ours to enjoy. God saves us out of all our troubles and delivers us from our fears. All who hope in Christ are purified. Those who are mourning find comfort. The humble-minded, meek, and merciful are blessed. The pure in heart see God. Rejoice, for what we are is but a hint of what we shall yet become, through Christ.

COLLECT

God of Blessing and Hope, whose love in Christ teaches us day by day, shape our souls this day, by your word and Spirit, so we may become a people who know your righteousness and share your love. May we be peacemakers and carriers of your blessing to all who seek you and all who would deny you, that the realm of heaven may be the dwelling place of all your saints within time and for all eternity. Amen.

OFFERTORY INVITATION

We praise God, not just with our lips, but with our substance. Our offerings are sacrifices of devotion, gladly given in response to the riches of God's blessing poured out on us in such abundance. We celebrate God's love through our service to all God's children. So much that is good will be accomplished as we give.

OFFERTORY PRAYER

In joyful thanksgiving, we bring our gifts to feed the hungers of others and quench their thirst. We present ourselves with our money, for you have appointed us to wipe away tears and offer hope in Christ. As we have been blessed, so may we be a blessing to others. In gratitude and rejoicing, we dare to risk our all to honor and serve you. Amen.

COMMISSION AND BLESSING

We go forth to worship God through our service;
blessing and glory and wisdom be to our God.
   We will bless God at all times;
   God's praise will continually be in our mouths.
We have been purified and equipped for our tasks;
thanksgiving and honor be to our God forever!
   Let us magnify our God in all we do and say;
   may God be exalted as the community scatters.
We go forth to listen and to help those who need us;
power and might be to our God forever and ever.
   God is our refuge in all times and places;
   God will continue to feed us wherever we go.
Amen. **Amen.**

(See hymns nos. 116, 117.)

Thanksgiving Day

Lesson 1:   Deuteronomy 8:7–18
               Psalm 65
Lesson 2:   2 Corinthians 9:6–15
Gospel: Luke 17:11–19

CALL TO WORSHIP

Praise and thanksgiving are due to God this day;
let us glorify our God together.
God has fed us in the wilderness with manna;
God has led us to this time of plenty and promise.
The year is crowned with God's bounty;
we have received abundance to be shared.
God visits the earth and waters it;
God scatters blessings to nourish the poor.
Surely God is touching and healing us;
give thanks that we are called to God's service.
God will direct us in new ways of living;
God will confirm in us our covenant in Christ.

INVOCATION

Gracious God, who supplies us with every blessing in abundance, lift up
our hearts in gratitude and thanksgiving. Open us to remember the gifts
we seldom notice, the bounty we take for granted, the rich possibilities
you provide. For bread without scarcity, for water that is pure, for houses
to live in and friends to enjoy, we give you humble thanks. For beauty and
bounty, for healing and hope, for the gospel of Christ, we lift our voices in
joyful praise. Dwell with us now. Amen.

CALL TO CONFESSION

How soon we forget the grace of God and the faith that makes us well!
How easily we take credit for the gifts that God alone provides! In wonder at God's patience with us, we are drawn back to the One who blesses
and empowers us. Let us pray that God will once more deliver us from
ingratitude and false pride.

PRAYER OF CONFESSION

We are unprepared to meet you, Gracious God. We have pursued our own
concerns day after day and night after night. We scarcely know how to talk
with you. We have eaten well without being grateful. We enjoy clothing
and shelter, mindless of the multitudes who lack these necessities. We take
good health for granted, as our due. Forgive our ingratitude. Have mercy
on us now. Amen.

ASSURANCE OF FORGIVENESS
Rise, let us go our way, living by the faith that makes us whole. God will multiply our resources and supply our needs. When transgressions prevail over us, God forgives. Surely the covenant God swore to our spiritual ancestors is confirmed in us. God hears our prayers and blesses us, delivering us from our fears and affirming our hope.

COLLECT
Accessible God, whose surpassing grace is available to all who call on you, feed us with that spiritual food we so desperately need. Plant the seeds of your truth among us to provide a rich harvest we can share. We would enlist again in your service, not for our own gratification but to spread the gospel of Christ, that the world may know your love. Amen.

OFFERTORY INVITATION
Those who sow sparingly will also reap sparingly, and all who sow bountifully will also reap bountifully. Give, then, as you have been blessed, recognizing the abundance God has so richly supplied. Give in joyful thanksgiving for the inexpressible gifts of God.

OFFERTORY PRAYER
We bless you, O God, for life and for all experiences that have helped to make us whole. Thank you for feeding and housing us, for multiplying our possessions, and for leading us through difficult times and places. Now, in these moments, we pour out our praise and renew our vows of faithfulness. You have enriched us for great generosity. Therefore, we dedicate, with joy, these contributions that symbolize our loyalty to Christ. May they proclaim good news, even as we live out the gospel in other places. We praise you, O God, for setting us free from limitations and from our ingratitude. Amen.

COMMISSION AND BLESSING
Get up and go on your way; your faith has made you well.
Return to your homes with joy and thanksgiving.
   We have been cleansed and healed;
   let us go our separate ways with great rejoicing.
God will increase the harvest of your righteousness;
through you, many lives will be blessed.
   We have been equipped to render service;
   let us join with all God's saints in thankful labor.
The grace of God goes with you and dwells in you;
thanks be to God for this inexpressible gift!
   Praise God, whose strength has established mountains;
   praise God, whose power stills the roaring seas.
Amen. **Amen.**

(See hymns nos. 118, 119.)

RELATED HYMN TEXTS

In this volume, I continue to address our need for hymns that mirror the scriptures used in worship. For each occasion in the church year, at least one new text is suggested. The particular biblical passage(s) that inspired each poem is noted. A specific tune is listed, but you may want to substitute another with the same meter.

Most hymnals contain a metrical index which can be a very helpful resource. Hymns are identified according to the number of syllables in each line. Thus, a common meter hymn (C.M. 8.6.8.6.) has eight syllables in the first and third lines, and six syllables in lines two and four. The notation, 7.6.7.6.D, means that the alternating pattern of seven and six syllables per line is doubled. In other words, this is an eight-line hymn with the first, third, fifth and seventh lines including seven syllables, and the even numbered lines in between having six syllables each. Except on those rare occasions when musical accents differ, you can usually substitute any tune with the same meter for the one suggested.

Tunes are also identified by name. These names are not always consistent in different hymnals. I have tried to use the name most commonly attached to tunes I had in mind when writing. If you cannot find the tune I have listed or it is unfamiliar to you, look for another tune with the same meter. Always check out the new lyrics in advance with a musician who can advise you about the appropriateness of a tune you select. Perhaps a choir can practice the new hymn ahead of time.

The one hundred twenty hymns in this book are directly related to specific lections or scripture readings in Year A of the *Common Lectionary*. Several texts are based on scriptures also used in Years B and C. In addition, there are four hymn texts written for other occasions, for a youth retreat, an outdoor ministry dedication, and a conference annual meeting.

Hymn-writing has proved to be a challenging and satisfying enterprise. I have learned a lot since I dared to try it just a few years ago. It's not easy to put scripture themes into rhyme and meter, with all the right accents, but I would encourage you to try your hand at it. Add some "fresh winds" to the hymnody of your church. And, please, use language that embraces all people and aims to reflect as fully as possible the amazing breadth and depth and variety of our experience of God!

1   Our Feet Are Standing

First Sunday of Advent — A   10.10.10.10.
Lavon Bayler   (TOULAN)

Our feet are standing in your courts, O God
Here you have led us from the path we trod.
Drawn from our warring ways we gather here,
Held in your peaceful love that casts out fear.

Long has your judgment challenged our pretense,
Called us away from senseless violence.
"Peace be within you," we have heard you say —
Help us to claim that peace along life's way.

Dwelling in peace, we know security
And, with companions, growing harmony.
Hear now the prayer of thanks our hearts express,
Glad to be in your house, in faithfulness.

(Psalm 122)

2   Hope Is a Gift

Second Sunday of Advent — A   10.10.10.10.
Lavon Bayler   (EVENTIDE)

Hope is a gift God offers us today
As we prepare to follow Jesus' way.
Sharing Christ's welcome as we enter in,
We seek once more forgiveness from our sin.

Hear, Gracious God, the wrong that we repent;
Grant us the fruit befitting our intent.
Hope, joy, and peace abound as we believe;
These, in humility, we now receive.

Baptized once more by Holy Spirit's fire,
We sing our gratitude with heaven's choir.
Summoned to share God's generosity,
We seek to help the poor find equity.

Fill all the earth with knowledge of your care,
God of all nations, God beyond compare.
May your dominion reach from sea to sea,
Shaping our will to live in harmony.

(Isaiah 11:1–10, Psalm 72:1–8, Romans 15:4–13, Matthew 3:1–12)

Happy Are Those Who Hope   3

Third Sunday of Advent — A
Lavon Bayler

8.6.8.6. (C.M.)
(ST. ANNE)

Happy are those who hope in God,
Who made both heaven and earth,
Who formed the seas and all within
And gave all creatures worth.

Through all the years our God keeps faith,
And justice reigns supreme.
Despite oppression, God will act
The prisoners to redeem.

God causes sightless eyes to see,
And feeds the hungry poor.
Those once bowed down are lifted up
To walk and to endure.

God watches over sojourners,
Upholds the ones bereaved,
Brings ruin to the wicked ones,
And will not be deceived.

O God, whose advent in the flesh
We welcome with our praise,
Reign now and ever in our midst,
Redeeming all our days.

(Psalm 146:5–10)

4   Come, O Sovereign One

Third Sunday of Advent — A   8.7.8.7.8.7.
Lavon Bayler   (REGENT SQUARE)

Come, O Sovereign One, in glory,
Come in all your healing power;
Come to change our wayward story
As we gather in this hour.
Grant us sight and ears to know you;
Bring our faith to fuller flower.

Grant us patience in our waiting,
Grant new strength to feeble knees;
Fearful hearts are celebrating
Advent news that lifts and frees.
Save us from the judgment due us;
Cleanse us as our sorrow flees.

Save us for the realm of heaven,
Save us from our grumbling ways,
As to us your gift is given:
Christ among us all our days.
Come once more in vital newness;
Bless, transform, break forth, amaze.

(Isaiah 35:1–10, James 5:7–10, Matthew 11:2–11)

We Lift Our Heads

Fourth Sunday of Advent — A
Lavon Bayler

5

6.6.8.6. (S.M.)
(ST. THOMAS)

We lift our heads to see
Your Word in flesh brought near.
Immanuel, your chosen one,
O God, will make all clear.

The fullness of your earth
Proclaims the news we need,
That one uniquely your own child
Has come our lives to lead.

You bless us day by day
Amid the trials we face.
Your cleansing power refreshes us
And helps us grow in grace.

O purify our hearts
And strengthen faith within
That we, as Christ's apostles, may
A fuller life begin.

(Psalm 24, Romans 1:1–7)

6   O God, to You Be Glory

Christmas Eve/Day — A, B, C   7.6.7.6.D.
Lavon Bayler   (WEBB)

O God, to you be glory
And praise from all the earth,
As we relive the story
Of Jesus' holy birth.
We bless your name with singing,
Your glorious works proclaim;
Our full devotion bringing,
We tell of One who came.

Let heavens be glad as shepherds,
Empowered by angel choirs,
Rush humbly to the manger
With trust your love inspires.
Good news of joy and peace, may
Our faith, like theirs, discern,
And take us to the Savior
To kneel, to hope, to learn.

The tiny child of Mary
In wonder we behold.
We come, enthralled yet wary,
As seekers to your fold.
O God, this mystery beckons,
Yet fills our hearts with fear.
What will it mean to follow
The One we worship here?

(Psalm 96, Luke 2:1–20)

7   As Light Breaks Forth

Christmas Eve/Day — A, B, C   8.8.8.8. (L.M.)
Lavon Bayler   (VOM HIMMEL HOCH)

As light breaks forth, we sing our praise
To you, Redeemer of our days,
For we have found in Jesus' birth
Good news of peace and human worth.

As shepherds from a hillside came,
Their hearts by music set aflame,
So we respond, rejoicing here,
In wonder of our God brought near.

As you, great God, in glory reign,
We cannot long in sin remain,
For by your righteousness and grace
The path to Bethlehem we trace.

As saving love transforms our fear,
And notes of hope and joy appear,
We rise, as saints, preparing ways
To live our thanks through all our days.

(Isaiah 9:2–7, Psalm 96, Titus 2:11–14, Luke 2:1–20)

Rejoicing, We Gather   8

Christmas Day (Alternate 1) — A, B, C   11.11.11.11.
Lavon Bayler   (MUELLER)

Rejoicing, we gather in reverence and awe,
For God is revealing what shepherds once saw.
In Bethlehem's manger, salvation appears,
Renewing our spirits and calming our fears.

So long we have watched for God's glorious reign
And listened to hear angel songs once again,
But evil surrounds us and idols abound
Where goodness and justice are meant to be found.

How welcome the sign of God's mercy and grace
That gathers the world in a kindly embrace.
We ponder, with Mary, in wonder before
The great invitation to come and adore.

With joy we respond and in gladness proclaim
Our grateful thanksgiving to God's holy name.
The Light of the world dwells within and among
God's children who heed what the angels have sung.

(Isaiah 62:6–7, 10–12, Psalm 97, Titus 3:4–7, Luke 2:8–20)

Word of Life

Christmas Day (Alternate 2) — A, B, C
Lavon Bayler

8.7.8.7.D.
(ST. ASAPH)

Word of Life, we bow before you,
Light of lights, we sing your praise.
Shine upon the darkness round us,
Turn our nights to glorious day.
We would clap our hands with singing,
Worshiping your Child and Heir,
Making joyful noises ever
For your steadfast love and care.

Grace and truth are freely given
Through the Word made flesh for all.
You have granted us the power
To respond to heaven's call.
Lead us from the wasted places
With good tidings for the earth.
We aspire to be your children
As your love proclaims our worth.

Faithfully, you offer comfort
To your people in distress,
Pouring out the saving wholeness
That dissolves our loneliness.
We believe your changeless promise,
Granting life abundantly.
May your joy and peace surround us
And your Word bring unity.

(Isaiah 52:7–10, Psalm 98, Hebrews 1:1–12, John 1:1–14)

Great the Works of God 10

First Sunday After Christmas — A
Lavon Bayler

8.7.8.7.8.7.
(DULCE CARMEN)

Praise to God from all the people,
Praise to God with all our hearts;
We will sing our thanks forever
For the gifts God's love imparts.
Great the works of One who saves us,
Glorious is God's righteousness.

God has claimed us and equipped us
In our dull bewilderment,
Sent redemption mid our falseness,
Offered as a covenant.
Great the works of One who saves us,
Glorious is God's righteousness.

When in fear and awe we gather,
Mercy greets us, lifts us high;
Wisdom dawns and love embraces,
All our thoughts to purify.
Great the works of One who saves us,
Glorious is God's righteousness.

(Psalm 111, Isaiah 63:7–9)

We Will Trust Our Savior

First Sunday After Christmas — A
Lavon Bayler

7.7.7.7. with refrain
(GLORIA)

God, by whom all things exist,
Sent the Christ in human form,
Claiming us as next of kin,
Leading us through every storm.
Refrain:
Brothers and sisters of Jesus who calls us,
we will trust our Savior. (*Repeat*)

Jesus pioneered for us
Ways to face our deepest woes,
Battling doubts and fears within,
Facing death and human foes.
Refrain

We are freed to claim our best
By the Babe of Bethlehem,
Who, as man of Nazareth,
Would not scorn us or condemn.
Refrain

How shall we repay our debt
To the one whose faithfulness
Wiped away the curse of sin,
Offering us true blessedness?
Refrain

(Hebrews 2:10–18)

One Dreadful Night

First Sunday After Christmas — A
Lavon Bayler

8.6.8.6.7.6.8.6.
(ST. LOUIS)

One dreadful night in Bethlehem,
Where Magi had appeared,
To Joseph came a fitful dream
Of one his people feared.
"You must escape from Herod;
His anger is intense.
Your child, who came to reign in love,
Will suffer violence.

So Joseph dared to travel far,
To flee to lands unknown,
To trust the inner voice he heard,
To go where he was shown.
We too would seek to follow
The paths that God intends,
To hear the voice, to see the dream,
To go where'er God sends.

So may the Babe of Bethlehem
Our loyalty inspire.
May we discern the prophet's voice
And join the angels' choir.
The promises of Christmas,
We'll carry through the year
In hope-filled words and living deeds
Which show that God is near.

(Matthew 2:13–15, 19–23)

13   The Human One Comes

New Year's Day — A
Lavon Bayler

8.6.8.6.D. (C.M.D.)
(FOREST GREEN)

The Human One in glory comes
With angels round about.
All nations gather at the throne
With faith and hope, yet doubt.
Then, shepherdlike, the Human One
Divides the goats and sheep,
And those whose lives reflect God's realm
Find God's surprises deep.

Come, blessed ones, for you shall know
More fully than before
The realm that God prepared for you,
Fulfillment now in store.
For when I knew not where to turn,
Too hungry to endure,
You offered food and drink and, more,
A welcome, warm and pure.

Oh, you must be mistaken, Lord;
You never came to me.
Oh, yes, in suffering ones I knew
Your hospitality.
But those excluded from the realm,
Denying their neglect,
Discover that I came to them
In folks they didn't expect.

How then shall we in this new day
Become God's dwelling place?
Will hurting ones and pris'ners find
In us God's love and grace?
And will our arms be open wide,
In greeting and embrace,
Our eyes discern the mark of Christ
In every human face?

(Matthew 25:31–46, Revelation 21:1–6a)

Jesus Comes, Jesus Comes 14

January 1 — Holy Name of Jesus and Mary — A, B, C
Lavon Bayler

7.7.7.4.7.
(JOSEF, LIEBER)

Jesus came as Mary's child,
Humble, poor, and undefiled,
Sheltered rudely in a stall,
God's love to share.
Fill all the air with greetings.

Jesus came to bless the earth,
Showing us life's highest worth,
Claiming us as next of kin,
Not slaves, but heirs.
Come, cast your cares on Jesus.

Jesus comes to bring us peace,
In his name to find release
From our selfishness and sin,
From numbing fear.
Oh, may we hear Christ's message.

Jesus comes to bring us joy,
As we all our gifts employ,
Praising God with thankful hearts,
For love's increase.
May we not cease our praises.

(Psalm 67, Galatians 4:4–7, Philippians 2:9–13, Luke 2:15–21)

15   Sing Praises and Be Joyful

Second Sunday After Christmas — A, B, C   Irregular
Lavon Bayler   (ADESTE FIDELES)

Praise God, who has blessed us
With the joys of Christmas.
Praise God, who has claimed us as children of hope.
Praise, all you people, news of God's appearing.
Refrain:
Sing praises, and be joyful,
Sing praises, and be joyful;
Sing praises, and be joyful: our Savior has come.

Christ came, and is coming,
Making peace among us.
Christ came to enlighten eyes and fill us with love.
Christ is revealing wisdom yet unfathomed.
Refrain

God's Spirit is blowing
Through our coldest winters.
God's Spirit is melting hearts, that faith may emerge.
Spiritual blessings come with grace abounding.
Refrain

(Psalm 147:12–20, Ephesians 1:3–6, 15–18)

16   The Word Was God

Second Sunday After Christmas — A, B, C   8.6.8.6.6. (C.M. with repeat)
Lavon Bayler   (CHRISTMAS)

The Word was God, the Word became
Good news to light our way.
The Word was Life, the Word was Light,
God's wonders to display,
God's wonders to display.

The Light has come in Jesus Christ
To overcome our night,
For Christ dispels the gloom and strife,
And calls us to unite,
And calls us to unite.

Christ seeks a place within our hearts,
To make a home therein.
Christ dwells in faith communities,
And calls us next of kin,
And calls us next of kin.

We seek to do the will of God,
To live by truth and grace,
For God is making known to us
Love's glorious embrace,
Love's glorious embrace.

(John 1:1–18)

Join the Magi 17

Epiphany — A, B, C
Lavon Bayler

8.7.8.7.
(DIJON)

Join the Magi at the manger,
Led by light to greater Light.
Come as friend, no longer stranger.
Come with neighbors you invite.

Know the joy that turns to singing;
Sense the mystery revealed.
Through the worship you are bringing,
May your wounded hearts be healed.

Kneel with Magi, offering presents,
Stewards of the grace of God,
Saints devoid of costly vestments,
Treading where disciples trod.

Walk in confidence and boldness,
Filled with faith that changes lives.
May we ever sense the closeness
God in Jesus Christ revives.

(Matthew 2:1–12, Ephesians 3:1–12)

18   How Shall We Come?

First Sunday After Epiphany — A (Baptism of Jesus)
Lavon Bayler

10.10.10.10.
(LANGRAN)

How shall we come to meet our God today?
How shall we know and follow Jesus' way?
In awe and fear, we seek the Spirit's power,
Reaching for healing grace within this hour.

How shall we grasp a faith that helps us grow?
How shall we witness to the truth we know?
Wait for the voice that calls us to proclaim:
Sins are forgiven now in Jesus' name.

How shall we preach to all good news of peace?
How shall our doing good bring love's increase?
Open our hearts, O God, to hear your voice,
That we may sing your praises and rejoice.

(Matthew 3:13–17, Acts 10:34–43)

Patiently, We Wait

19

Second Sunday After Epiphany — A
Lavon Bayler

7.7.7.7.7.7.
(DIX)

Patiently, we wait for God,
Who has heard our cries of pain.
From the pit, God rescues us,
Setting us on firm terrain.
We will sing our songs of praise,
Trusting God through all our days.

Blessed are all who trust in God,
Turning not to prideful ways,
Wondrous thoughts and deeds abound,
Setting hearts and lives ablaze.
Numberless, beyond compare,
Are God's deeds we now declare.

Sacrificial offerings
From the past are not required,
But we take God's law within,
Doing deeds we've long admired.
God, whose will is our delight,
Shares good news we now recite.

God, whose steadfast faithfulness
Grants salvation day by day,
Opens hearts and lips with love,
Spoken 'mid the world's decay.
Congregations shall declare
God's deliv'rance ev'rywhere.

(Psalm 40:1–10)

20   O God, Our Light

Third Sunday After Epiphany — A

Lavon Bayler

8.6.8.6.D. (C.M.D.)

(ST. MATTHEW)

O God, our light, whom shall we fear?
For you have saved and healed.
Your day has dawned in Jesus Christ,
Whose work your realm revealed.
O grant us strength to face all foes,
To break oppression's rod.
Increase our joy and confidence
In serving you, O God.

O God, the stronghold of our lives,
We will not be afraid
To follow in that unity
For which Christ Jesus prayed.
Tear down the barriers we erect
Between ourselves and you,
And draw us close to all you love
Through what we say and do.

O God, whose pardon we embrace,
Repenting all our sin,
Direct our lives in ways made new
By Christ's own reign within.
As Jesus preached and healed and taught,
We too would risk our all,
To right the world's inhuman woes
In answer to your call.

(Isaiah 9:1–4, Psalm 27:1–6, 1 Corinthians 1:10–17, Matthew 4:12–23)

What Does God Require?   21

Fourth Sunday After Epiphany — A
Lavon Bayler

8.6.8.6.8.8.8.6.
(THE STAFF OF FAITH)

What does our God require of us
When we have heard God's call?
How shall we live in faithfulness
Whatever may befall?
Will God be pleased with offerings,
With sacrifice and other things?
No, God prefers a faith that sings
Of justice meant for all.

What shall we bring before our God,
Whose saving acts we know?
How will our prayers and praise reveal
The awe that we would show?
God's kindness we are meant to share
With sisters, brothers everywhere,
In humble deeds that show our care,
Wherever we may go.

(Micah 6:1–8)

22   Jesus Taught

Fourth Sunday After Epiphany — A
Lavon Bayler

6.5.6.5.D.
(PENITENCE)

Jesus taught the people
From the mountainside
As disciples, listening,
Laid aside their pride:
Blessed, the poor in spirit
Live in heaven's realm;
Mourners, finding comfort,
Nought can overwhelm.

Meek the earth inherit,
Hungry ones are filled;
Mercy is obtained for
Those in mercy skilled;
People pure in heart shall
See the God they love;
One who works for peace shall
Be God's child above.

Blessed are those who suffer,
Righteous to the end;
All who live for Jesus
Evil shall transcend.
Come, rejoice with gladness,
Your reward is great.
For the wrong you suffered,
God will compensate.

(Matthew 5:1–12)

Come to the Fast

23

Fifth Sunday After Epiphany — A
Lavon Bayler

6.6.8.6.D. (S.M.D.)
(DIADEMATA)

Come to the fast of God,
Designed by God's intent:
Not ashes, sackcloth, sacrifice,
Nor ritual we invent,
Not shows of humbleness
To please our own conceit,
But acting out our covenant,
Oppression to defeat.

Come to the fast of God,
Put wicked fists away,
For quarrels and fighting have no place
Within God's dawning day.
Loose bonds of wickedness,
Undo the thongs of yokes,
And free the people long oppressed:
The poor and hungry folks.

Come to the feast of God,
For all are welcome here
To share the bread that God provides
And bring the homeless near.
God's glory brings new light,
And healing grace appears.
Then God will answer when you call
From mercy's vast frontiers.

(Isaiah 58:3–9a)

24   O God of Gracious Wisdom

Fifth Sunday After Epiphany — A   7.6.8.6.8.6.8.6.
Lavon Bayler   (ST. CHRISTOPHER)

O God of gracious wisdom,
We trust your righteousness;
Your mercy grants us light each day,
As we our need confess.
We fear no foe, nor tidings grave,
Nor rulers of this age;
Your Spirit searches all our thoughts
Along life's pilgrimage.

You light our lamps with goodness,
Our neighbors' needs to see;
Your love inspires our just intent
And generosity.
You take our weakness, make us strong,
Embolden all our speech;
Our hearts are firm in your embrace,
Enabling us to teach.

We thank you for the vision
That makes your mission clear.
We seek to act as salt and light,
That others may revere
Good works that you empower each day,
And glorify your name.
May we, in Christ, serve faithfully,
Your wonders to proclaim.

(Psalm 112:4–9, Matthew 5:13–16, 1 Corinthians 2:1–11)

How Shall We Choose?   25

Sixth Sunday After Epiphany — A
Lavon Bayler

8.8.8.8. (L.M.)
(GERMANY)

How shall we choose what God intends?
Follow the way of life and good.
How shall we walk where Jesus sends?
Make God's commands our livelihood.

When death and evil stalk our ways,
When hearts are turned away from right,
Our God invites each one who strays
To flee from shadows to the light.

God, bless our land and dwell therein,
That we may, steadfast, keep your laws.
Divert our minds from grievous sins,
From other gods and tragic flaws.

Help us to hear your caring voice;
Help us to praise with upright hearts.
In fond obedience, we rejoice
In promises your love imparts.

(Deuteronomy 30:15–20, Psalm 119:1–8)

26   We Seek Your Ways

Sixth Sunday After Epiphany — A   Irregular, with refrain
Lavon Bayler   (NEED)

We seek your ways, O God,
Your law and grace.
Fulfill your prophet's word
With love's embrace.
    Refrain:
    O feed us, as your children,
    Growing and maturing.
    We seek to live as neighbors
    To all we meet.

We seek the realm of heaven,
Where anger is assuaged,
Where righteousness abounds
And pardon is engaged.
    Refrain

We seek an end to strife,
To jealousy and pain,
That by the Spirit's power
We may be whole again.
    Refrain

We seek to live in peace,
Fulfilling your command,
Co-workers with our God,
In this and every land.
    Refrain

(Matthew 5:17–26, 1 Corinthians 3:1–9)

Seventh Sunday After Epiphany — A
Lavon Bayler

11.10.11.9.
(RUSSIAN HYMN)

Living in covenant with our Creator,
We have been saved from our sin and distress.
God offers freedom for dungeons we cling to,
Coming in Christ to forgive and bless.

Let none deceive themselves with foolish wisdom,
With crafty schemes that the world calls success.
God knows our thoughts and our futile endeavors,
Coming in Christ to forgive and bless.

Called from our busyness, we are invited,
In silent trust, our concerns to express.
God is our refuge, our rock, and our fortress,
Coming in Christ to forgive and bless.

Summoned to build on Christ's solid foundation,
We grow within at the Spirit's behest,
Fashioning temples for God's holy service.
Sharing good news: all in Christ are blessed.

(Psalm 62:5–12, Isaiah 49:8–13, 1 Corinthians 3:10–11, 16–23)

28 — In Christ, Be Strong

Seventh Sunday After Epiphany — A
Lavon Bayler

2.10.10.10.4.
(JULIAN)

Say yes,
For God directs our paths in faithful ways,
While granting light and hope through all our days.
Turn from each evil deed and harmful phrase.
In Christ, be strong.

Say no
To lustful glances and adulterous deeds,
Committing self to live by higher creeds,
In partnership to go where Jesus leads.
In Christ, be strong.

Say no
To falsehoods and to oaths that demonstrate
Self-righteousness or honor overrate.
Speak simply, as for God your spirits wait.
In Christ, be strong.

Say yes
To God, who calls for purity and grace,
Who claims our faith amid the commonplace.
Turn now from harmful habits that debase.
In Christ, be strong.

(Matthew 5:27–37)

Teach Us, O God

Eighth Sunday After Epiphany — A
Lavon Bayler

7.6.7.6.D.
(LANCASHIRE)

Teach us, O God, your statutes,
That we may keep your law,
For you alone are holy —
You fill our lives with awe.
In covenant, we serve you
And seek your way to find.
Go with us in our struggles
To live your love most kind.

As stewards of your mysteries,
As servants called to bring
Your light to things now hidden,
We would your praises sing.
You turn us from our striving
For things that pass away,
To sharing with out neighbors
The goods that we survey.

Let love of neighbor send us
To go the extra mile,
To pray for those who hate us,
Who slander and revile.
May we your justice render
In true equality,
While turning from all vengeance
To generosity.

(Leviticus 19:1–2, 9–18, Psalm 119:33–40, Matthew 5:38–48, 1 Corinthians 4:1–5)

30   Come to This Hour

Last Sunday After Epiphany — A (Transfiguration)   8.6.8.6. (C.M.)
Lavon Bayler   (ST. AGNES)

Come to this bright and shining hour,
Witnessing majesty;
Come and discern the Spirit's power,
Moving to set us free.

High from the mountaintop, God speaks
Like a devouring fire:
You are my child, the one earth seeks,
Faithfulness to inspire.

Listen and wait; the morning star
Rises within our hearts.
Fear not the unfamiliar;
Cherish what God imparts.

Come that your face may shine in Christ,
Until that day dawns clear
When all that Jesus sacrificed
Shall in full truth appear.

(Exodus 24:14–18, Psalm 2:6–11, Matthew 17:1–9, 2 Peter 1:16–21)

God, Whose Steadfast Love

Ash Wednesday — A, B, C
Lavon Bayler

8.7.8.7.D.
(BEECHER)

God, whose steadfast love surrounds us,
Meet us in our fast, we pray.
In your mercy so abundant,
Wash away our sins today.
Living in the gloom and shadow
Of transgressions we confess,
We would rid our hearts of evil,
Purged from wrong and emptiness.

In our weeping, in our mourning,
We return, O God, to you.
Seeking grace and full forgiveness,
Cleansed from guilt to trust anew.
Sanctify the congregation,
That together we may be
Open to your Holy Spirit,
Filled with joy and unity.

On this day of our salvation,
Granted wisdom you impart,
Come, O God, equip your people
With a full and gen'rous heart.
We are ready now to serve you
In our wealth or poverty.
Make us truthful, honest, open,
In a faithful ministry.

(Psalm 51:1–12, Joel 2:1–2, 12–17a, Matthew 6:1–6, 16–21, 2 Corinthians 5:20b–6:10)

32   Led by the Spirit

First Sunday in Lent — A   10.9.9.9.
Lavon Bayler   (EUCHARISTIC HYMN)

Led by the Spirit, tempted by devils,
Jesus, in hunger, longed to be fed;
But he gained strength on other levels,
Tasting God's word as nourishing bread.

Seeing God's people, longing to win them,
Jesus gave thought to leaping from towers.
Rescue by God would be no problem,
Only a grave mistreatment of power.

Glimpsing the lure of worldly dominions,
Longing to bring God's reign on the earth,
Jesus, rejecting small opinions,
Opted for love as life's fullest worth.

We will be tempted, much as was Jesus,
Lured to misuse the faith we confess.
Let us join hands, that all who see us
May in Christ's strength defy sin's distress.

(Matthew 4:1–11)

33   Author of Heaven and Earth

First Sunday in Lent — A   6.6.4.6.6.6.4.
Lavon Bayler   (SERUG)

Author of heaven and earth,
Granting to all their worth,
Your name we praise.
Let not our greed intrude
On vistas we have viewed,
For you provide our food
And light our ways.

Out of the depths we cry.
When we your voice defy;
Lord, who could stand?
Yet you forgive and bless,
Holding in tenderness
All who in dark distress
Grasp for your hand.

When we deny your word,
And our complaints are heard,
Teach us to pray.
Waiting in hope, our souls
Focus on higher goals.
When grace your love extols,
We find your way.

(Genesis 2:4b–9, 3:1-7, Psalm 130, Romans 5:12–19)

God, Who Calls 34

Second Sunday in Lent — A
Lavon Bayler

7.7.7 7.D.
(MARTYN)

God, who calls to worlds unknown,
May our journey be with you.
When we feel bereft, alone,
Grant us hope to see us through.
Let your steadfast love abound,
Promising new life and hope.
Bless us with a faith profound;
Teach us how to trust and cope.

Send your Spirit to renew
Souls weighed down with fear of death.
Let us now be born anew,
Granted here the Spirit's breath.
Lift us up on love's strong wings,
Saving us from dull routines,
As the risen Savior brings
Visions bright of heavenly scenes.

(Genesis 12:1–8, Psalm 33:18–22, John 3:1–17, Romans 4:1–17)

35 Make Joyful Noise

Third Sunday in Lent — A
Lavon Bayler

6.6.8.6. (S.M.)
(MERCERSBURG; LAKE ENON)

Make joyful noise today;
O come, and let us sing.
Raise voices high in sounds of praise,
And glad thanksgiving bring.

The depths of earth are God's,
The heights of mountains too.
God formed the land, and seas below,
As gifts for me and you.

O come to worship now;
Bow down to God in prayer.
And, kneeling at the Shepherd's feet,
Know love in present there.

O harden not your hearts,
Complaining of God's ways.
Seek not for proofs no one can give,
But rest in God always.

(Psalm 95)

The Wells of God

Third Sunday in Lent — A
Lavon Bayler

8.6.8.6.D. (C.M.D.)
(MATERNA)

Come, weary people, to the well
And rest a little while.
There's water here, and truth to tell,
And welcome, with a smile.
This place can be a house of prayer,
Of worship and of care.
The wells of God are everywhere,
And Christ will meet us there.

Come, people bent beneath the weight
Of sin's distressing load;
Bring all complaints, mistakes, and hate
For pardon God bestowed
In Jesus Christ, who quenches thirst,
And loves us at our worst.
The wells of God are everywhere,
And Christ will meet us there.

Come, people seeking ways to serve,
To sow good deeds, or reap.
In harvest fields that test your nerve,
Connect with those who weep.
In thirsty, hungering neighbors see
Your larger family.
The wells of God are everywhere,
And Christ will meet us there.

(Exodus 17:3–7, John 4:5–42)

37   Have Peace with God

Third Sunday in Lent — A   10.10.10.10.
Lavon Bayler   (SINE NOMINE)

Have peace with God since, justified by faith,
We hope in glory, standing in God's grace.
We will rejoice, though suffering we may face.
Come, Holy Spirit, with love to save us.

We learn endurance through our suffering;
Character forms amid our wandering,
And hope becomes God's special offering.
Come, Holy Spirit, with love to save us.

While we were weak, Christ died for one and all;
While we were sinners, would not let us fall.
As enemies, we would not hear God's call.
Come, Holy Spirit, with love to save us.

For whom would we be willing now to die?
What would we do for Christ, not asking why?
God's reconciling love is ever nigh.
Come, Holy Spirit, with love to save us.

(Romans 5:1–11)

Compassionate Shepherd 38

Fourth Sunday in Lent — A
Lavon Bayler

11.11.11.11.
(ST. DENIO)

Compassionate Shepherd, whose care we have known,
Whose goodness and mercy among us has shown
Straight paths and still waters, restoring our souls,
We dwell in your household, pursuing your goals.

The light you have promised around and within
Shines brightly, revealing our pretense and sin.
We judge by appearances, not from the heart,
Ignoring the wholeness your love would impart.

You come in our blindness to cleanse and to heal;
You conquer our darkness, your will to reveal.
Prepare us today for surprises in store
When grace, unexpected, appears at our door.

O God, who have chosen the youngest and least
To eat at your table and serve at your feast,
Awaken our spirits; inspire us to share
Ourselves and our substance, your way to declare.

(1 Samuel 16:1–13, Psalm 23, John 9, Ephesians 5:8–14)

39   O God, Who Gives Life

Fifth Sunday in Lent — A

Lavon Bayler

6.6.8.6.D. (S.M.D.)

(TERRA BEATA)

O God, who gives us life,
Who fills our lungs with breath,
Send now your Spirit in our midst
To save our souls from death.
How shall our dry bones live,
Where hear your word anew?
Amazing God, our lives are changed
Whene'er your winds blow through.

O God, who grants us hope
When we are sore distressed,
Hear supplications of our hearts,
And lead our souls to rest.
How bountiful your ways;
You listen when we call.
Your strength directs our stumbling feet,
Supports us, lest we fall.

O God, who bids us speak
Of your unfailing grace,
In valleys where your people lie
Defeated, in disgrace,
We seek to walk with you,
To share your Spirit's power.
Equip us now to prophesy
In this and every hour.

(Psalm 116:1–9, Ezekiel 37:1–14)

Fifth Sunday in Lent — A
Lavon Bayler

8.8.8.8.8.8.4.4.4. (L.M. with alleluias)
(LASST UNS ERFREUEN)

Come, all who follow Jesus' way;
See God's surprises every day.
Celebrating life abundant,
Meet here the friend who conquers death.
Welcome from God renewing breath,
Singing praises, singing praises.
Alleluia! Alleluia! Alleluia!

Set not your minds on mortal things,
Rather on peace the Spirit brings.
Celebrating life abundant,
Dare to be witnesses to light,
Helping those stumbling in the night.
Singing praises, singing praises.
Alleluia! Alleluia! Alleluia!

Hear once again the Teacher's word,
Letting your life by Christ be stirred.
Celebrating life abundant,
Join in the resurrection song,
Freeing all people bound by wrong,
Singing praises, singing praises.
Alleluia! Alleluia! Alleluia!

(John 11:1–45, Romans 8:6–11)

41   Bowing in Shame

Sixth Sunday in Lent — A (Passion Sunday)
Lavon Bayler

8.8.8.8. (L.M.)
(HAMBURG)

Bowing in shame, O God, we come,
Washing our hands, but still unclean,
As evil reigns while we are mum
And Jesus dies again, unseen.

Open our ears to hear once more
Voices within shouting, "Crucify!"
Help us to feel the thorns Christ wore,
Sensing anew his lonely cry.

Why, O God, did you forsake?
Why must my Savior die for me?
Knowing the cross is our mistake,
We, in its shadow, make our plea.

When we avoid the cross of pain
And turn away from neighbors' need,
When we your suff'ring once disdain
Come, Gracious God, to intercede.

(Matthew 27:11–50)

42   Emptied of Self

Sixth Sunday in Lent — A, B, C (Passion or Palm Sunday)
Lavon Bayler

4.8.4.8.
(GOLGOTHA)

Emptied of self,
The Christ of God, in human form,
Came to our earth,
Our minds to shape, our hearts to warm.

Taught to sustain
The wearied servants in their toil,
Christ stood with God,
And did not from crowds' jeers recoil.

In Jesus' name,
We gather here amid earth's cries,
To bow our knees,
As God awakens ears and eyes.

How shall we praise
The one obedient unto death?
We will exalt
With joyous tongues, with every breath!

(Isaiah 50:4–9a, Philippians 2:5–11)

Ride to Jerusalem 43

Sixth Sunday in Lent — A (Palm Sunday) 10.10.10.10.10.
Lavon Bayler (OLD 124TH)

Ride to Jerusalem, O prophet, Christ.
Go where the lambs of God are sacrificed.
We will applaud you, raise our branches high,
Fully believing you will never die.
Ride to Jerusalem, O prophet, Christ.

Ride on your donkey, thus proclaiming peace,
Spreading the word that love will never cease.
We lay our choicest gifts before your feet,
Willing commitment that shall be complete.
Ride on your donkey, thus proclaiming peace.

Ride through our homes and churches every day;
We need to shout, "Hosanna!" come what may.
Hear us rejoicing as your praise we sing,
And all our stewardship before you bring.
Ride through our homes, and churches every day.

(Matthew 21:1–11)

44   What Shall We Render?

Maundy Thursday — A, B, C
Lavon Bayler

8.6.8.6. (C.M.)
(ST. ANNE)

What shall we render to our God,
For all the bounty given?
We lift the cup salvation brings
And call the name from heaven.

Before God's people gathered here,
We pay our vows of praise.
Most precious in the sight of God
Are saints who gave their days.

Their servanthood your will reveals.
O help us, God, to be
The thankful ones whose faithfulness
Shines bright for all to see.

Praise God within the house of prayer;
Praise God in marketplace.
Praise God as people celebrate;
O praise the God of grace!

(Psalm 116:12–19)

We Gather

Maundy Thursday — A
Lavon Bayler

7.6.7.6.D.
(PASSION CHORALE)

We gather with our Savior,
Invited here to share
Our heritage of favor
In our Creator's care.
Remembering together
The goodness God imparts,
We face the question whether
We love with all our hearts.

To love means being open
To what another gives.
It presses us to listen
And actively forgives.
In others, Jesus greets us
And offers what we need,
Yet often guilt impedes us,
Or pride resists their deed.

O wash our feet, dear Sovereign,
That we too learn to serve
Through words and deeds most genuine
And love without reserve.
In broken bread, we know you;
In cup poured out, we feel
The depth of your compassion.
Now fill us with your zeal.

(John 13:1–15, 1 Corinthians 11:23–26)

46 Good Friday Comes

Good Friday — A, B, C
Lavon Bayler

10.4.10.4.10.10.
(SANDON)

Amid our best and worst, through all our years,
Good Friday comes.
In all our sorrow, grief, and hidden fears,
Good Friday comes.
One who among us lived as God intends
Is cruelly killed, deserted by his friends.

Living as servant, smitten and despised,
Our Savior comes.
Dying to heal the poor and victimized,
Our Savior comes.
Though we like sheep have often gone astray,
God offers us, in Christ, a better way.

Yet do we use the sword instead of love,
And Jesus cries.
Once more deny a loyalty above,
And Jesus cries.
Then when the cock announces day is here,
We join our Lord to weep a bitter tear.

Guilt on our hands we cannot wash away,
Yet Christ forgives.
Though we desert and often disobey,
Yet Christ forgives.
So now we stand before the cross today
In humble trust, invited here to pray.

(Isaiah 52:13–53:12, John 18–19)

Hear Me, God

Good Friday — A, B, C
Lavon Bayler

8.8.8.5.
(JACOB'S LADDER)

Hear me, God; I feel forsaken.
Answer, God, my words of groaning.
Day and night I cry, not resting;
Listen, God of love.

You delivered all my parents;
They who trusted found you faithful.
Yet I hear a mocking torment
Saying, All is vain.

Be not far from all my trouble
As the roaring lions encircle,
As my strength is slowly emptied;
Answer when I call.

I have nothing left to offer:
Starving, bruised, and stripped of power.
Where is One who bore this sorrow?
Let me stand with Christ!

(Psalm 22:1–18)

48   In Confidence, We Seek

Good Friday — A, B, C
Lavon Bayler

8.6.8.6. (C.M.)
(AZMON)

In confidence before the throne
Of grace, so freely given,
We seek the mercy we have known
And are by challenge driven.

We would confess our fallen ways;
Our weaknesses we own.
Temptation stalks and sin betrays,
Yet we are not alone.

As Jesus prays, we know our needs
Are raised in godly fear
To One who hears and ever heeds
Our broken hearts, sincere.

We look to Jesus, God's own child,
Our great high priest and friend,
Obedient and oft reviled,
Eternal life to send.

(Hebrews 4:14–16, 5:7–9)

God Is Our Strength

49

Easter Day — A, B, C

Lavon Bayler

6.6.8.6. (S.M.)

(BOYLSTON)

God is our strength and song,
Salvation, freely given.
Here in this place where we belong,
We catch a glimpse of heaven

We sing of victory,
Assured by God's right hand.
Great deeds of God are history
That we would understand.

We shall not die, but live,
And give to God our praise.
Worship is our imperative,
With thanks through all our days.

The stone, rejected, stands
As head of all the earth.
On this glad day, our lives expand,
Rejoicing at new birth.

(Psalm 118:14–24)

50   Hear the Good News

Easter Day — A, B, C   8.8.8. with alleluias
Lavon Bayler   (VICTORY)

Alleluia! Alleluia! Alleluia!
Hear the good news: Our Savior lives.
Receive the peace God freely gives.
All who believe know God forgives.
Alleluia!

Life can no longer be the same;
The risen Christ has called our name.
Our hearts, like Mary's, set aflame:
Alleluia!

God shows no partiality,
Granting new life that sets us free,
Healing the wounds of history.
Alleluia!

Jesus commands us now to preach,
Witnessing by the ways we teach,
Seeking the whole wide world to reach.
Alleluia!

(John 20:1–18, Acts 10:34–43)

When Christ Appears 51

Easter Day — A
Lavon Bayler

8.6.8.6.D. (C.M.D.)
(ELLACOMBE)

When Christ, who is our life, appears
A new day dawns, with grace.
We set our minds on things above
To shape our daily pace.
We shall not fear new life Christ brings,
But meet this time with joy,
For everlasting love abounds
And sin cannot destroy.

We worship at the feet of Christ,
Who bids us tell the earth
That God has made us family
And celebrates our worth.
We shall appear in glory with
The Christ, whose radiance
Inspires our humble faithfulness
And sends us forth to dance.

Arise to join the risen Christ,
Who builds us from within,
To live as resurrection folks
Who know their origin.
Go quickly now to plant and tend
The world in Jesus' name.
Arise, for Zion is our home
As we God's goals reclaim.

(Jeremiah 31:1–6, Matthew 28:1–10, Colossians 3:1–4)

52   God, We Would Praise You

Easter Evening   11.11.11.6.
Lavon Bayler   (INTEGER VITAE)

God, we would praise you, celebrating Easter,
Singing of mighty deeds throughout earth's history
Hear all our voices, blended now in chorus,
Making one melody.

God, we would praise you, for the resurrection,
For Jesus' sacrifice and day of triumph.
Cleanse us from evil, take away our boasting,
That we, in Christ, may live.

God, we would praise you in our daily living,
Humbly obeying truth that you have given.
Help us to witness in our daily actions,
Shining like stars for you.

God, we would praise you with both strings and cymbals,
Blending together trumpet, harp, and timbrel.
Use all our varied weaknesses and powers,
That all the world may sing.

(Psalm 150, Daniel 12:1–3, Acts 5:29–32, 1 Corinthians 5:6–8)

Come, Walk with Us

Easter Evening (or Third Sunday of Easter)
Lavon Bayler

8.8.8.8. (L.M.)
(CANONBURY)

Come, walk with us along life's way,
O Risen Christ we cannot see.
Inspire our thoughts and all we say,
That we may find true unity.

Surprise us here with life made new,
With vision cleansed and hope re-formed.
May faith and trust guide all we do,
That humankind may be transformed.

Commune with us at tables spread
With daily bounty from above.
With open eyes, may we be led
To speak our joy and share your love.

Reorder our priorities
And set our hearts aflame once more.
In confidence that stirs and frees,
May we, your church, take wing and soar.

(Luke 24:13–49)

54   Our Hearts Are Glad

Second Sunday of Easter — A   8.6.8.6.8.6. (C.M.)
Lavon Bayler   (CORONATION)

Our hearts are glad, let souls rejoice,
Our bodies dwell secure,
For God gives counsel, grants us choice,
And helps us to endure;
For God gives counsel, grants us choice,
And helps us to endure.

With mighty works and wondrous signs
God proves our hope is sure,
As resurrection glory shines
And helps us to endure;
As resurrection glory shines
And helps us to endure.

Our goodly heritage evokes
A faith both strong and pure,
Equips us for life's heavy yokes,
And helps us to endure;
Equips us for life's heavy yokes,
And helps us to endure.

We wake or dream, still God imparts
A love to heal and cure.
God's presence warms and fills our hearts
And helps us to endure;
God's presence warms and fills our hearts
And helps us to endure.

(Psalm 16:5–11, Acts 2:14a, 22–32)

Jesus, We Have Gathered 55

Second Sunday of Easter — A
Lavon Bayler

7.7.7.7.D.
(ST. GEORGE'S WINDSOR)

Jesus, we have gathered here
In this quiet atmosphere,
Waiting patiently to know
Peace and power you would show.
Born to living hope once more,
We would worship and adore
God, whose mercy opens wide
Doors once closed to those outside.

May we live no more in fear;
Breathe your Spirit on us here.
Take away the doubts we nurse;
Come among us to reverse
Sin's allure and pride's disgrace,
That we may your signs embrace.
By God's mercy born anew,
We would praise and honor you.

Our inheritance we claim
As you set our hearts aflame.
We, your resurrection church,
Give our lives to join the search
For that new and better way
God reveals to us each day.
May we find in your employ
Healing grace and fullest joy.

(John 20:19–31, 1 Peter 1:3–9)

56   What Shall We Contribute?

Third Sunday of Easter — A
Lavon Bayler

8.7.8.7.D.
(AUSTRIAN HYMN)

What, O God, shall we contribute
For the bounty you have lent?
How can we begin to thank you
For new life that you have sent?
We will pay our vows before you,
Lifting high salvation's cup,
Gathering around your Table,
There within your love to sup.

We, your servants, come together,
Calling now upon your name;
In the presence of your people,
Our rich heritage reclaim.
We remember saints among us
Who were faithful unto death.
We would offer our thanksgiving,
Praising you with every breath.

(Psalm 116:12–19)

We're Born Anew

Third Sunday of Easter — A
Lavon Bayler

6.6.6.6.6.6.
(LAUDES DOMINI)

In awe and joy we bring
Good news we're uttering:
In Christ, we're born anew.
Our God has glorified
The one we crucified;
In Christ, we're born anew.

When we our sins repent,
While truly penitent,
In Christ, we're born anew.
Baptized, forgiven, blest;
God's love is manifest;
In Christ, we're born anew.

Our souls are purified
As we in truth abide;
In Christ, we're born anew.
In faith and hope we grow,
And seek God's word to know;
In Christ, we're born anew.

God's promises are sure
To all, both rich and poor:
In Christ, we're born anew.
May we God's gifts impart
While loving from the heart;
In Christ, we're born anew.

(Acts 2:14a, 36–41, 1 Peter 1:17–23)

58   God of Abundant Life

Fourth Sunday of Easter — A
Lavon Bayler

6.4.6.4.6.6.6.4.
(ST. EDMUND)

God of abundant life,
We sing your praise,
Healed by the wounds of Christ,
Through all our days.
Trusting our Shepherd's care,
We would our faith declare.
Though fear and pain intrude,
Wonders amaze.

God of community,
As we return
With all who seek your signs,
Help us to learn.
Let your apostles teach
Ways still beyond our reach.
Draw back your straying flock,
Truth to discern.

God of the table spread
For all to feast,
May we break bread, in love,
With great and least.
Help us to be the church;
Gladden our earnest search,
As in your care we grow,
From sin released.

(Psalm 23, John 10:1–10, Acts 2:42–47, 1 Peter 2:19–25)

59   Seeking a Refuge

Fifth Sunday of Easter — A
Lavon Bayler

10.10.10.10.
(BREAD OF LIFE)

Seeking a refuge, God, coming to you
We claim your righteousness to see us through.
As you deliver us, save us from shame,
Hear us and rescue us, in Jesus' name.

You are a fortress strong, ready to save;
Yours is the guidance we desire and crave.
Keep us from idols vain; teach us to trust.
Free us to do your will through causes just.

Receive our spirits, God, as we commit
All that we have and are, not counterfeit.
You have redeemed our lives, giving us voice,
Blessed by your steadfast love, we now rejoice.

Faithful are you, O God, through all our days,
Leading us by the hand to better ways,
Through all adversities, heeding our cry,
Setting us on our feet, and lifting high.

(Psalm 31:1–8)

O Living Stone

60

Fifth Sunday of Easter — A
Lavon Bayler

11.10.11.10.
(WELWYN)

O Living Stone, with eagerness we greet you;
Teach us your word that meets our spirits' needs.
Build up your church in truth that leads to virtue;
Grant us the milk for which an infant pleads.

May we look up to sense your sovereign glory,
Through all your works, to let God grant us sight.
As chosen people, living our faith's story,
May we arise into your wondrous light.

Filled by the Spirit, we would not be troubled;
You are the way, the truth, the life we seek.
Studying scripture, we are now persuaded:
We are a royal priesthood, called to speak.

You have prepared for us a place where mercy
Reigns in a world turned upside down by trust,
Where transformed people taste your knowledge early
And do your greater works for causes just.

(John 14:1–14, Acts 7:55–60, 17:1–12, 1 Peter 2:2–10)

61 Come, Hear

Sixth Sunday of Easter — A
Lavon Bayler

6.6.8.6. (S.M.)
(DENNIS)

Come, hear what God has done.
God's promises are true.
New life in Christ has just begun,
And love will see us through.

We seek and feel and find
God's presence with us here,
Transforming all of humankind
And canceling our fear.

The One who made this world
Is near to us as breath.
God listens to our prayers unfurled
And lifts us up from death.

Let reverence and zeal
Be joined with gentleness.
The Holy Spirit will reveal
God's love and will to bless.

We'll suffer for the right,
While seeking only good,
God lifts us daily to the light
To form one neighborhood.

(Psalm 66:8–20, John 14:15–21, Acts 17:22–31, 1 Peter 3:13–22)

For Joy, We Clap

62

Ascension — A, B, C
Lavon Bayler

6.6.6.6.8.8.8.
(RHOSYMEDRE)

For joy, we clap our hands
And shout and sing our songs.
God rules o'er all the lands;
Our best to God belongs.
For goodly heritage and grace,
That keep our lives in your embrace,
We thank you, God, within this place.

May we, with joy, go forth
With praises ev'rywhere,
To east, west, south, and north,
Our Ruler to declare.
O God of nations, hear our prayer,
That we may in your goodness share
And show to all the world your care.

(Psalm 47)

63   Who Can Believe

Ascension — A, B, C   14.14.4.7.8.
Lavon Bayler   (LOBE DEN HERREN)

Who can believe the good news that the witnesses tell us?
How shall we listen with hearts that are hardened and jealous?
Come now to hear
All that the Spirit makes clear,
Offering pardon and wellness.

When God's forgiveness is showered on people repenting,
Surely our doubts and our skeptical views are relenting.
Hope in the light,
Using your God-given sight,
Now to your mission consenting.

Baptized with water and spirit, in great expectation,
Gladly we wait for God's promise to find confirmation,
That we may teach
All whom God calls us to reach,
Making God's love our vocation.

(Mark 16:9–16, 19–20, Luke 24:46–53, Acts 1:1–11, Ephesians 1:15–23)

Keep Us in Your Name   64

Seventh Sunday of Easter — A
Lavon Bayler

10.10.11.11.
(HANOVER)

Keep us in your name, that we may be one,
Engaged in the work that Christ has begun.
O teach us to pray with a jubilant joy,
Set free by the Spirit, your gifts to employ.

O may we unite in work and in song,
Proclaiming the right, resisting the wrong.
Great God of all nations, we reach out our hands
To link people here and in faraway lands.

Send quickly your Spirit, fill us with power
To witness and share your love in this hour.
We lift up our praises for goodness outpoured
In Jesus, our Savior, Redeemer, and Lord.

Keep us in your world, and grant us your word,
That in all we say your truth may be heard.
Grant life at its fullest, eternal and blest,
To meet every challenge and pass every test.

(Psalm 68:1–10, John 17:1–11, Acts 1:6–14)

65   Beloved, Rejoice

Seventh Sunday of Easter — A

Lavon Bayler

8.6.8.6.D. (C.M.D.)

(ALL SAINTS NEW)

Beloved, do not be surprised
When suffering comes your way;
All who in Christ resist the wrong
Face danger every day.
Rejoice, be glad, for you are blest,
God's Spirit rests on you.
Christ's glory shines within your heart;
God's promises are true.

Under the mighty hand of God,
Move humbly through each day;
God's care will lighten all your loads,
Your troubles to allay.
Be sober, watchful, firm in faith,
Resisting wrong and sin.
Cast all anxieties on God;
Experience grace within.

Reach out to children everywhere
Who bear indignity;
Throughout the world, God's people wait
For true community.
May God restore, establish you
With strength, whate'er befalls.
Eternal glory shall be yours
In Christ, who claims and calls.

(1 Peter 4:12–14, 5:6–11)

Pour Out Your Spirit 66

Pentecost — A
Lavon Bayler

8.8.8.8. (L.M.)
(DUKE ST.)

Pour out your Spirit, God of Power;
Send peace to strengthen us this hour.
May we in all your works rejoice,
And faithful service be our choice.

Come to us now in wind and fire;
Let varied gifts our work inspire.
Sharpen our vision, draw us nigh,
That we may dream and prophesy.

Help us to hear and understand
All of the best that you have planned.
We are your people, called to be
One body, joined in unity.

Glory to God forevermore!
Singing your praise, we now adore
You, who forgive and quench our thirst.
Reign in our lives, acknowledged first.

(Psalm 104:24–34, Isaiah 44:1–8, John 7:37–39, 20:19–23, Acts 2:1–21,
1 Corinthians 12:3b–13)

67   While We Have Life

Pentecost — A, B, C
Lavon Bayler

8.8.8.8.8.8.
(ST. CATHERINE)

Pour out your Spirit on all flesh,
That young and old may visions see.
Let sons and daughters prophesy
As they discern your wonders free.
   Refrain:
   While we have life, your praise we sing;
   We will rejoice in everything.

Come, mighty wind and tongues of fire,
Filling our lives that we may speak
In language all can understand,
For we, as one, life's meaning seek.
   Refrain

Help us believe your Spirit's power,
As on your works we meditate.
We would be open to your gifts,
For you renew and re-create.
   Refrain

In every season you provide
Wisdom and food on which we thrive.
May your great glory be proclaimed
Through actions strong and faith alive.
   Refrain

(Psalm 104:24–34, Acts 2:1–21)

Come, All Who Thirst

68

Pentecost — A
Lavon Bayler

11.10.11.10.
(ALBANY)

Come, all who thirst, to drink the living water,
Come with your faith to meet the God of peace,
For you are chosen, here before God's altar,
To hear good news, announcing sins' release.

Come to remember it was God who made you,
Come to experience all the help God gives,
For you are gifted servants, of great value,
Using your talents for the Christ who lives.

Come to receive once more the Holy Spirit,
Come that descendants may through you be blessed,
For you are sent that others may inherit
A vital church, one body, at its best.

Come now to celebrate your varied service.
Come to rejoice in work that God inspires,
For you are given blessings full of promise:
Faith, wisdom, tongues to do what God desires.

(Isaiah 44:1–8, John 7:37–39, 20:19–23, 1 Corinthians 12:3b–13)

69   We Rejoice, O God

Trinity Sunday — A
Lavon Bayler

8.7.8.7.7.7.
(UNSER HERRSCHER)

We rejoice, O God, and praise you,
Praise you with a song that's new,
With our instruments and voices,
Show our thanks in all we do.
Hear our shouts of joy and trust
For your righteousness most just.

All your work, O God, is faithful;
In your steadfast love we dwell.
May we evermore be grateful
As we seek to serve you well.
Let the earth now stand in awe,
Seeking ways to keep your law.

Give your counsel to the nations,
Speak, O God, to change our plans.
Let us live in imitation
Of the best your love commands.
All our thoughts and deeds engage;
Choose us as your heritage.

(Psalm 33:1–12)

The Grace of Jesus Christ   70

Trinity Sunday — A
Lavon Bayler

6.6.8.6.D. (S.M.D.)
(LEOMINSTER)

The grace of Jesus Christ
Is with us in this place;
The love of God, revealed to us,
No testing can erase.
The Holy Spirit comes
With peace, to which we cling.
The Three in One unites our hearts,
Community to bring.

When we reside in doubt
And find that hope has failed,
When we are tested for our faith,
God's kindness has prevailed.
Our weakness turns to strength
Before God's mighty hand;
We worship One who speaks to us,
And bids us take our stand.

The grace of Jesus Christ
Goes with us through our days.
The love of God expressed in us,
Helps others know God's ways.
The Holy Spirit grants
Empowering truth and joy;
The Three in One will send us forth
As saints in God's employ.

(Deuteronomy 4:32–40, Matthew 28:16–20, 2 Corinthians 13:5–14)

71 O Help Us Build

May 29–June 4 — A
Lavon Bayler

7.6.7.6.D.
(MUNICH)

O help us build, dear Savior,
On rock that you provide.
May steadfast love surround us
And be to us a guide.
Protect us from the rains, and
Defend us from the gale,
That we may never waver,
Our service never fail.

Your heritage has formed us;
Your righteousness imparts
Great blessings without number,
And joy to all our hearts.
Keep us from false allegiance
To human strength and might,
And arm us with the courage
To follow truth and right.

Now justified by grace, we
Go out to work and play,
To use the gifts you give us
In thankfulness each day.
May families find blessing
Through what we have to share,
And all of us find meaning
In daring acts of care.

(Genesis 12:1–9, Psalm 33:12–22, Matthew 7:21–29, Romans 3:21–28)

God of Great Promises   72

June 5–June 11 — A
Lavon Bayler

6.6.9.6.6.8.
(SCHÖNSTER HERR JESU)

God of great promises,
God whom our forebears heard,
Answer us now as we cry to you.
How long will you forget?
How shall we bear our pain
When you seem far away from view?

We trust your steadfast love
Making our hearts rejoice,
As we remember how bountifully
You have provided for
People in all their need.
We praise and thank you joyfully.

We hear Christ calling us:
"Come, people, follow me;
Learn of the mercy my love desires."
We answer, "Here am I,"
In glad obedience
And worship that full trust inspires.

(Genesis 22:1–18, Psalm 13, Matthew 9:9–13, Romans 4:13–18)

Our God Has Shown

June 12–June 18 — A   8.6.8.6. (C.M.)
Lavon Bayler   (WINCHESTER OLD)

Our God has shown great love for us
In Christ, who dared to die
While we were sinners, poor and weak,
To cleanse and purify.

God sent us Christ to reconcile
And claim our origin.
God is our refuge and our strength,
A present help within.

We will not fear though earth should change,
For Christ has died to save.
We celebrate the gift of life
And joy that Jesus gave.

Be still and know that God is one,
Who makes all wars to cease,
Whose name is raised above the earth,
Who offers us true peace.

(Psalm 46, Romans 5:6–11)

God of All Nations

74

June 12–June 18 — A
Lavon Bayler

10.10.10.10.10.10.
(YORKSHIRE)

God of all nations struggling to be first,
Speak to your people on this changing earth.
We will not fear, for you will quench our thirst,
Granting our bodies food, our spirits worth.
We will rejoice and open up our hearts
To know compassion that your love imparts.

When we despair and lose the will to live,
When our divisions lead to strife and war,
Show us a refuge and alternative,
Your reconciliation to explore.
We will rejoice, for you have set us free
From lesser loyalties and rivalry.

When we were sinners, we did not deserve
Love's healing pardon you in Christ conferred.
Now, by the strength of Christ, empowered to serve,
We see the harvests waiting for your word.
We will rejoice to teach and preach and heal,
Enriched by prayer, your purpose to reveal.

(Genesis 25:19–34, Psalm 46, Matthew 9:35–10:8, Romans 5:6–11)

75   Savior, Abide

June 19–June 25 — A
Lavon Bayler

8.8.8.8. (L.M.)
(MARYTON)

Savior, abide through night and day;
Teach us to follow Jesus' way.
Whether in dreams or work or prayer,
Your presence comforts everywhere.

We trust in your deliverance
From death and fear and ignorance.
When we must face deceit and wrath,
Grant us your truth to light our path.

We bow before your faithfulness,
Opening all our hiddenness;
We have been quick to disobey,
To nurse our sins and go astray.

When you forgive, you cleanse and lift,
Our guilt, by grace, your boundless gift.
O lift us now beyond our wrong
That we may join in heaven's song.

How awesome is your dwelling place
Where we behold you face to face!
We would be true in all we say,
And faithful in the ways we pray.

(Genesis 28:10–17, Psalm 91:1–10, Romans 5:12–19, Matthew 10:24–33)

Give Ear, O God

June 26–July 2 — A
Lavon Bayler

6.6.4.6.6.6.4.
(ITALIAN HYMN)

Give ear, O God, to me;
Hear my integrity;
See me aright.
Know that my cause is just;
Know that in you I trust;
With guileless lips, I must
Walk through the night.

Let vindication from
Violent actions come
Once more to me.
My mouth does not transgress;
In me no wickedness
Causes me to confess
Dishonesty.

Yet, O my God, I seek
Refuge, for I am weak;
You know my heart.
Waking to steadfast love
I am not master of,
I sense true life above,
Which you impart.

(Psalm 17:1–7, 15)

Bless Us, O Christ

June 26–July 2 — A   7.6.7.6.D.
Lavon Bayler   (WEBB)

Bless us, O Christ, our Savior,
For we have wrestled long
To find your will and purpose,
That we may sing your song.
We take your cross and follow
Where you would have us go.
We risk our lives, to find them
In ministries you show.

Free us from sin's cruel slavery
To see you face to face,
O God, who offers newness
Of life in your embrace.
Old selves destroyed and buried,
We rise with Christ to live
United as disciples,
In Christ our all to give.

We take the name of Christian
With true sincerity.
Our love of Christ surpasses
All other loyalty.
To offer cups of water
To quench another's thirst,
To spend our lives for Jesus,
In life and death, comes first.

(Genesis 32:22–32, Matthew 10:34–42, Romans 6:3–11)

O God, Our Source

July 3–July 9 — A
Lavon Bayler

8.6.8.6. (C.M.)
(SERENITY)

O God, from whom we draw our strength,
O Source of all things good,
We bless you that, through stormy days,
You by our side have stood.

O God, you see our suffering,
O Rescuer and Friend,
We seek your revelation now
Oppression to transcend.

O God, who made the earth and heaven,
O Lover of each child,
We thank you for the saving grace
That on the poor has smiled.

O God, whose gracious will we seek,
O Parent of us all,
We turn from labor to your love
In answer to your call.

O God of gentle, lowly hearts,
O Giver of our rest,
We take the yoke of Jesus Christ,
And seek to do our best.

(Exodus 1:6–2:10, Psalm 124, Matthew 11:25–30)

79   Thanks Be to God

July 3–July 9 — A   10.10.10.10.10.10.
Lavon Bayler   (FINLANDIA)

Thanks be to God through Jesus Christ our Lord,
Who rescues us from death and wretchedness,
Who stills the war that rages oft within
And makes us captives of our sinfulness.
We find delight, O God, in faithfulness
To you, whose love is meant to save and bless.

We seek to do those things your law commands;
We want to be the people you intend,
But all the good to which we would aspire
Is lost in evil ways that we befriend.
O save us from life's meaningless distress
To find delight, O God, in faithfulness.

Remove us from our slavery to flesh,
That what is spiritual may reign within.
Help us to understand our harmful deeds
That violate our creed and lead to sin.
Strengthen our will, and let our lives express
The joy we find, O God, in faithfulness.

(Romans 7:14–25a)

80   Surely Your Goodness

July 10–July 16 — A   11.10.11.10
Lavon Bayler   (CONSOLATION)

Surely your goodness, God, is ever with us;
Surely in Christ we are your family.
When we consider all your deeds so wondrous,
We can no longer live in slavery.

Surely you waken faith and hope within us;
Surely your patient care is always near.
When we strike out in ways that are injurious,
You call us back to face a new frontier.

Surely your Spirit falls on all your children;
Surely you raise us to a fuller life.
When by your word you strengthen and embolden,
We dare to witness in the face of strife.

Surely you call us into humble service;
Surely you make us heirs with Christ above.
And when our zeal outruns our prayers and practice,
You are a faithful help, a steadfast love.

(Exodus 2:11–22, Psalm 69:6–15, Romans 8:9–17)

A Sower Went to Sow   81

July 10–July 16 — A   6.6.8.6. (S.M.)
Lavon Bayler   (FESTAL SONG)

"A sower went to sow,"
Said Jesus to the crowd.
"Some seeds there are that will not grow
Though they are well endowed.

"Some fall along the path;
Some land on rocky ground,
Where birds devour a quick repast,
And depth cannot be found.

"Some put down shallow roots
And wither in the sun.
Still others simply bear no fruits,
By treacherous thorns outdone.

"Some fall on fertile soil
And yield abundant grain,
Responding to the sower's toil,
A hundredfold to gain."

What kind of soil are we,
Who hear this parable?
Will we bear fruit unsparingly,
In actions worshipful?

(Matthew 13:1–9, 18–23)

82   God of Fire

July 17–July 23 — A
Lavon Bayler

8.7.8.7.8.7.7.
(CWM RHONDDA)

God of fire and burning bushes,
We would bless your holy name;
On the ground where we are standing,
We your benefits proclaim.
You are merciful and gracious,
As you set our hearts aflame,
As you set our hearts aflame.

You have rescued and delivered
People from the depths of sin;
You have healed our broken spirits
That we may new life begin.
In your steadfast love, we're living,
Praising you, our origin,
Praising you, our origin.

You are with us as we serve you,
Day by day and hour by hour,
As we work for truth and justice
In your awesome strength and power.
From affliction to renewal,
You are freeing lives to flower,
You are freeing lives to flower.

(Exodus 3:1–12, Psalm 103:1–13)

83   Reveal to Your Children

July 17–July 23 — A
Lavon Bayler

12.11.12.11.
(KREMSER)

Reveal to your children your glory and promise,
That from the Creation we're longing to know,
The life you intend we would put into practice,
To see the realm of heaven from good seed you sow.

Consider our suffering and hope for salvation;
Consider the harvest we patiently wait.
Both weeds and good grain we now find in each nation,
Yet, in the realm of heaven, the least can be great.

Shape us like the mustard seed, truly amazing,
From tiny beginnings to show forth your reign,
That we may provide for community praising,
And in every place now proclaim your domain.

Grant us to be leaven in worship and service;
Use us to influence your church and your earth.
Firstfruits of the Spirit, proclaiming your promise,
We live now in hope, recognizing our worth.

(Matthew 13:24–43, Romans 8:18–25)

Give Thanks to Our God   84

July 24–July 30 — A   10.10.11.11.
Lavon Bayler   (LYONS)

Give thanks to our God, and call on God's name;
All wonderful works, God's glory proclaim.
Let hearts who are seeking God's presence rejoice,
For God gives the strength for our hands and our voice.

God's miracles stand; God's judgments are true.
God chooses to work through me and through you;
And, just as our ancestors followed God's call,
We too are committed to giving our all.

God's covenant stands through thousands of years,
A witness to joys, a comfort through tears;
For we have inherited God's saving grace
That brought us from slavery and gave us a place.

The Sovereign "I AM" remembers our names,
And week after week our loyalty claims.
God promises freedom no other can give,
As listening and serving, we learn how to live.

(Exodus 3:13–20, Psalm 105:1–11)

85   How Shall We Pray?

July 24–July 30 — A   8.6.8.6. (C.M.)
Lavon Bayler   (NUN DANKET ALL UND BRINGET EHR)

How shall we pray, O Holy One?
We know not what to say.
Yet will your Spirit give us strength,
And lead us to your way.

Where shall we find life's treasure hid?
How shall we know its joy?
You search our hearts and know our minds,
And will our strength employ.

Come, saints of God, to give your all,
The realm of heaven to know.
Like treasures, pearls, and bursting nets,
It will God's wonders show.

God, who alone can judge our works,
Cooperates for good
With all who love God's purposes
In daily livelihood.

(Matthew 13:44–52, Romans 8:26–30)

Deliver Us, O God

July 31–August 6 — A
Lavon Bayler

8.8.8.8.8.8.
(MELITA)

Deliver us, O God, this day
From spirits fainting in distress,
For we would learn your better way
Of faithfulness and righteousness.
Through generations, you have blessed
Your people, threatened and oppressed.

We live in faith that you will feed
Your hungering children when we share,
For Christ has met us in our need
With healing touch and living care.
May we, from selfishness released,
Enjoy your great memorial feast.

We meditate on all you've done,
On all your steadfast love has wrought.
In Christ, our victory is won,
O'er every peril we have fought.
In life and death, we shall not fear,
For we can sense your Spirit near.

No height nor depth can separate
Your children from their faith and trust.
No principality or power
Can thwart in this or any hour
God's will for true community
And all creation's unity.

(Exodus 12:1–14, Psalm 143:1–10, Matthew 14:13–21, Romans 8:31–39)

87 God of All People

August 7–August 13 — A   11.12.12.10.
Lavon Bayler   (NICAEA)

Praise and high thanksgiving, God of all people,
We would sing about you, for we believe your word.
As you have delivered Israel from Egypt,
Come to us now, fulfilling all we've heard.

God of cloud and darkness, God of all people,
We rejoice with gladness and worship in this hour.
We would now remember all your saving actions,
Fearing your awesome majesty and power.

When we have forgotten, God of all people,
When hidden wickedness denies your watchful care,
Turn us from rebellion to a glad obedience;
Lead through the desert, making us aware.

Faithfully each morning, God of all people,
Your loving-kindness stretches out another day.
We will trust your mercy, praising all the wonders
Each day will bring to followers of your way.

(Exodus 14:19–31, Psalm 106:4–12)

Come to the Mountaintop 88

August 7–August 13 — A
Lavon Bayler

6.6.8.6. (S.M.)
(ST. ANDREW)

Come to the mountaintop;
O come away to pray.
Pour out the anguish of your heart;
Find solace for the day.

Come to a quiet place
To meet Christ face to face;
Let go of sorrow, guilt, and pain
In Jesus' kind embrace.

Come to the restless sea,
Where people cringe in fear;
Take heart, for Christ is also there,
Your fervent prayers to hear.

Come to the marketplace;
There claim the covenant
That binds us not to things, but God,
In outreach jubilant.

Come to a needy world,
Where worship is reviled.
Come, grow in faith and love and zeal,
With Jesus, God's own child.

(Matthew 14:22–33, Romans 9:1–5)

89 God Has Heard

August 14–August 20 — A
Lavon Bayler

10.8.10.8.8.8.
(MARGARET)

"God has heard your cries and your murmuring,"
Moses said to those who complained.
And in our day, too, our complaints will bring
Answers clear that are God-ordained.
Refrain:
God's blessings are so abundant
For those living in covenant.

"Be it done for you as your heart desires,"
Jesus answered a woman's faith.
Now the healing word that our trust inspires
Can be known as we pray and wait.
Refrain

"Give your ears, O people, to what I teach,"
God implored those forgetful ones,
And today God's truth is within the reach
Of all loyal daughters and sons.
Refrain

"All the gifts of God cannot be denied,"
The apostle Paul once proclaimed,
And today that mercy is amplified,
In the people whom Christ has named.
Refrain

(Exodus 16:2–15, Psalm 78:1–3, 10–20, Matthew 15:21–28, Romans 11:13–16, 29–32)

Salvation Comes

August 21–August 27 — A
Lavon Bayler

8.8.8.8. (L.M.)
(MENDON)

Salvation comes from God, our rock.
How shall we show our gratitude?
Will we still trust while others mock?
Will joy remain our attitude?

When Moses struck a rock, in trust,
God sent fresh water, pure and clear.
How can we think our God unjust?
How can we fail to see and hear?

Peter confessed his faith, and found
Jesus the Christ, who called him rock.
Yet this great leader, so renowned,
Once heard the crowing of a cock.

What kind of rock of certainty
Do we, the church, make known today?
Are we a vital entity,
Bringing the flocks to Jesus' way?

The Rock of our Salvation praise;
May our thanksgiving fill the air.
With joyful noise, our hymns we raise,
Daring to follow anywhere.

(Exodus 17:1–7, Psalm 95, Matthew 16:13–20, Romans 11:33–36)

91   All God Has Said

August 28–September 3 — A
Lavon Bayler

8.6.8.6. (C.M.)
(DUNDEE)

All that our God has said to us
We seek, each day, to do;
We keep in mind the covenant
And promises renew.

The presence of our God is sure;
We tremble when we think
Of all God's majesty and power
That bid us come and drink.

Death has no power to threaten us,
And losses lead to gain.
Temptation we have put behind,
That Christ, in us, may reign.

Denying self before the cross,
God's voice we would obey;
God bears us up on eagles' wings,
And grants new life today.

We seek to be God's holy ones,
A congregation strong,
To follow Christ in care and love,
And stand against all wrong.

(Exodus 19:1–9, Psalm 114, Matthew 16:21–28)

Live, by Grace

August 28–September 3 — A
Lavon Bayler

7.7.7.7.7.7.
(REDHEAD 76)

Live, by grace, the will of God,
Treading where our Savior trod,
Willingly to pay the price
As a living sacrifice.
Let your holy worship be
Claiming all God's mercies free.

Once conformed to worldly claims,
Living now by higher aims,
You will see as perfect norms
Minds renewed as good transforms
All we call acceptable
and most truly spiritual.

Live most humbly day by day,
As God's grace in you holds sway;
Think with sober judgment true,
By the faith assigned to you.
May the church one body be,
Joined in perfect unity.

Use the gifts unique to you
And, with love and zeal, outdo
Everyone in honoring
All whom Christ is gathering.
By the Spirit set aglow,
May your hope and patience grow.

(Romans 12:1–13)

93   We Trust in You

September 4–September 10 — A   10.10.10.10.
Lavon Bayler   (BREAD OF LIFE)

> We put our trust in you, our Help and Shield.
> You, God, have challenged us through truth revealed.
> Idols we leave behind as powerless;
> You offer steadfast love and faithfulness.
>
> We glorify your name, seeking your face.
> Through cloud and stormy trial, we know your grace.
> Whether by trumpet sound or warning fire,
> You draw us back to life, and faith inspire.
>
> Walk with us day by day, lest we withdraw.
> Teach us to live by love that keeps your law.
> Seeking our neighbor's good, we will invest
> Effort and loyalty, and give our best.
>
> When there is conflict, and we disagree,
> Help us to listen with integrity.
> Let now your church unite in Jesus' name,
> Your reconciling love by deeds proclaim.

(Exodus 19:16–24, Psalm 115:1–11, Matthew 18:15–20, Romans 13:1–10)

God of Law

September 11–September 17 — A

Lavon Bayler

8.7.8.7.D.

(HYMN TO JOY)

God, whose law revives our spirits,
With a testimony sure,
Grant your simple children wisdom
And a faith both strong and pure.
In your precepts now rejoicing,
We look up in awe and fear,
With enlightened eyes perceiving
Righteous ways you're making clear.

May we all desire your guidance
And the warning signs you give;
Speak once more your great commandments,
Showing us the way to live.
You discern our hidden errors,
All the faults we never claim;
Keep us from presumptuous sinning,
That your will may be our aim.

May your love have full dominion
In our words and deeds, we pray.
Help us celebrate the holy
With our neighbors every day.
Loyalty and honest labor,
Overcoming human strife,
Dominate our high intentions,
With a reverence for life.

(Exodus 20:1–20, Psalm 19:7–14)

95 Our Tongues Utter Praises

September 11–September 17 — A
Lavon Bayler

11.11.11.11.
(ST. DENIO)

Our tongues utter praises; our knees bow, in awe
To you, God most holy, whose word is our law.
We live in community, never alone;
In living or dying, your presence is known.

How varied our precepts, how different our views,
Yet Christ seeks our multiple talents to use,
Uniting us all, lest our judgments divide,
Inviting all people in love to abide.

When jealousy, anger, and wrong hold full sway,
Beclouding our vision and leading astray,
God's judgment is sure; we are called to account,
Our envy, impatience, and sin to surmount.

Forgiveness unlimited Christ offers now
To people who vengeance and hate disavow.
If we, from our hearts, pardon those in our debt,
God promises mercy, our sins to forget.

All praise be to God in whatever we do;
All honor to Christ in the work we pursue.
Abstaining or eating, thanksgiving our goal,
We gladly forgive as the Spirit makes whole.

(Matthew 18:21–35, Romans 14:5–12)

Where Is Our Loyalty?   96

September 18–September 24 — A
Lavon Bayler

6.6.8.6.D. (S.M.D.)
(DIADEMATA)

Where is our loyalty?
What claims our faith and trust?
Distracting idols we create
Deny a God most just.
Yet all God's wondrous works
Surround us every day;
The steadfast love of God abounds
To show a better way.

Surely the wrath of God
Is what we oft deserve;
A stiff-necked people, we forget
Our gospel call to serve.
Yet still the summons comes
To vineyards, where our work
Can join with those already there
To show God's handiwork.

Living in partnership
And seeking unity,
We find in Christ the grand design
Of who we're meant to be.
While we are here on earth,
Our highest joy will come
In helping others learn to love
In outreach venturesome.

(Exodus 32:1–14, Psalm 106:7–8, 19–23, Matthew 20:1–16, Philippians 1:21–27)

97 O Reigning God

September 25–October 1 — A
Lavon Bayler

7.6.7.6.D.
(ANGEL'S STORY)

O Reigning God, most holy,
We tremble as we bow
To praise your name, and worship;
Have mercy on us now.
Your justice is established,
With equity for all.
We cry to you, our Helper;
Defend us, lest we fall.

You know our names and call us
To faithful partnership;
The favor of your presence
Inspires our leadership.
Your goodness and your glory
Are manifest each day;
O grant us eyes to see you
And follow in your way.

We seek to keep your statutes,
To do your holy will,
To live as ones forgiven,
Your purpose to fulfill.
Through times of doubt, restore us;
When we are weak, make strong
The ties that join your people
In work that conquers wrong.

(Exodus 33:12–23, Psalm 99)

Many Are Called
98

September 25–October 1 — A
Lavon Bayler

11.10.11.10., with refrain
(TIDINGS)

Many are called to work within God's vineyard;
Who will respond, the realm of God to claim?
Will we reach out, as well as journey inward,
Bound by God's love, for all of us the same?
Refrain:
Sing of God's glory, bow ev'ry knee,
Finding a common faith through loyal ministry.

Share in the Spirit's active work among us,
Learning from Christ encouragement and joy;
Seeking to find together true consensus,
Let no conceit or selfishness destroy.
Refrain

Focus concern each day on others' welfare,
Emptying self to serve, as Christ has done;
When other suffer, take the time to be there,
Sharing the healing work by Christ begun.
Refrain

In true humility and glad obedience,
Know God is working day by day in you,
Carving from fears and pain a strong endurance
That through the years will always see you through.
Refrain

(Matthew 21:28–32, Philippians 2:1–13)

99 O God, Our Strength

October 2–October 8 — A
Lavon Bayler

6.7.6.7.6.6.6.6.
(NUN DANKET ALLE GOTT)

O God, our strength and song,
Whose hand is laid upon us,
We ask that you will be
Our Shepherd, great and wondrous.
Commission us again
To seek a worthy goal,
And guide along the way
To change and make us whole.

We seek maturity
And faith to catch the vision
Of Jesus' upward call
That asks for our decision.
With minds on earthly things,
We find the cross unreal;
O draw us to yourself,
Its power and grace to feel.

Grant us a forward look,
Forgetting past distresses.
May we your vineyard tend
With joy that love expresses.
Inspire our stewardship
As we live out your care.
Stay with us in the church;
Go with us everywhere.

(Numbers 27:12–23, Psalm 81:1–10, Matthew 21:33–43, Philippians 3:12–21)

This Land, O God

October 9–October 15 — A
Lavon Bayler

8.6.8.6.D. (C.M.D.)
(MATERNA)

This land, O God, is ours to see,
To cherish for each child,
For we are not inheritors,
But stewards, reconciled
To live in harmony and peace
With all that you create.
To you, O God, we all belong;
We know that you are great.

You make the sun and clouds arise;
You send the wind and rain.
By signs and wonders all around,
This planet you sustain.
You give to us a heritage
That we may use and share,
For it is not for us alone;
Your love goes everywhere.

Your invitation reaches us;
Your feast is spread for all.
Throughout your realm, doors open wide
To all who heed your call.
Grant us the faith and strength each day,
Not only to reply,
But by our active words and deeds
To draw your children nigh.

(Deuteronomy 34:1–12, Psalm 135:1–14, Matthew 22:10–14)

101 — We Rejoice!

October 9–October 15 — A
Lavon Bayler

7.6.7.6.7.7.7.6.
(JESUS SAVES)

Called to labor, side by side,
We rejoice, we rejoice!
In the gospel to abide,
We rejoice, we rejoice!
Share good news that God is here;
Shun anxiety and fear;
Live in peace and joy brought near.
We rejoice, we rejoice!

As our praise and prayers abound,
We rejoice, we rejoice!
Giving thanks on holy ground,
We rejoice, we rejoice!
Asking God for what we need,
Seeking here our souls to feed,
We will serve in word and deed.
We rejoice, we rejoice!

In whatever things are true,
We rejoice, we rejoice!
Giving honor that is due,
We rejoice, we rejoice!
We have learned God's grace is sure;
What is lovely, just, and pure
Shall in excellence endure.
We rejoice, we rejoice!

(Philippians 4:1–9)

All Our Praise

102

October 16–October 22 — A
Lavon Bayler

7.7.7.7.D., with refrain
(MENDELSSOHN)

All our praise, O God, we sing
As, in trust, to you we bring
Longing hearts and searching minds,
Honest doubts, surprising finds.
Pardon our desire to test
If your ways are really best.
We would give you all we owe,
Asking you to help us grow.
> *Refrain:*
> All our thanks to you we bring,
> Praising you for everything.

Happy in the help you give,
We are hopeful while we live.
May our work for truth be blessed,
Seeking right for those oppressed.
You, who set the prisoners free,
Helping those, once blind, to see,
Lift the burdens people bear,
Pain and loss, so oft unfair.
> *Refrain*

(Psalm 146)

103

Gracious God

October 16–October 22 — A
Lavon Bayler

8.7.8.7.D.
(IN BABILONE)

Gracious God, whose kindly dealing
Draws us near to those we love,
Weave a harmony among us
That partakes of joys above.
Walk with us along life's journey,
Lifting hearts and minds as one,
Drawing ever-wider circles
Through the church, by Christ begun.

May all people be our people,
For your love unites us all;
Even death cannot divide when
We have shared a common call.
Hear the prayers and praise we offer,
Giving thanks, remembering
All who live and labor with us,
All who cause our hearts to sing.

By the Holy Spirit's guidance,
We have sensed the gospel's power;
Lift us up to full conviction
As we worship you this hour.
Send your word once more among us,
Teaching us like Christ to care;
We would welcome all your children
In the faith and hope we share.

(Ruth 1:1–19a, 1 Thessalonians 1)

For Steadfast Hope 104

October 16–October 22 — A   8.8.8.8.8.8.
Lavon Bayler   (MELITA)

For steadfast hope and works of love,
For all that lifts our hearts above,
We thank you, God, and praise your name
For grace, forevermore the same.
We thank you for our friends who care,
And all who in your mission share.

We pray for all whose faithfulness
Inspires a lingering joyousness,
Who live the gospel day by day
In all they think and do and say.
May we receive the Spirit's power
To bring our lives to glorious flower.

Send forth the news to every land,
That all may hear and understand:
The true and living God extends
A welcome that forgives and mends.
O may we serve in joy and peace,
With praises that will never cease.

(1 Thessalonians 1)

105   May We Be Blessed

October 23–October 29 — A   8.6.8.6. (C.M.)
Lavon Bayler   (FINGAL)

May we be blessed who fear you, God,
And call upon your name,
And may we walk in ways you send,
Your wonders to proclaim.

We labor for the common good,
Not just our own delight,
But, to your glory, helping all
Find favor in your sight.

We share with those enjoying less
Of all your grace imparts,
As servants, happy in the fruits
Of peace within our hearts.

May all who venture forth in faith
Enjoy prosperity,
While reaching out with love for all,
In true sincerity.

O gather all your children near,
Their children's children too,
That we may share a vision, and
Community renew.

(Ruth 2:1–13, Psalm 128)

Test Us, O God 106

October 23–October 29 — A
Lavon Bayler

10.10.10.10.
(SINE NOMINE)

Test us, O God, to know our hearts and minds,
Cleansing from error all your goodness finds.
Entrust us with good news for all to share,
That your commandments may prosper everywhere.

To love you, God, as we are loved by you;
That is the quest we're seeking to renew,
With all our soul and strength your love to show,
Letting your gospel set hearts and minds aglow.

To love ourselves, rejoicing in your care,
Knowing our value nothing can impair,
We celebrate the courage you impart,
To live life boldly, with gentleness of heart.

To love our neighbors, be they friend or foe,
Wanting for them the best their life can know;
We dare to risk ourselves for others' sake,
Serving with gladness, in joyous give-and-take.

Approved by you, we live in confidence,
With true affection, without violence.
No need for glory, flattery, or greed,
For you are with us and meet our every need.

(Matthew 22:34–46, 1 Thessalonians 2:1–8)

107   Lead Us, God

October 30–November 5 — A
Lavon Bayler

7.8.7.8.8.8.
(LIEBSTER JESU)

Lead us, God as you intend,
As we labor in your service.
We would thank you without end,
Day and night in faithful witness.
Help us tell the gospel story,
Living in your realm and glory.

Rising early, we would build
Cities that reflect your purpose,
Sharing wealth, as you have willed,
Giving substance, not just surplus.
As your family, may we flourish,
Seeking to restore and nourish.

Save us from anxiety,
As we rest within your keeping,
Teaching simple piety,
Confident, awake or sleeping.
May our children learn self-mastery,
Finding joy within your mercy.

(Ruth 4:7–17, Psalm 127, 1 Thessalonians 2:9–13, 17–20)

108   Teach Us, O Christ

October 30–November 5 — A
Lavon Bayler

6.6.8.6.(S.M.)
(TRENTHAM)

Teach us, O Christ, to live
In humble honesty,
That we may learn from you each day
The grace of modesty.

No honors would we seek,
Not fame or deference,
But find in you the strength we need
For simple confidence.

We would not add more weight
To burdens people bear,
But rather seek to lift their loads
And in their sorrows share.

May all our deeds reflect
The best our words can tell,
That we may live authentically
And seek to serve you well.

(Matthew 23:1–12)

Listen Well 109

November 6–November 12 — A   7.8.7.8.7.7.
Lavon Bayler   (RATISBON)

Listen well, God bids us hear
Words that summon us from grieving;
Let the voice of God make clear
Messages for our receiving.
There is comfort for our pain;
Jesus meets us once again.

Look around that we may see
Those who face despair and misery;
May our minds and hearts be free
To respond and live more justly.
As we feel another's plight,
Lead us, God, to do what's right.

Worship in God's warm embrace,
Not with empty forms or pretense.
We are gathered by God's grace,
Rather than our own convenience.
God will hear our thanks and praise,
Joined with sacrificial ways.

(Psalm 50:7–15, Amos 5:18–24, 1 Thessalonians 4:13–18)

110   Keep Watch

November 6–November 12 — A
Lavon Bayler

8.6.8.8.6.
(REST)

Keep watch, the realm of heaven is near,
The day and hour unknown.
The wise prepare to see and hear
The one who comes to make all clear
And claim us as God's own.

Each one is given a task to do,
And gifts to use each day.
Christ bids us to our work be true,
And grants us hope to see us through
The blows that come our way.

Prepare your lamps, and keep them lit,
With faith to feed the flame.
Be watchfully alert and fit
As to the Christ we now commit
Our best to God's acclaim.

Come, meet the Christ with hearts aglow;
God welcomes great and least.
Now, as we worship, God will know
The many ways we seek to grow.
Come, join the joyful feast!

(Matthew 25:1–13)

The Day of God

November 13–November 19 — A
Lavon Bayler

7.6.7.6.D.
(ST. THEODULPH)

The Day of God is coming,
A time of judgment sure;
Its great distress and anguish
No sinner can endure.
No wealth can stay God's verdict,
No pleading still God's wrath,
When, in our wasteful stupor,
We choose destruction's path.

Be silent, then, O people
Whose ears no longer hear;
Observe the sights around you
That show that God is near.
The earth's oppressed are crying
For help that you can give;
In darkness, they are dying
While you could help them live.

Rise up, in new commitment,
As children of the day,
Who, making vows, perform them
And follow Jesus' way.
May faith inspire our actions
And hope encourage all
To love through deeds of mercy,
In answer to God's call.

(Psalm 76, Zephaniah 1:7, 12–18, 1 Thessalonians 5:1–11)

112   Sovereign and Owner

November 13–November 19 — A
Lavon Bayler

11.10.11.10.
(CUSHMAN)

Sovereign and Owner of the whole creation,
You have entrusted us with talents wide;
Surely their use involves an obligation
Daily to do our best, as you provide.

Whether the fortunes given are extensive,
Or our endowment is more limited,
All our responses are to be expressive
Of joyous thanks for gifts unmerited.

We would not hide the talents you have given,
For fear we cannot do as others do;
Grant us the courage, by commitment driven,
Ever to take new risks and follow through.

Help us be faithful over much or little,
That we may hear your welcome words, "Well done!"
Grant us success as slothfulness we battle,
Living our thankfulness for victories won.

(Matthew 25:14–30)

113   Come, God, Our Shepherd

November 20–November 26 — A
Lavon Bayler

8.8.8.8. (L.M.)
(FEDERAL STREET)

Come, God, our Shepherd, lead us now;
Speak to the trust that we avow.
We have been lost, and we have strayed,
Yet we can turn to you for aid.

Crippled and weak your comfort seek;
Victims, oppressors hear you speak.
Surely your justice will prevail,
Meant to restore both strong and frail.

When we are scattered, bring us home
Rescue from places where we roam.
Move through the shadows where we grieve;
Let us, in you, new life receive.

Feed us once more as you console;
May your acceptance make us whole.
Led by your mercy, we would dwell
Safe in your house, your love to tell.

(Psalm 23, Ezekiel 34:11–16, 20–24)

When You Come 114

November 20–November 26 — A
Lavon Bayler

11.11.11.11.
(LYNDHURST)

When you come in glory, Christ our Lord, to reign,
Nations will be gathered, blessings to obtain.
But we face your judgment of our faithfulness,
Knowing we deny you and your will to bless.

Shall we be as goats or sheep before your throne?
Did we always give the best that we have known?
How has your compassion shown itself in us?
Have our actions made your gospel luminous?

Daily you have met us when we did not know
It was you who hungered, had no place to go
When you came as stranger, were we slow to greet?
Did we clothe and house you, give you food to eat?

When you suffered illness, pain and grief and loss,
Did we come to listen, help you bear your cross?
Jesus, we would free you from the prison cell
Where injustice casts you. Come, to make us well.

How could we deserve the goodness of your realm
While our sins deceive, and seem to overwhelm?
"Come, blest one," you beckon; we cannot believe
You are ready, waiting, eager to receive.

(Matthew 25:31–46)

115   Raise Us Now

November 20–November 26 — A   7.7.7.7.7.7.
Lavon Bayler   (PILOT)

Raise us now, Almighty God;
Lift us from the ruts we've trod.
As, by Adam, came our death,
So, in Christ, we gain new breath.
Resurrect us from the sod;
Raise us now, Almighty God.

Every rule and power below
Is destroyed, Christ's reign to know.
Soon there'll be no enemies,
As we seek our God to please.
Faithfulness will need no prod;
Raise us now, Almighty God.

Even death's authority
Is subjected, without plea.
You will be, O God, to me,
And to everyone I see
All in all, in glory shod.
Raise us now, Almighty God.

(1 Corinthians 15:20–28)

Bless God, Exalt Together — 116

All Saints–November 1 — A (or first Sunday in November) 7.6.7.6.D.
Lavon Bayler (MEIRIONYDD)

Bless God, exalt together,
Sing praises to God's name.
Beloved saints, rejoicing,
Be glad; God's love proclaim.
May all who are afflicted
With troubles hard to bear
Cry out to greet their Savior,
Who rescues from despair.

Bless God, who gives us refuge;
Be radiant with joy.
O taste eternal goodness,
False hungers to destroy.
Let all find living water
To quench their every thirst,
That, prideful boasting ended,
Their love of God comes first.

Bless God, with great thanksgiving;
All honor, power, and might
Ascribe to God forever,
And honor with delight.
The Lamb will be our shepherd
And wipe away our tears.
Come, all beloved children,
To live with hope, not fears.

(Psalm 34:1–10, 1 John 3:1–3, Revelation 7:9–17)

117 As Jesus Taught

All Saints — A   7.6.7.6.D.
Lavon Bayler   (LANCASHIRE)

As Jesus taught disciples the blessedness of trust
And called for true rejoicing despite attacks unjust,
We seek to learn and follow in joyous confidence,
The paths where Christ still leads us to make a difference.

The realm of heav'n is promised to humble-minded folk,
Whose poverty of spirit all pretenses revoke.
How blessed, too, is meekness made strong as we obey,
In selfless dedication, the One who leads the way.

May all who mourn find comfort, and thirsty be refreshed;
May those whose spirits hunger be filled with righteousness.
In purity of heart shall we see and truly live
In One whose grace and mercy we know when we forgive.

How blessed now are all who proclaim God's word of peace,
Who reconcile with neighbors, and work that wars may cease.
Rejoice, be glad, Christ calls us to live within God's realm,
Beginning now among us, that naught can overwhelm.

(Matthew 5:1–12)

Praise to You, O God

Thanksgiving Day — A
Lavon Bayler

8.7.8.7.8.7.
(REGENT SQUARE)

Praise to you, O God, in Zion,
You, who hear our every prayer,
We have made our vows before you;
Now forgive the sins we share.
You have chosen us for blessing,
Brought us near in sheltering care.

In your courts we dwell, rejoicing;
In your temple, know our place.
You have satisfied with goodness
Saints of every age and race.
Come, O God of our salvation,
May we know your healing grace.

By your strength, the seas and mountains
Took their shape, to shout for joy.
Waters flow in great abundance,
Meant to nourish, not destroy.
As you crown the year with bounty,
We would all your praise employ.

Hope of earth and distant heavens,
By whose gifts we prosper here,
We would join with all creation
Singing joyous praise sincere.
May we be forever growing,
Day by day and year by year.

(Psalm 65)

119   Forget Not

Thanksgiving Day — A
Lavon Bayler

8.6.8.6. (C.M.)
(ST. PETER)

Forget not all that God has done,
Providing this good land;
The valleys, hills, and rushing streams
Are from God's mighty hand.

Abundant crops from soils so rich
Provide our daily bread;
Remember that our God provides
The means by which we're fed.

Throughout the years, our God has led
Through dangers and distress;
We live by gracious providence,
Drawn from the wilderness.

Beware of claiming as our own
The power to create,
As if the bounty we enjoy
Were ours to orchestrate.

God draws us into covenant,
And grants us strength and power,
That we may live with faithfulness
In every day and hour.

(Deuteronomy 8:7–18)

Cheerfully Giving

120

Thanksgiving Day — A
Lavon Bayler

11.11.11.6.
(INTEGER VITAE)

Cheerfully giving, thanking God, we worship,
Grateful that God supplies what we are needing.
Surely the gospel is our greatest treasure;
We would obey and serve.

Bountifully sowing, we will reap the harvest
God has intended all the world enjoy.
Deeds that we do, God multiples and blesses;
We are enriched with love.

Seeking God's mercy, praying for deliverance,
Asking for healing, we approach the Savior.
Teacher, have mercy, save us from our suffering;
Help us to show our thanks.

From God's abundance, we have gifts for sharing,
That generosity may be our temper.
Surely our faith has offered strength and wholeness;
Thanks be to God, from all!

(Luke 17:11–19, 2 Corinthians 9:6–15)

121   A Youthful Vision

Youth, Young Adults
Lavon Bayler

8.7.8.7.D.
(HYMN TO JOY)

God, we bring our youthful vision,
Seeking better worlds than ours.
Walk beside us on our journey
Through the minutes and the hours,
When we're faced with grievous choices,
Knowing not which way to go.
Bridge the gaps that separate us
From the best your love would show.

We are troubled by the suffering
Of your children, far and near.
Why, O God, do you allow so
Many folk to live in fear,
Burdened down by war and hunger,
Shelterless and robbed of hope?
In this world of problems, help us
Face the pain and learn to cope.

Draw us into your intentions
For a loving, peaceful earth.
We would celebrate the oneness
That acknowledges our worth.
Linking with our sisters, brothers,
In the work you'd have us do,
Help us share ourselves with others,
Taking risks in service true.

God, Our Guide and Leader 122

Youth, Young Adults
Lavon Bayler

11.11.11.11., with refrain
(ST. GERTRUDE)

God, our guide and leader, meet us here, we pray.
As we face the future, and decisions weigh.
Stretch and use our talents as we live each day,
Overcome temptation, and pursue your way.
   Refrain:
   God of love and mercy, show us paths to take.
   Help us make the choice you would have us make.

What shall we believe, O God? How shall we express
Faith that lies within us, pain that brings distress?
When doubts overwhelm us, when we suffer loss,
Will Christ's living presence reach us from the cross?
   Refrain

What works shall we do, O God? Who will be our guide
As we view vocations, trying to decide?
What will satisfy us? What meet wider needs?
Will the gifts we're sharing reach where Jesus leads?
   Refrain

Who will share our lives, O God? Who will help us feel
Times of deepest caring, knowing love is real?
Guide our life commitments through all joy and woe.
May we grow in faithfulness, changing as we go.
   Refrain

God, our guide and leader, send us forth, we pray,
Facing brighter futures, following your way.
Childhood is behind us as our faith grows strong,
As we choose the work we'll do, as love becomes our song.
   Refrain

123   The Hills and Forest Beckon

Outdoor Ministry
Lavon Bayler

7.6.7.6.D.
(AURELIA)

The hills and forest beckon
As we return once more
To sense your whispered stillness,
O God, whom we adore.
The beauty that surrounds us
Reveals your splendid care;
The holy ground beneath us
Says you are everywhere.

This sacred place of memories
Has seen us laugh and cry;
The friendships we have made here
Will last until we die.
By witnesses surrounded
From generations past,
We're building for the future
New structures that will last.

Our dreams and aspirations
Have brought us to these hours,
In joyous affirmation
Of all your love empowers
For lives are touched and changed here
At Pilgrim Park* each year.
Our leap of faith allows for
New programs to appear.

---

* Substitute your own name. This song was sung at groundbreaking for a new retreat center at Pilgrim Park, near Princeton, Illinois.

People United   124

U.C.C. Identity   10.11.11.11.10.11.
Lavon Bayler   (JUDAS MACCABEUS)

People united, all one family,
We affirm together who we're meant to be:
Followers of Jesus, seeking God's high way,
By the Holy Spirit, granted power today.
People united, all one family,
We affirm together who we're meant to be.

Daily we rise to sing our joy and praise,
As God's gift of pardon sets our hearts ablaze
To confront the evil deep within our hearts,
And proclaim the gospel God's great love imparts.
People united, all one family,
We affirm together who we're meant to be.

Within the universal church, we state
How our faith has led us to participate
In God's worldwide mission, living out our call,
Sharing peace and justice meant for one and all.
People united, all one family,
We affirm together who we're meant to be.

Teaching and preaching all the Living Word,
We repent our cowardly witness yet unheard.
Open all our senses to receive and give,
That your suffering children may be freed to live.
People united, all one family,
We affirm together who we're meant to be.

May the United Church of Christ sustain
Present celebrations of God's coming reign.
As we work for justice, may the world be healed,
And your will for wholeness be once more revealed.
People united, all one family,
We affirm together who we're meant to be.

INDEXES

Alphabetical Index of Hymns

(by hymn number)

Topical Index of Hymns

(by hymn number)

Index of Scripture Readings

Psalms (*continued*)

67	January 1
	(Holy Name)
68:1–10	Easter 7
69:6–15	Pentecost 8
72:1–8	Advent 2
72:1–14	Epiphany
76	Pentecost 26
78:1–3, 10–20	Pentecost 13
81:1–10	Pentecost 20
89:20–21,	
24, 26	Maundy Thursday
91:1–10	Pentecost 5
95	Lent 3
	Pentecost 14
96	Christmas Eve/Day
97	Christmas Day,
	Second Proper
98	Christmas Day,
	Third Proper
98:1–5	Holy Cross
99	Pentecost 19
103:1–13	Pentecost 9
104:24–34	Pentecost
105:1–11	Pentecost 10
106:4–12	Pentecost 12
106:7–8,	
19–23	Pentecost 18
111	Christmas
112:4–9	Epiphany 5
114	Pentecost 15
115:1–11	Pentecost 16
116:1–9	Lent 5
116:12–19	Maundy Thursday
	Easter 3
117	New Year's Day
118:14–24	Easter Day
118:19–29	Palm Sunday, Lent 6
119:1–8	Epiphany 6
119:33–40	Epiphany 8
122	Advent 1
124	Pentecost 7
127	Pentecost 24
128	Pentecost 23
130	Lent 1
135:1–14	Pentecost 21
143:1–10	Pentecost 11
146	Pentecost 22
146:5–10	Advent 3
147:12–20	Christmas 2
150	Easter Evening

Proverbs

31:10–13,	
19–20, 30–31	Pentecost 26

Isaiah

2:1–5	Advent 1
7:10–16	Advent 4
9:1–4	Epiphany 3
9:2–7	Christmas Day/Eve
11:1–10	Advent 2
35:1–10	Advent 3
42:1–9	Epiphany 1
	(Baptism of Jesus)
44:1–8	Pentecost
49:1–7	Epiphany 2
49:8–13	Epiphany 7
50:4–9a	Passion and Palm
	Sunday, Lent 6
52:7–10	Christmas,
	Second Proper
52:13—53:12	Good Friday
58:3–9a	Epiphany 5
60:1–6	Epiphany
62:6–7, 10–12	Christmas,
	Second Proper
63:7–9	Christmas

Jeremiah

31:1–6	Easter Day
31:7–14	Christmas

Ezekiel

34:11–16,	
20–24	Pentecost 27
37:1–14	Lent 5

Daniel

12:1–3	Easter Evening

Joel

2:1–2, 12–17a	Ash Wednesday

Amos

5:18–24	Pentecost 25

Micah

6:1–8	Epiphany 4

Zephaniah

1:7, 12–18	Pentecost 26

Matthew

1:18–25	Advent 4
2:1–12	Epiphany
2:13–15,	
19–23	Christmas 1
3:1–12	Advent 2
3:13–17	Epiphany 1
	(Baptism of Jesus)

4:1–11	Lent	2:15–21	January 1
4:12–23	Epiphany 3		(Holy Name)
5:1–12	Epiphany 4	17:11–19	Thanksgiving Day
	All Saints	24:13–35	Easter 3
5:13–16	Epiphany 5	24:13–49	Easter Evening
5:17–26	Epiphany 6	24:46–53	Ascension
5:27–37	Epiphany 7		
5:38–48	Epiphany 8	**John**	
6:1–6, 16–21	Ash Wednesday	1:1–14	Christmas,
7:21–29	Pentecost 2		Second Proper
9:9–13	Pentecost 3	1:1–18	Christmas 2
9:35—10:8	Pentecost 4	1:29–34	Epiphany 2
10:24–33	Pentecost 5	3:1–17	Lent 2
10:34–42	Pentecost 6	4:5–42	Lent 3
11:2–11	Advent 3	7:37–39	Pentecost Sunday
11:25–30	Pentecost 7	9	Lent 4
13:1–9, 18–23	Pentecost 8	10:1–10	Easter 4
13:24–43	Pentecost 9	11:1–45	Lent 5
13:44–52	Pentecost 10	13:1–15	Maundy Thursday
14:13–21	Pentecost 11	14:1–14	Easter 5
14:22–33	Pentecost 12	14:15–21	Easter 6
15:21–28	Pentecost 13	17:1–11	Easter 7
16:13–20	Pentecost 14	18:1—19:42	Good Friday
16:21–28	Pentecost 15	20:1–18	Easter Day
17:1–9	Epiphany,	20:19–23	Pentecost
	Last Sunday	20:19–31	Easter 2
	Lent 2		
18:15–20	Pentecost 16	**Acts**	
18:21–35	Pentecost 17	1:1–11	Ascension
20:1–16	Pentecost 18	1:6–14	Easter 7
21:1–11	Palm Sunday, Lent 6	2:1–21	Pentecost
21:28–32	Pentecost 19	2:14a, 22–24	Easter 2
21:33–43	Pentecost 20	2:14a, 36–41	Easter 3
22:1–14	Pentecost 21	2:42–47	Easter 4
22:15–22	Pentecost 22	5:29–32	Easter Evening
22:34–46	Pentecost 23	7:55–60	Easter 5
23:1–12	Pentecost 24	10:34–43	Epiphany 1
24:36–44	Advent 1		(Baptism of Jesus)
25:1–13	Pentecost 25		Easter Day
25:14–30	Pentecost 26	17:1–12	Easter 5
25:31–46	January 1	17:22–31	Easter 6
	(New Year's Day)		
	Pentecost 27	**Romans**	
26:14—27:66	Passion Sunday, Lent 6	1:1–7	Advent 4
28:1–10	Easter Day	3:21–28	Pentecost 2
28:16–20	Trinity Sunday	4:1–17	Lent 2
		4:13–18	Pentecost 3
Mark		5:1–11	Lent 3
16:9–16,		5:6–11	Pentecost 4
19–20	Ascension	5:12–19	Lent 1
			Pentecost 5
Luke		6:3–11	Pentecost 6
2:1–20	Christmas Eve/Day	7:14–25a	Pentecost 7
2:8–20	Christmas,	8:6–11	Lent 5
	Second Proper	8:9–17	Pentecost 8

Romans (*continued*)

1 Corinthians

2 Corinthians

Galatians

Ephesians

Philippians

Colossians

1 Thessalonians

Titus

Hebrews

James

1 Peter

2 Peter

1 John

Revelation

Index of Words and Themes

Ancestors (*continued*)
Maundy Thursday
Pentecost 3, 5, 7
Thanksgiving

Anger
Advent 3
Epiphany 4, 8
Pentecost 9, 14, 26
All Saints

Anguish
Epiphany 3
Lent 5
Pentecost 26

Anticipation
Advent 1
Lent 4
Easter Day
Easter 2
Pentecost 25

Anxiety
Easter 4, 7
Pentecost 21, 24

Apathy
All Saints

Appearance(s)
Epiphany, Last Sunday
Lent 4
Easter Sunday
Ascension Day
Pentecost 14

Arrogance
All Saints

Ascension
Ascension Day

Assurance
Christmas Season 2
Ash Wednesday
Lent 3
Easter Evening
Pentecost 6, 10, 11, 13, 25

Attitude(s)
Advent 1

Authenticity
Pentecost 25

Authority(ies)
Trinity Sunday
Pentecost 2, 16, 20

Awake(n)
Lent 4
Palm Sunday
Easter Evening
Pentecost 26, 27

Awe and Wonder
January 1 (Jesus and Mary)
Epiphany
Epiphany 1, 2, 8, Last Sunday
Ash Wednesday
Passion Sunday
Maundy Thursday
Easter Day
Easter 2, 7
Pentecost
Trinity
Pentecost 2, 4, 5, 6, 7, 9, 17, 23

Baptism
Advent 2
Epiphany 1, 2
Easter 3, 6
Pentecost
Trinity
Pentecost 6, 20
All Saints

Bearing Fruit
Advent 2
Pentecost 8, 20

Beatitudes
Epiphany 4
All Saints

Beauty
Christmas Eve/Day
Epiphany 3
Thanksgiving

Becoming
Epiphany 7
Pentecost 18
All Saints

Believe(rs)
Advent 4
Christmas Eve/Day
Epiphany 1, 4
Passion Sunday

Good Friday
Easter Sunday
Easter Evening
Easter 3, 5
Ascension Day
Pentecost 9, 10, 16, 19

Best
Christmas Day 2
Epiphany 7, 8
Pentecost 3, 4, 6, 24, 25, 26

Betrayal
Passion Sunday
Good Friday
Pentecost 17

Better Way
Christmas Season 1
Epiphany 8
Palm Sunday
Easter Evening
Pentecost 4, 18

Bewilderment
Good Friday
Pentecost

Birth(day)
Advent 4
Christmas Eve/Day
Christmas Day II
Pentecost

Bitter(ness)
Epiphany 8
Maundy Thursday
Pentecost 26

Bless(ing)
Advent 2, 4
Christmas Season 1, 2
New Year's Day
January 1 (Jesus and Mary)
Epiphany 1, 2, 4, 6, 8, Last Sunday
Lent 2, 3
Palm Sunday
Easter 2, 4, 7
Trinity Sunday
Pentecost 2, 3, 5, 6, 7, 9, 10, 11, 12,
    13, 14, 17, 18, 19, 20, 21, 22, 23,
    24, 25
All Saints
Thanksgiving

Blindness
Advent 3
Christmas Season 2
Lent 4
Pentecost 22, 26

Boasting
Pentecost 2
All Saints

Body of Christ
Christmas Eve/Day
Lent 4
Pentecost
Pentecost 15, 16

Bondage
Christmas Season 1
Lent 5
Pentecost 6, 7, 9, 21

Boredom
Pentecost

Born Anew
Christmas Season 2
Lent 2
Easter 2, 3

Bounty
Epiphany 3, 6, 8, Last
    Sunday
Lent 5
Easter 7
Pentecost 3, 13, 21
Thanksgiving

Bread
Christmas Season 2
New Year's Day
Epiphany 5
Lent 1
Maundy Thursday
Easter Evening
Easter 3, 4, 7
Pentecost 3, 8, 13
Thanksgiving

Breath(e)
Epiphany 1, 6
Lent 1, 5
Easter Evening
Easter 2, 5
Pentecost 22, 23

Brightness
Epiphany
Easter Evening

Brokenness
Christmas Day 2
Christmas Season 1
Epiphany 1
Lent 1, 5
Good Friday
Pentecost

Brothers and Sisters
Christmas Day 2
Christmas Season 1
New Year's Day
Epiphany
Epiphany 5, 6, 7
Lent 3
Passion Sunday
Palm Sunday
Maundy Thursday
Easter 4, 5
Pentecost 4, 8, 9, 15, 17, 20, 22, 23, 24, 25, 26, 27
All Saints

Building
Epiphany 7
Trinity Sunday
Pentecost 2, 4, 8, 24, 26

Burden(s)
Advent 2, 3
Christmas Eve/Day
Lent 2
Easter
Pentecost 7, 8, 15, 24

Busyness
Maundy Thursday
Pentecost 18, 21

Call(ed)
Christmas Eve/Day
Epiphany 2, 3, 4
Easter Sunday
Easter 4, 5
Passion Sunday
Good Friday
Pentecost 10
Thanksgiving

Calm
Lent 4
Pentecost 27

Care, Caring
Advent 2, 4
Christmas Season 1
New Year's Day
Epiphany 2, 3
Lent 1, 3
Passion Sunday
Maundy Thursday
Easter 3, 5, 7
Pentecost 3, 5, 8, 11, 13, 15, 17, 20, 23, 26

Celebration
Advent 4
New Year's Day
January 1 (Jesus and Mary)
Lent 1, 5
Palm Sunday
Maundy Thursday
Easter Sunday
Easter Evening
Easter 5, 7
Pentecost
Trinity
Pentecost 10, 11, 14, 21, 25

Challenge(s)
Epiphany 8
Lent 4
Trinity
Pentecost 9, 12, 14, 16, 24

Change
Epiphany
Epiphany 5
Ash Wednesday
Lent 2, 3
Pentecost 4, 8, 13, 15, 23

Cheer(ful)
Pentecost 14, 15

Child(ren) (of God) (of Light)
Advent 2, 4
Christmas Eve/Day
Christmas Day 2
Christmas Season 2
January 1 (Jesus and Mary)
Epiphany 3, 5, 6, 8
Trinity
Lent 3, 4
Pentecost 2, 6, 7, 8, 9, 12, 13, 16, 19, 23, 24, 26
All Saints

Commendation
Pentecost 20

Commission(ed)
Ascension Day
Pentecost 6, 20, 21

Commitment
Christmas Eve/Day
Christmas Day 2
Christmas Season
Epiphany 2, 4, 6
New Year's Day
Palm Sunday
Maundy Thursday
Good Friday
Easter Sunday
Easter Evening
Easter 5
Trinity Sunday
Pentecost 3, 4, 6, 11, 15, 17, 18

Commonplace
Christmas Day 1
January 1 (Jesus and Mary)
Epiphany
Pentecost Sunday

Commonwealth
Pentecost 20

Communion
Epiphany
Maundy Thursday
Easter 3
Pentecost 23, 24

Community
Advent 2
Christmas Day 1
Epiphany
Epiphany 1, 2, 4, 6, 7
Passion Sunday
Maundy Thursday
Easter Sunday
Easter 4, 5, 7
Ascension Day
Trinity Sunday
Pentecost 4, 10, 13, 15, 16, 17, 18, 19,
    21, 23

Companion(ship)
Easter 7
Pentecost 2, 25

Comparisons
Pentecost 2

Compassion
Epiphany
Epiphany 5, 7
Easter 6
Pentecost 4, 9, 11, 19, 21, 24,
    27

Complacency
Lent 3
Pentecost 15

Complaint(s)
Epiphany 8
Lent 3
Maundy Thursday
Pentecost 13, 25

Concern
Christmas Day 1
Pentecost 22
Thanksgiving

Condemn(ation)
Lent 1
Pentecost 25

Confess(ion)
Christmas Eve/Day
Christmas Day 2
Christmas Season 1
Epiphany 2, Last Sunday
Lent 1, 3,
Passion Sunday
Good Friday
Pentecost 9, 11, 14, 15, 18, 27

Confidence
Christmas Season 1
Epiphany
Epiphany 3
Lent 2, 4
Passion Sunday
Palm Sunday
Maundy Thursday
Easter Evening
Easter 3
Pentecost 9, 10, 11, 23, 24

Confirmation, Confirm
Epiphany 2, 8
Pentecost 20

Conformity
Palm Sunday
Pentecost 15, 18

Confront(ation)
Trinity Sunday
Pentecost 16

Confusion
Epiphany 3, 5
Pentecost 4, 25, 27

Contemplation
Pentecost 18

Conversation
Pentecost 14

Conviction
Pentecost 2

Cornerstone
Pentecost 20

Correction
Pentecost 25

Counsel(or)
Christmas Eve/Day
Easter 6
Trinity Sunday

Courage
Advent 3
Christmas Eve/Day
Epiphany 1, 2, 3
Lent 3
Passion Sunday
Maundy Thursday
Easter 4
Pentecost 2, 6, 7, 11, 12, 15, 19, 23, 24

Covenant
Christmas Season 1
Epiphany 1, 7
Maundy Thursday
Easter 3
Pentecost 10, 12, 13, 15, 17
Thanksgiving

Creation, Creator, Creative
Advent 2, 4
Christmas Day 2
Epiphany 5, 6, 7
Ash Wednesday

Lent 1, 3, 5
Palm Sunday
Easter 2, 3, 5
Pentecost
Trinity Sunday
Pentecost 3, 9, 10, 11, 14, 15, 16, 19,
20, 21, 22, 25

Cries, Cry
New Year's Day
Epiphany
Epiphany 1, 2, 5, 6, Last Sunday
Good Friday
Easter 5
Pentecost 6, 9, 13

Cross
Epiphany 3, 4
Good Friday
Easter Sunday
Pentecost 6, 15, 20

Crucifixion
Good Friday
Pentecost 20

Cruelty
Passion Sunday
Good Friday
Pentecost 20

Cup
Maundy Thursday
Easter 3
Pentecost
Pentecost 27

Cut Off
Advent 3

Cynics
Advent 3

Daring
Christmas Eve/Day
Christmas Season 1
Epiphany 2, 5, 6, Last Sunday
Lent 2, 3, 5
Easter 3
Pentecost
Pentecost 3, 6, 9, 12, 13, 16, 25

Darkness
Christmas Day 1, 2
Christmas Season 2

Devotion
Easter 4
Pentecost 3, 5, 8, 15, 17, 22
All Saints

Difference(s)
New Year's Day
Epiphany 3, 4, 6
Passion Sunday
Easter Sunday
Easter 6
Pentecost 4, 21

Difficult(ies)
Christmas Eve/Day
Lent 4
Thanksgiving

Direct(ion)
Christmas Day 2
Epiphany 6
Lent 1
Pentecost 3, 27
Thanksgiving

Disciple(ship)
Epiphany 1, 3, Last Sunday
Lent 4
Passion Sunday
Palm Sunday
Maundy Thursday
Good Friday
Easter Sunday
Easter 3, 4
Pentecost
Trinity Sunday
Pentecost 3, 4, 5, 6, 8, 19, 23

Discipline(s)
Advent 1
New Year's Day
Ash Wednesday
Lent 4
Palm Sunday
Trinity Sunday
Pentecost 5, 9

Disobedience
Advent 4
January 1 (Jesus and Mary)
Pentecost 13

Distortion
Epiphany 5
Passion Sunday
Pentecost 11

Distress
Epiphany 5
Lent 5
Passion Sunday
Pentecost 11, 20, 16

Distrust
Advent 3
Passion Sunday

Divisions, Divisive
Easter 6
Pentecost
Pentecost 6, 27

Dogmatic Certainty
Pentecost 11

Domination
Advent 1

Doubt
January 1 (Jesus and Mary)
Epiphany 5
Lent 5, 6
Passion Sunday
Good Friday
Easter Evening
Easter 2
Ascension Day
Pentecost
Trinity Sunday
Pentecost 3, 6, 10, 11, 12, 14, 16,
    17, 27

Dreams
Advent 3
Epiphany 4
Pentecost
Pentecost 5, 6

Drink
Pentecost 14

Dry (Bones)
Lent 5
Pentecost 14

Eager(ness)
Advent 2, 3
Lent 1
Pentecost 9

Eagle's Wings
Pentecost 15

Ears
Advent 2, 3
Christmas Day 1
Epiphany 5
Lent 1
Easter 3, 4, 5
Ascension Day
Pentecost 2, 4, 6, 9, 13 19

Elderly
Pentecost 27

Emmanuel
Advent 4

Empowerment
Advent 2
Christmas Day 2
New Year's Day
Christmas Season 2
Epiphany
Epiphany 1, 2, 3, 5, 6, 7, Last Sunday
Ash Wednesday
Lent 1, 3, 4, 5
Easter 7
Pentecost 4, 6, 7, 16, 17, 29, 22, 23
Thanksgiving

Emptiness, Empty
Lent 5
Passion Sunday
Palm Sunday
Pentecost 3, 14, 19, 21, 23, 25

Encouragement
Pentecost 19, 20, 24, 26

Endurance
Ash Wednesday
Lent 3
Pentecost 17

Enemies
Epiphany 3, 8
Lent 4
Passion Sunday
Easter 5, 7
Pentecost 4, 11, 20, 27

Energy
Christmas Day 1
Pentecost 4, 7, 25

Enlighten(ment)
Christmas Day 2
Christmas Season 2

Lent 4
Ascension Day
Pentecost 17

Enrich(ment)
Thanksgiving

Entrust(ed)
Christmas Season 2
Epiphany 3, 7
Pentecost 12, 15, 16, 17, 20, 25, 26

Equality
Advent 1
Passion Sunday

Equip(ped)
Advent 1
Epiphany 1, 6
Lent 1, 3, 4
Good Friday
All Saints

Equity
Christmas Eve/Day
Christmas Day 2
January 1 (Jesus and Mary)
Pentecost 19

Eternal Life, Eternity
Passion Sunday
Easter Evening
All Saints

Eternal Values
Epiphany 6
Pentecost 16, 21

Evil
Advent 1, 4
Christmas Day 1
Christmas Season 1
Epiphany 3, 4, 6, 8
Ash Wednesday
Lent 4
Good Friday
Easter Evening
Pentecost 7, 15, 27

Excellence
Pentecost 21

Excitement
Pentecost 18

Feeding, Fed, Food (*continued*)
Pentecost
Pentecost 4, 11, 21, 22, 24, 27
All Saints
Thanksgiving

Feet
Christmas Day 1, 2
Epiphany 1, 4
Lent 2
Easter Sunday
Easter 5
Pentecost 16

Fire, Flames
Advent 2
Christmas Day 2
Epiphany 1, 8
Easter 6
Pentecost
Pentecost 16

Flesh
Christmas Day 2
Lent 5
Pentecost
Pentecost 8

Follow(ers)
Epiphany 3, 4
Lent 5
Passion Sunday
Palm Sunday
Maundy Thursday
Good Friday
Easter
Easter 4
Pentecost 3, 6, 12, 15, 22

Foolishness
Epiphany 4
Lent 5
Pentecost 3

Foot-washing
Maundy Thursday

Forget, Forgotten
New Year's Day
Lent 3
Maundy Thursday
Easter Sunday
Pentecost 3, 12, 13, 14, 18, 20
Thanksgiving

Forgiveness
Advent 4
Christmas Eve/Day
New Year's Day
January 1 (Jesus and Mary)
Epiphany
Epiphany 1, 6, 8, Last Sunday
Ash Wednesday
Lent 1, 2, 4, 5
Passion Sunday
Maundy Thursday
Good Friday
Easter Evening
Easter 2, 3, 4
Ascension Day
Pentecost
Trinity Sunday
Pentecost 5, 6, 7, 8, 9, 12, 13, 14, 15,
16, 17, 19, 20, 21, 22, 23, 24, 27
Thanksgiving

Forsaken
Good Friday

Fortress
Easter 5
Pentecost 5

Foundation(s)
Epiphany 7
Pentecost 2, 4

Fountain
New Year's Day
Pentecost 14

Free(dom)
Advent 3
Christmas Eve/Day
New Year's Day
Epiphany 1, 5, 7
Lent 1, 5
Palm Sunday
Easter 6
Trinity
Pentecost 6, 7, 8, 9, 10, 11, 14, 16, 22,
27
Thanksgiving

Friends
Christmas Day 1
New Year's Day
January 1 (Jesus and Mary)
Epiphany 5, 6
Lent 1

Maundy Thursday
Good Friday
Easter Sunday
Easter 3, 6, 7
Trinity Sunday
Pentecost 2, 3, 4, 5, 8, 10, 11, 12, 13,
  14, 16, 17, 18, 19, 20, 22, 23, 24,
  25, 26
All Saints
Thanksgiving

God's Majesty
Advent 3
Christmas Day 2
Epiphany 1, Last Sunday
Pentecost
Pentecost 2, 26
All Saints

God's Peace
Advent 1
Christmas Day 2

God's Power
Christmas Season 1
January 1 (Jesus and Mary)
Epiphany 1, 5, 7
Ash Wednesday
Lent 2
Ascension Day
Easter 7
Pentecost
Trinity Sunday
Pentecost 15, 18, 23
All Saints

God's Presence
Advent 1, 2, 4
Christmas Day 2
Christmas Season 1, 2
Epiphany
Epiphany 1, 2, 4, 6, Last Sunday
Ash Wednesday
Lent 1, 3, 4, 5
Palm Sunday
Good Friday
Easter Sunday
Easter 2, 3, 4, 5, 6, 7
Pentecost
Trinity Sunday
Pentecost 4, 5, 6, 8, 9, 10, 11, 12, 13,
  14, 15, 16, 17, 18, 19, 21, 22, 23,
  25, 27
All Saints

God's Promise(s)
Advent 2, 3, 4
Christmas Eve/Day
New Year's Day
Epiphany 1, 8
Ash Wednesday
Lent 2
Good Friday
Easter Evening
Easter 3, 6
Ascension Day
Trinity Sunday
Pentecost 2, 3, 5, 6, 7, 8, 10, 11, 12,
  18, 21

God's Protection
Christmas Season 1
Lent 4
Good Friday
Pentecost 5, 6, 7

God's Purposes
New Year's Day
Epiphany 5, Last Sunday
Lent 1, 3
Good Friday
Ascension Day
Pentecost 3, 8, 10, 13, 16, 17, 18, 19, 26

God's Realm (Reign, Rule)
Advent 2
Christmas Eve/Day
Christmas Day 1, 2
New Year's Day
Epiphany
Epiphany 3, 7, 8, Last Sunday
Lent 2, 3, 5
Passion Sunday
Palm Sunday
Easter 5, 6, 7
Ascension Day
Pentecost 4, 8, 9, 10, 16, 17, 18, 19, 20,
  21, 22, 23, 24, 25, 27
All Saints

God's Saving Acts
Epiphany 2
Good Friday
Pentecost 9, 10, 13, 21

God's Voice
Advent 2, 3
Christmas Day 2
Epiphany 1, 6, Last Sunday
Lent 2, 3
Pentecost 3, 14, 15, 19, 20, 27

God's Ways
Advent 2
January 1 (Jesus and Mary)
Epiphany 4, 5, 6, 7
Lent 1, 4
Easter 5
Pentecost 2, 12, 14, 15, 16, 17, 18,
  22, 23

God's Will
Advent 4
Christmas Season 2
Epiphany 2
Easter Sunday
Easter 5
Trinity Sunday
Pentecost 2, 3, 5, 6, 7, 9, 13, 14, 15,
  19, 26

God's Word
Advent 4
New Year's Day
Christmas Season 2
Epiphany 2, 5, 6, Last Sunday
Lent 1, 3, 5
Easter Evening
Pentecost
Pentecost 4, 8, 9, 10, 12, 13, 16, 17,
  20, 21
All Saints

God's Work(s)
Advent 1
Christmas Eve/Day
Christmas Season 1
New Year's Day
January 1 (Jesus and Mary)
Epiphany
Epiphany 1, 5, 8, Last Sunday
Lent 3, 4
Easter Sunday
Pentecost
Trinity Sunday
Pentecost 4, 10, 11, 12, 18, 19, 24,
  27

God's Wrath
Pentecost 18, 19

Good Deeds
Christmas Eve/Day
Christmas Season 1
Epiphany 5
Pentecost 2

Good News (Tidings)
Advent 2, 3, 4
Christmas Eve/Day
Christmas Day 1, 2
Christmas Season 1
New Year's Day
January 1 (Jesus and Mary)
Epiphany
Epiphany 1, 2, 3, 7, Last Sunday
Lent 1, 2, 3, 4
Palm Sunday
Good Friday
Easter Sunday
Easter Evening
Easter 2, 3, 5, 7
Ascension Day
Trinity Sunday
Pentecost 2, 4, 22, 23, 24, 25, 26
All Saints
Thanksgiving

Good Shepherd
Easter 4
Pentecost 4

Goodness
Epiphany 4, 6
Lent 4
Good Friday
Easter 4
Pentecost 2, 15, 27

Gospel
Advent 4
Epiphany
Epiphany 3
Pentecost 3, 18, 21, 22, 23
Thanksgiving

Grace, Gracious
Advent 4
Christmas Eve/Day
Christmas Day 1, 2
Christmas Season 2
New Year's Day
Epiphany
Epiphany 2, 4, 5, 7
Lent 1, 2, 3, 5
Passion Sunday
Palm Sunday
Good Friday
Easter Sunday
Easter Evening
Easter 5
Trinity Sunday

Pentecost 2, 3, 5, 6, 9, 13, 17, 19, 21,
22, 26
Thanksgiving

Gratitude
Advent 3
New Year's Day
January 1 (Jesus and Mary)
Epiphany 1
Lent 1, 4
Ash Wednesday
Maundy Thursday
Good Friday
Easter 3, 7
Pentecost
Pentecost 3, 8, 11, 12, 13, 17, 18, 19,
25, 27
All Saints
Thanksgiving

Greed
Trinity Sunday
Pentecost 13, 23

Green Pastures
Pentecost 27

Growth
Epiphany 6, 7
Lent 3
Pentecost 4, 6, 7, 9, 18, 27
All Saints

Grief
Good Friday
Easter 2
Pentecost 25, 27

Grumble
Advent 3

Guests
Maundy Thursday

Guilt
Epiphany 2, 8
Lent 2
Maundy Thursday
Good Friday
Easter 6
Pentecost 8

Hand(s)
Advent 4
Epiphany 1, 5, 7, 8

Lent 1, 5
Easter 5
Pentecost Sunday
Pentecost 11, 13, 14, 16, 20, 21

Happy
Pentecost 22, 24
All Saints

Harmony
Advent 2

Harp, Lyre, Strings
Trinity Sunday

Harvest
Advent 2
Christmas Eve/Day
Pentecost 4, 9, 18
Thanksgiving

Healing, Health
Advent 1, 3
Christmas Day 1
New Year's Day
Christmas Season 2
Epiphany 1, 3, 5, 6, 7, 8
Ash Wednesday
Lent 1, 3, 4, 5
Maundy Thursday
Good Friday
Easter Sunday
Easter 4, 6, 7
Pentecost 3, 4, 8, 11, 13, 17, 22
Thanksgiving

Hear(ing)
Advent 1, 2, 3
Christmas Season 1
Epiphany
Epiphany 2, 5, Last Sunday
Lent 1, Z, 5
Good Friday
Easter Sunday
Easter 4, 5, 6
Pentecost 3, 6, 9, 11, 15, 19, 20, 21, 24,
25

Heart(s)
Advent 4
Christmas Eve/Day
Christmas Day 1, 2
Christmas Season 1, 2
January 1 (Jesus and Mary)
Epiphany 2, 4, 5, 6, 7, 8

Hospitality
Lent 4
Easter 3
Pentecost 6, 21

Humility
Advent 2
New Year's Day
January 1 (Jesus and Mary)
Epiphany 1, 4, 5
Ash Wednesday
Passion Sunday
Palm Sunday
Good Friday
Easter 7
Trinity Sunday
Pentecost 2, 5, 7, 12, 14, 24
All Saints
Thanksgiving

Hunger
New Year's Day
Epiphany 4, 5, 6, 7
Palm Sunday
Easter 5
Pentecost
Pentecost 4, 13, 22, 24, 25, 27
All Saints

Hurt(s)
Epiphany 6, 8
Lent 1
Maundy Thursday
Easter 5, 6

Identity
Pentecost 15, 19

Idols
Christmas Eve/Day
Christmas Day 1
Lent 1
Easter 5
Pentecost 11, 16, 18, 22, 23

Image (of Christ)
Epiphany
Epiphany, Last Sunday
Pentecost 10

Imagine(ation)
Maundy Thursday
Pentecost 14, 18

Impatience
Advent 3
Epiphany 4

Incarnation
Advent 4

Individuality
Pentecost 18

Indulgence
Pentecost 26

Influence
Pentecost 7

Inheritance
New Year's Day
Christmas Season 2
Epiphany 4
Lent 2
Easter 2

Inner Being
Pentecost 19

Insensitivity
Pentecost 12

Intentions
Christmas Season 2
Epiphany 1, 6, 7
Easter 5, 6

Invest
New Year's Day
Epiphany 3
Pentecost 26

Invitation
Epiphany 3
Ash Wednesday
Lent 1
Palm Sunday
Pentecost 25

Isolation
Pentecost 8, 15

Jealousy
Epiphany 6
Easter 5, 6
Pentecost 20

Epiphany 4
Ash Wednesday
Pentecost 25
All Saints

Multiply
Thanksgiving

Mystery of God
Christmas Eve/Day
Epiphany
Epiphany 4, 8, Last Sunday
Easter 5
Pentecost 9

Name(s)
Epiphany, Last Sunday
Palm Sunday
Easter Sunday
Pentecost 6, 19
All Saints

Narrowness
Epiphany
Lent 1, 3, 4
Easter 2, 6
Pentecost 7, 25

Need(s)(y)
Advent 2
Christmas Day 1
New Year's Day
Epiphany
Epiphany 5
Lent 1, 3
Good Friday
Easter 6, 7
Pentecost Sunday
Pentecost 4, 9, 11, 14, 15, 22, 25, 26, 27
Thanksgiving

Neglect
New Year's Day
Epiphany
Maundy Thursday
Pentecost 3, 9, 11

Neighbors
Epiphany 2
Lent 3
Palm Sunday
Pentecost 16
All Saints

New Commandment
Maundy Thursday

New Day
Christmas Day 1, 2
New Year's Day
Epiphany 1, Last Sunday

New Life
Advent 4
Christmas Day 1
Christmas Season 1
New Year's Day
Epiphany 1, 4, 6, 8
Ash Wednesday
Lent 2, 5
Maundy Thursday
Good Friday
Easter Sunday
Easter Evening
Easter 2, 3, 5, 6
Pentecost 6, 7, 8, 9, 10, 11, 12, 26

New Possibilities
New Year's Day
Epiphany 8
Lent 2
Ascension Day
Pentecost Sunday

New Song
Trinity Sunday

New Ways
New Year's Day
Epiphany
Easter 7
Pentecost 2
Thanksgiving

Night
Advent 1
Christmas Season 2
Good Friday

Now
Easter Sunday

Obedience
Advent 2, 4
January 1 (Jesus and Mary)
Epiphany 6
Lent 1
Easter 3
Pentecost Sunday
Pentecost 3, 15, 16, 19, 20

Redemption
Christmas Eve/Day
Christmas Day 1
Christmas Season 1
Epiphany 4
Lent 1
Easter 5
Pentecost 9, 12, 17

Reform
Easter Evening
Pentecost Sunday

Refuge
Epiphany 7
Easter 5
Pentecost 4, 5, 6, 23
All Saints

Rejoicing
Christmas Eve/Day
Christmas Day 1
New Year's Day
January 1 (Jesus and Mary)
Epiphany 2, 3, 4
Ash Wednesday
Lent 3, 4, 5
Palm Sunday
Easter Sunday
Easter 2, 5, 7
Ascension Day
Pentecost Sunday
Trinity Sunday
Pentecost 4, 10, 11, 12, 16, 17, 21, 22, 24
All Saints
Thanksgiving

Relationships
Advent 2
Christmas Eve/Day
Epiphany 5, 6
Lent 1
Passion Sunday
Palm Sunday
Easter 3
Pentecost Sunday
Pentecost 2, 3, 7, 10, 13, 15, 16, 17, 22, 23, 24

Remembrance
Christmas Season 1
Ash Wednesday
Lent 5

Maundy Thursday
Ascension Day
Pentecost 3, 10, 11, 12, 13, 14, 15, 16, 18, 22, 27
Thanksgiving

Renewal
Advent 4
Christmas Day
New Year's Day
Epiphany 1
Ash Wednesday
Lent 2, 3, 5
Easter 4
Pentecost Sunday
Pentecost 6, 7, 8, 9, 10, 11, 14, 15, 16

Repentance
Advent 2
Epiphany 3
Good Friday
Pentecost 2, 19

Reproof
Pentecost 25

Rescue
January 1 (Jesus and Mary)
Epiphany 3
Good Friday
Pentecost 7, 8, 27

Resistance
Christmas Eve/Day
Epiphany 8, Last Sunday
Pentecost Sunday
Pentecost 6, 9, 13

Resources
Advent 2, 4
Christmas Season 1, 2
New Year's Day
Epiphany, Last Sunday
Lent 1, 2, 3, 4
Passion Sunday
Pentecost 5, 25, 26, 27
Thanksgiving

Responsibility
Palm Sunday
Maundy Thursday
Easter 3
Pentecost 2, 20, 26

Responsiveness
Christmas Eve/Day
Christmas Season 1
Epiphany, Last Sunday
Ascension Day
Pentecost 3, 4, 12, 17, 18, 22, 27

Rest
Lent 5
Passion Sunday
Good Friday
Pentecost 7, 24, 27

Restoration
Lent 4
Pentecost 8, 24, 27

Results
Pentecost 18

Resurrection
Lent 5
Easter Sunday
Easter Evening
Easter 2, 6
Ascension Day
Pentecost 25

Revelation
Christmas Eve/Day
Epiphany
Epiphany 5, Last Sunday
Lent 3, 4
Maundy Thursday
Good Friday
Easter 7
Pentecost 2, 5, 7, 9, 10, 13, 16, 24

Reverence
Epiphany 1
Ash Wednesday
Easter 6

Reward(ing)
Ash Wednesday
Pentecost 18

Rich(es)
Advent 2
Christmas Season 2
Epiphany
Ash Wednesday
Maundy Thursday

Pentecost 14, 19, 22, 27
Thanksgiving

Right
Epiphany 1
Ash Wednesday
Lent 2
Easter Sunday
Easter 5, 6
Pentecost 7

Righteous(ness)
Advent 2
Christmas Eve/Day
Christmas Day 1, 2
Epiphany
Epiphany 1, 4, 5, 6
Lent 1, 5
Easter Evening
Easter 4, 5, 6
Trinity Sunday
Pentecost 3, 5, 17, 25, 27
All Saints
Thanksgiving

Rise(n)
Lent 1
Easter Sunday
Easter 4, 6

Risk
Epiphany 2
Passion Sunday
Palm Sunday
Ascension Day
Pentecost 13
All Saints

Ritual(s)
Pentecost 3, 25

Rivalry
Pentecost 4, 22

Rock
Epiphany 1
Lent 3
Easter 5
Pentecost 2, 14, 17

Rod and Staff
Easter 4

Roots
Advent 2

Soul
Advent 4
Lent 2
Easter 4, 5
Pentecost 9, 11, 17, 19, 22, 27
All Saints

Sower
Pentecost 8
Thanksgiving

Sparingly
Thanksgiving

Spirit(s)
Christmas Season 2
Epiphany 1, 5, 6
Ash Wednesday
Lent 2, 3, 5
Passion Sunday
Ascension Day
Pentecost 5, 6, 7, 8, 11, 16, 19, 23, 25, 27

Spiritual Ancestors
Pentecost 8, 11, 13
Thanksgiving

Spiritual Blessings
Christmas Season 2

Spiritual Depths, Heights
Pentecost 7, 9, 11, 14

Spiritual Nourishment
Christmas Season 1
Lent 1, 5
Easter 5

Standards
Pentecost 6, 18

Star(s)
Christmas Day 2
Epiphany
Epiphany, Last Sunday
Easter Evening
Pentecost 9

Steadfast Love
Advent 2
Christmas Season 1
New Year's Day
Epiphany 1, 2, 7
Ash Wednesday

Lent 1, 2
Passion Sunday
Palm Sunday
Maundy Thursday
Easter 5, 6
Trinity Sunday
Pentecost 2, 6, 8, 9, 11, 12, 16, 17, 18

Steward(ship)
Advent 4
Epiphany
Epiphany 8, Last Sunday
Easter 4
Pentecost 16, 18, 26

Still (Small Voice)
Advent 4
Epiphany 4,7
Pentecost 4

Still Waters
Lent 4
Pentecost 27

Stone(s)
Lent 5
Easter Sunday
Easter 5

Story
Advent 4
Christmas Eve/Day
January 1 (Jesus and Mary)
Maundy Thursday
Pentecost 13

Strangers
Christmas Day 1
New Year's Day
Palm Sunday
Easter Evening
Pentecost 23, 27

Strength
Advent 3, 4
Christmas Season 1, 2
Epiphany 1, 2, 3, 4, 5
Ash Wednesday
Lent 2, 5
Good Friday
Easter Sunday
Easter 4, 5, 7
Pentecost 4, 6, 7, 10, 13, 16, 17, 18, 20, 21, 22, 25, 27
Thanksgiving

Strife
Epiphany 3, 6
Pentecost 20

Struggle
Advent 2
Passion Sunday
Pentecost 6, 8

Stumbling (Block)
Epiphany 8
Lent 4, 5
Good Friday

Success
Christmas Day 1

Suffering
Christmas Season 1
Maundy Thursday
Good Friday
Passion Sunday
Easter Sunday
Easter 4, 5, 7
Pentecost 4, 9, 21, 22, 24

Swords (and Plowshares)
Advent 1
Pentecost 11

Table
Maundy Thursday
Easter 3, 4
Pentecost 3, 21

Teach(er, ing)
Christmas Season 1
Epiphany 6, 8
Passion Sunday
Trinity Sunday
Pentecost 5, 10, 11, 12, 13, 14, 19,
21, 24

Tears
New Year's Day
Christmas Season 2
Good Friday
All Saints

Temptation
Christmas Season 1
New Year's Day
Lent 1
Passion Sunday

Terror
Pentecost 26, 27

Test
New Year's Day
Trinity Sunday

Testify, Testimony
Epiphany 2, 6, 8
Pentecost 8

Thanks(giving)
Christmas Day 1
Christmas Season 1, 2
New Year's Day
Epiphany 2, 3, 6, 7
Lent 2, 3, 4, 5
Palm Sunday
Maundy Thursday
Easter Sunday
Easter 3
Ascension Day
Pentecost Sunday
Pentecost 2, 6, 7, 8, 10, 11, 12, 13, 14,
16, 17, 20, 22, 24, 25, 26, 27
All Saints
Thanksgiving

Thirst
New Year's Day
Epiphany 4, 7
Lent 3
Pentecost Sunday
Pentecost 11, 23
All Saints

Time and Space
Christmas Day 2
Lent 3
Easter Sunday
All Saints
Thanksgiving

Time, Talent, Treasure
Christmas Season 2
Ash Wednesday
Lent 1, 5
Passion Sunday
Easter 4, 6
Pentecost 10, 16, 26

Tithes and Offerings
New Year's Day
Epiphany 5, 8
Passion Sunday
Pentecost 7, 11, 24

Togetherness
Advent 2, 4
Christmas Season 2
Pentecost Sunday
Pentecost 3, 6, 7, 18, 21, 22, 26
Thanksgiving

Tongue(s)
Passion Sunday
Pentecost Sunday

Touch
Advent 3
Lent 4
Easter Sunday
Pentecost Sunday
Pentecost 16

Tradition
Pentecost 27

Transformation
Advent 3
Christmas Eve/Day
Christmas Day
New Year's Day
Epiphany 4, 8
Ash Wednesday
Lent 3, 5
Pentecost 6, 15, 18

Tremble
January 1 (Jesus and Mary)
Pentecost Sunday
Pentecost 9, 19

Trinity
Trinity Sunday

Trouble(s)
Epiphany 3
Easter Evening
Easter 5, 6
Pentecost 4, 7, 25
All Saints

Trumpets, etc.
Christmas Day 2
Easter Evening

Trust
Advent 2
Christmas Season 1
Epiphany 1, 2, 4, 5, 7, 8
Lent 2, 4, 5

Passion Sunday
Good Friday
Easter Evening
Easter 3, 4, 5
Ascension Day
Pentecost Sunday
Trinity Sunday
Pentecost 2, 3, 5, 7, 8, 10, 11, 12, 13, 16, 22, 23

Truth
Advent 2, 3, 4
Christmas Eve/Day
Christmas Day 2
Christmas Season 2
Epiphany
Epiphany 1, 2, 6
Ash Wednesday
Lent 3
Maundy Thursday
Good Friday
Easter Evening
Easter 3, 5, 6, 7
Trinity Sunday
Pentecost 7, 8, 12, 17, 20, 21, 22

Turned Away
Epiphany, Last Sunday
Good Friday
Pentecost 3

Understanding
Christmas Season 1
Epiphany 4, 6, 7, 8
Lent 1
Palm Sunday
Easter Sunday
Pentecost Sunday
Pentecost 3, 8, 10, 13, 21, 23
Thanksgiving

Unexpected
Christmas Eve/Day
Christmas Season 1
January 1 (Jesus and Mary)
Trinity Sunday
Pentecost 3, 13

Unity
Advent 2
Epiphany 3, 4, 6
Passion Sunday
Easter 6, 7

Pentecost Sunday
Pentecost 7, 8, 21, 23, 27

Valleys
Epiphany 4, Last Sunday
Lent 5
Pentecost 3, 27

Values(ed)
Christmas Eve/Day
Epiphany 8
Easter 2, 4
Pentecost 20, 23, 27

Venture(s)
Pentecost 12

Victory
Easter Sunday

Vineyard
Epiphany 8
Pentecost 18, 19, 20

Vision(s)
Advent 1, 2
Christmas Day 1, 2
Christmas Season 1
January 1 (Jesus and Mary)
Epiphany 7, Last Sunday
Lent 5
Easter Evening
Easter 5, 6
Pentecost Sunday
Pentecost 6, 7, 9, 11, 15, 22, 25, 27
All Saints

Visit(s)
Advent 1
Thanksgiving

Voice(s)
Christmas Eve/Day
Christmas Season 1
Epiphany 6
Lent 5
Easter 4, 5
Trinity Sunday
Pentecost 2, 27
Thanksgiving

Vows
Pentecost 25, 26
Thanksgiving

Walk
Advent 1
Christmas Eve/Day
Christmas Season 1
Epiphany 3, 4, 5, 6
Ash Wednesday
Passion Sunday
Lent 4, 5
Maundy Thursday
Easter 5
Pentecost

War(riors)
Advent 1
Christmas Eve/Day
Epiphany 4
Pentecost 25

Waste(land)
Lent 5
Pentecost 26

Watch(ful)
Advent 1
Christmas Day 1
Good Friday
Pentecost 12, 25, 27

Water
Christmas Season 2
Epiphany 6, 7
Lent 3
Easter 4, 6
Pentecost 6, 7, 8, 13, 14, 23, 27
Thanksgiving

Way (Truth, Life)
Christmas Day 2
Epiphany 6
Easter 5
Pentecost 14, 15, 17, 21

Weakness
Advent 3
Epiphany 4, 5
Pentecost 4, 27

Wealth
Christmas Season 2
Epiphany
Epiphany 4
Lent 2, 3
Pentecost 15

Weapons
Pentecost 25

Weariness
Advent 4
Christmas Season 2
Epiphany
Passion Sunday
Palm Sunday
Good Friday
Easter 4
Pentecost 7, 25

Weeping
Ash Wednesday
Easter Sunday

Welcome
Advent 2
Christmas Eve/Day
Epiphany 6, Last Sunday
Easter Sunday
Easter 2
Pentecost 2, 6, 16, 17, 20, 21, 24

Well(s)
Lent 3

Well-being
Pentecost 17
Thanksgiving

Whisper(s)
Lent
Palm Sunday
Pentecost 15

Wholeness
Christmas Eve/Day
Christmas Day 1
January 1 (Jesus and Mary)
Epiphany 5, 8
Ash Wednesday
Lent 1, 2, 4
Palm Sunday
Good Friday
Easter 6
Pentecost Sunday
Pentecost 4, 11, 15, 16, 23, 26, 27
Thanksgiving

Wickedness
Pentecost 12

Wilderness
Advent 2, 3
Easter 7

Pentecost 14
Thanksgiving

Wind(s)
Christmas Season 2
Lent 2, 5
Pentecost Sunday
Pentecost 2

Wings
Pentecost 15

Wisdom
Christmas Season 1, 2
Epiphany
Epiphany 4, 5, 7, Last Sunday
Easter 4
Pentecost Sunday
Pentecost 7, 14, 17, 23
All Saints

Witness
Christmas Eve/Day
Christmas Day 2
New Year's Day
Christmas Season 2
Epiphany 1, 2, 4, 5
Ash Wednesday
Lent 2
Palm Sunday
Maundy Thursday
Good Friday
Easter Sunday
Easter Evening
Easter 2, 7
Ascension Day
Pentecost Sunday
Trinity Sunday
Pentecost 5, 6, 8, 12, 15, 22, 24, 25

Wolf and Lamb
Advent 2

Wonder(s, ful, ing)
Advent 2
Christmas Eve/Day
New Year's Day
Pentecost Sunday
Trinity Sunday
Pentecost 5, 9, 10, 13, 14, 15, 18, 21

Wondrous Deeds (Works)
Epiphany 2
Pentecost 10, 12

ABOUT THE AUTHOR

In the Bayler household, a light in the study at 4 A.M. usually means that Lavon is engaged in devotions, preparing for the day. A frequent part of her spiritual discipline is the writing of worship materials related to the ecumenical common texts lectionary. *Fresh Winds of the Spirit, Book 2* is her fourth book of resources. The regular practice of immersing herself in the Scriptures that so many other pastors are studying keeps her in touch with their journey, even on those Sundays when she is not called upon to preach in one of the fifty churches in her association.

Lavon Bayler is minister of the new Fox Valley Association of the Illinois Conference, United Church of Christ. She has served on the conference staff since 1979, after twenty years as a pastor of congregations in Ohio and Illinois. Her husband, Robert Bayler, is vice president for religion and health of the U.C.C.-related Evangelical Health Systems, based in Oakbrook, Illinois. They met in seminary, married in New Albin, Iowa, were ordained together in Lebanon, Pennsylvania, and served as co-pastors for their first six years in ministry. Lavon is well known as a church educator, and Bob as a leader in health and human service ministries.

During a sabbatical in 1991, Lavon taught a worship course at Eden Theological Seminary, St. Louis, her alma mater, as minister-in-residence. She has led workshops for various denominations and ecumenical groups across the country. Over the years, she has been active in several peace, environmental, and human rights groups.

The Baylers are parents of three sons: David, a customer services representative for a major publisher (married to Jennifer, a special education teacher); Jonathan, who is director of student activities and programs at Elgin Community College, where he is also head baseball coach; and Timothy, who is a senior at the University of Arizona. Physical fitness buffs may be interested in Lavon's fourteen years of logging her early morning swims; she just passed the three-thousand-mile mark.